John Wise
EARLY AMERICAN DEMOCRAT

John Wise

EARLY AMERICAN DEMOCRAT

BY GEORGE ALLAN COOK

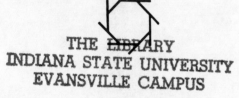

1966

OCTAGON BOOKS, INC.

New York

Copyright 1952 by George Allan Cook

Reprinted 1966
by special arrangement with George A. Cook

OCTAGON BOOKS, INC.
175 FIFTH AVENUE
NEW YORK, N.Y. 10010

LIBRARY OF CONGRESS CATALOG CARD NUMBER: 66-28373

Printed in U.S.A. by
NOBLE OFFSET PRINTERS, INC.
NEW YORK 3, N. Y.

To my mother and my father

Preface

I BECAME INTERESTED in John Wise several years ago when Professor Ralph L. Rusk, of Columbia University, suggested that a good edition of *The Churches Quarrel Espoused* or of *A Vindication of the Government of New England Churches* would be a contribution to scholarship. As I worked, I came to believe that both Wise's life and his books deserved serious study.

In writing the biography of John Wise I have found many libraries and their staffs helpful. I cite especially the Columbia University libraries—scarcely one of which has failed to contribute to this study—the library of Union Theological Seminary, the library of the New York Historical Society, and the New York Public Library, especially its Reserve, Local History, and Manuscript divisions. In tours of research I have consulted the Boston Athenæum Library, the James Blackstone Library, of Branford, Connecticut, the Boston Public Library, the John Carter Brown Library, of Brown University, the Burnham Public Library, of Essex, Massachusetts, the Houghton Library, of Harvard University, the Ipswich (Mass.) Public Library, the library of the Massachusetts Historical Society, the library of the Pennsylvania Historical Society, and the library of the Suffolk (Mass.) County Courthouse. I am grateful to Mr. Lawrence C. Wroth, librarian of the John Carter Brown Library, and to Mr. Stephen T. Riley, librarian of the Massachusetts Historical Society, for fruitful suggestions.

Church, school, town, county, and state records provided me with much material. The First Congregational Church, of

Essex, and the North Congregational Church, of Ipswich, Massachusetts, allowed me to examine their church records, and the Roxbury (Mass.) Historical Society gave me access to the records of the First Church of Roxbury. Roxbury Latin School kindly permitted me to study a number of manuscripts. The town records of Branford, Connecticut, and Ipswich, Massachusetts, and the court records of Essex County and Middlesex County, Massachusetts, made available numerous pertinent documents for my study. In the Archives Division of the Massachusetts Statehouse, where I spent many hours studying manuscripts, I found the personnel unfailingly courteous and helpful. Mr. John L. Dolan, town clerk of Ipswich, and Dr. W. E. Lowther, minister of the First Congregational Church of Essex, I thank for their kindness and encouragement. Also, I thank Mr. and Mrs. Charles H. Paull, of Essex, for allowing me to visit the John Wise house, which is their home.

Professors Richard B. Morris and James L. Clifford, of Columbia University, have read the typescript of this biography, and I am grateful for their interest and criticism. My friend Dr. Hal Bridges, of the University of Arkansas, has given me advice and guidance, and I am grateful to him.

I owe a very great debt of gratitude to Professor Rusk, under whose direction this study was carried out. He has shown an unflagging interest in its progress and has given freely of his time to its improvement.

G.A.C.

Wagner College
September, 1952

Contents

Introduction

DURING THE LAST HALF of the seventeenth century and the first quarter of the eighteenth an extraordinary country preacher by the name of John Wise lived in New England. He was chaplain in two military expeditions; leader of his town in protest against an arbitrarily imposed tax; spokesman for one of the earliest versions of the challenge "No taxation without representation";[1] petitioner for two of the most vigorously prosecuted victims in the Salem witchcraft trials; defender of democracy in the government of church and state; writer of satire and persuasive argument; first notable American advocate of the "natural rights" school of philosophy; and sponsor of paper money, singing by note, and smallpox inoculation. There are legends that he downed a neighborhood wrestling champion and prayed his parishioners free from pirates' hands; but whatever his physical and spiritual prowess may have been, he was indisputably a man of great force of mind and character.

John Wise was, for the times, a democrat both in action and in thought. Not only did he champion the right of the colonists to impose their own taxes but he also wrote two forceful and witty books in support of congregational autonomy in the New England churches. *The Churches Quarrel Espoused* treated in satire proposals that Wise saw as threats to the freedom of the individual church, and *A Vindication of the Government of New England Churches* rehearsed the democratic basis of church polity. Wise did not see democracy in the image of the English government. Though he looked upon that government with an approving eye, even calling it "an *Elisium*," still he saw it as a mixed government, combining two or more systems. Democracy was to Wise best for both church and state.

Wise wrote with perspicacity and ease. Although at times he tortured his arguments into division after division, after the manner of contemporary sermons, still he smoothed the reader's way with humor, wit, and eloquence. His discernment was remarkable for his day. He viewed man as endowed by nature with "many Enobling Immunities"—gifts of liberty and trust—that rendered him "the most August Animal in the World." Wise was here following after Baron Pufendorf, to be sure, but an unqualified enthusiasm often led him to a more exalted expression of idea than his master's.

No full-length study of Wise has hitherto been made. He has been only more or less briefly viewed in periodicals;[2] in histories of thought, literature, and the churches;[3] and in biographical reference works.[4] He deserves a greater name and a fuller record.

CHAPTER I

Ancestry and Early Life

JOHN WISE, though he was destined to live a full and vigorous life, came into the world quietly and obscurely. He was born into the second generation of Massachusetts Bay Puritans. His mother, Mary Thompson Wise, was recorded a member of the Roxbury church before 1647.[1] Though no similar information concerning his father has been found, still the earliest record mentioning Joseph Wise speaks for his integrity, for it states his rewards as an indentured servant to Deacon George Alcock, physician of Roxbury.

It has been suggested that Deacon Alcock brought Joseph Wise to America in 1636.[2] After Alcock came to America in the fleet that brought Governor Winthrop in 1630, he made two voyages to England. One of them he made in order to fetch his young son and Joseph Wise; the other, in order to bring back his second wife, his first having not survived the winter of her arrival.[3]

Perhaps 1636 is suggested as the year for Joseph Wise's coming to America because it would fit the usual length of an indenture period,[4] since the elder Wise is known to have been freed in midsummer of 1641. Whether or not he served fewer than the usual number of years, he received, according to George Alcock's will drawn up December 22, 1640, "his time, from after mid-somer next."[5]

At the time of Joseph Wise's period of service the practice of indenture was not new, and the contracts usually took set forms. The Virginia colony employed indentured servants extensively, and New England somewhat less.[6] Between the servant and his master was drawn up a legal contract, binding the one to faithful service for a number of years as payment for his passage, and the other to the provision of sufficient food, drink, clothing, and shelter during the period of service and, perhaps, a final specified reward, such as money, land, clothing, or tools.[7] The specified reward, or "freedom dues," granted Joseph Wise, while not usual, was nevertheless not unheard of. He received, in addition to his time, a young heifer.

Because his will and contemporary comment attest to the good character of Deacon Alcock, it may be supposed that Joseph Wise found his master congenial and his place in the Alcock home not unduly humbling. Deacon Alcock was important in the community. He had served as deacon at the Roxbury church from its gathering, and before that time had done similar duty in the Dorchester church for the Roxbury people who attended service there. He had been a member of the Massachusetts Bay Colony's first court, in 1634. According to the testimony of his minister, John Eliot, "he lived in a good & godly sort" and at his death "left a good savor behind him; the Pore of the church much bewailing his losse."[8] In his will Alcock canceled the debt of his brother Thomas, of Dedham, and made him and his children substantial gifts. He provided also for the bringing up of a young woman and for the education of his two sons. Among the overseers of the will were some of the great men of the Puritan community: the teacher of the Roxbury church, John Eliot, famed missionary to the Indians; the pastor of the church, Thomas Weld, collaborator with Eliot and Richard Mather in the composition of the Bay Psalm Book;[9] and Thomas Hooker, the brother of Alcock's first wife.[10] Though the will was drawn up only a few days before Alcock's death, it does not seem fair to ascribe its liberality to the stricken conscience of a dying man.[11]

Though New England was never to sponsor servitude with any heartiness, it was in this first decade of rapid settlement, 1630-1640, that the Puritans made the widest use of indentured servants. The loneliness of Wise's position, then, could not have particularly oppressed him.[12] In the same household with him he found another bound servant, and in the town there were several.

But burdensome or not, Joseph Wise's years of bondage came to an end, and he found himself a free man who had to make his way in a new country. Late in life he is said to have been a butcher,[13] and in 1647 he mortgaged his house, malthouse, and kiln.[14] The property he mortgaged would suggest another business venture—that of brewing beer and ale, or the dispensing of malt for other people's brewing. According to the records of Harvard University, he made payments several times during the 1650's for persons indebted to the college, and two of those payments were in malt.[15] Whatever his occupation, evidently he attained a position of respectability; in 1676 the Roxbury freemen elected him to jury duty.[16]

Joseph Wise may have had some portion of the fifty acres that Deacon Alcock was supposed to receive for bringing over an indentured servant.[17] But the problems his new freedom presented he did not long try to meet alone. He soon sought a wife to help him. In December following the summer of his release he wedded Mary Thompson.

She was probably the daughter of the Reverend William Tompson,[18] of Braintree, later Quincy, Massachusetts. The family had settled first at Agamenticus, now York, Maine, after their arrival from England, in 1637, but two years later removed to Braintree, where Tompson was installed as minister.

Two brothers of the Braintree family, William and Benjamin, were graduated from Harvard College. William became a minister, and Benjamin a schoolmaster-physician, who had as his pupil the celebrated Cotton Mather. Benjamin achieved some fame as a verse writer both in his own time and later. His chief work was *New Englands Crises,* a piece on King Philip's War, in which John Wise served as chaplain. It is reasonable to conjecture that if he was John Wise's uncle, he influenced his nephew to seek a college education, though an objection to such a conjecture is that it would not explain why John was the only college graduate in a family variously reported as comprised of ten, twelve, and thirteen children.[19]

John was the fifth of these children. Joseph, Jeremiah, Sarah, and Mary preceded him, and Henry, Bethia, Katherine, Benjamin, William, Benjamin again,[20] and Abigail followed. All the children started their lives with the benefit of baptism, John himself being baptized August 15, 1652.[21] Presumably he was born only a few days earlier, for it was customary to carry a child to church for baptism on the Sunday after his birth.

At the distance of centuries, the boy John can now be seen only as a hazy figure, by the dimly reflected light of his times and of fellowtownsmen who were his older contemporaries. When he began to talk with some degree of fluency and meaning and to have some understanding of what was said to him, he was doubtless set to learning the catechism, if not by his parents and neighbors, then by his minister. For the Roxbury church had as its teacher for nearly sixty years that zealous spirit of Puritan evangelism the Reverend John Eliot. He was a great believer in catechizing and "spent in it a World of time."[22]

While John Wise was growing up, Eliot was performing

prodigies of labor. He had come to New England in 1631; and when some of his friends gathered the church at Roxbury a few months later he became its senior minister; he remained so until his death, in 1690, at the age of eighty-six.[23] Twenty-five years of his ministry he served alone.[24]

But John Eliot served not only his parishioners. The inscription on the Parish tomb, a repository for the remains of the town's early ministers, called him "The Apostle to the Indians."[25] And so he was. When he looked upon the aborigines, he saw them as subjects for salvation. Eliot declared that God put into his heart "a compassion over their poor Souls, and a desire to teach them to know Christ, and to bring them into his Kingdome."[26] He could not, as some did, "grant that the Heathen might be saved without the Knowledge of the Lord Jesus Christ."[27]

Eliot's enthusiasm was well known, and it was not surprising that the ministers of Massachusetts Bay, instructed by the General Court in 1646,[28] designated him one of two missionaries to carry the Gospel to the Indians. So indefatigably did Eliot toil that the town of Natick, a refuge for Christian Indians, was established in 1650, and so vigorously did he publicize the needs of the missionary work that Cromwell himself, Lord Protector of the Commonwealth, helped in 1649 to form "The President and Society for the Propagation of the Gospel in New England," an organization which made very substantial contributions to Eliot's work. These things happened at the beginning of Eliot's apostleship to the Indians. In 1661 Eliot published in the Indian language the New Testament and in 1663 the Old Testament, the first Bible to be printed in America. New towns of "praying Indians" were established. In 1671 Eliot described nine such settlements,[29] and three years later, on an inspection tour with Major Daniel Gookin, the Indian commissioner, he found fourteen towns with a combined population of eleven hundred Christian natives.[30]

Though in the following year King Philip's War caused the disintegration of many of these communities and brought down upon the heads of Eliot and Major Gookin, because of their defense of the Christian Indians, the suspicions, threats, and insults of their neighbors, Eliot remained faithful to his missionary work.[31]

The works and personal vitality of Eliot could not have passed uncommented upon by his parishioners, and it would have been a dull boy of Roxbury town who would not have heard the talk. Contemporaries have attested to Eliot's attractive qualities. In *Wonder-Working Providence* Captain Edward Johnson, town clerk and military leader of Woburn and occasional surveyor for the General Court, has described Eliot as being "of a cheerful spirit, walking unblameable, of a godly conversation, apt to teach, as by his indefatigable paines both with his own flock, and the poore Indians doth appeare."[32] And Cotton Mather spoke of the agreeableness of Eliot's preaching, saying that it was so plain that "the very *Lambs* might wade, into his Discourses on those Texts and Themes, wherein Elephants might *swim*" and that it was so lively in its condemnation of sin that "his pulpit [was] another Mount *Sinai*," surrounded with "as many *Thunderbolts* as *Words*."[33]

The forthrightness of the man doubtless struck home. Certainly his convictions did not go unnoticed by the Massachusetts General Court. Eliot had his own ideas about government and had expressed them during the Puritan regime in a political work called *The Christian Commonwealth*. Here and in his Indian towns Eliot shaped a scheme of government, based on Jethro's advice to his son-in-law Moses,[34] that called for various levels of elected authority. Believing that his plan was a divine institution with Christ as the law-giver, Eliot declared that the Lord was "about to Shake all the Earth, and throw down that great Idol of Humane Wisdome in Governments, and set up Scripture-government in the room thereof."[35] Between the book's writing and its publication in London, in 1659, events had occurred that made its public appearance an indiscretion, one that Eliot himself would not have committed without the help of a friendly printer. Now his words rang so loudly in the ears of Massachusetts' elected authority that the General Court, apprehensive of the reception of Eliot's statements by Charles II's "Kingly Government," ordered the book's suppression and required a retraction of any statements suggesting that the government of England was anti-Christian.[36]

Samuel Danforth, pastor of the church from 1650 until his death in 1674, and remembered for his vehement discourses, probably also had his influence.[37] What seventeenth-century youngster would have been impervious to fear when he heard an exhortation that took this form?

Hasten you after your lecherous Kindred into the stinking Lake: sit down with your Brethren and Sisters in the depths of Hell. As you have partaken with them in their sordid Pleasures, partake with them also in their Plagues and Torments. Let thy lustful Body be everlasting Fuel for the unquenchable fire: Let thy lascivious Soul be eternal Food for the never-dying Worm. Let Indignation and Wrath, Tribulation and Anguish be thy portion world without end. Hell from beneath is moved to meet thee, and is ready to entertain thee.[38]

Still, Roxbury boys were not always attentive. At a town meeting January 15, 1666, it was "a complaint of several of the Inhabitance that they wanted convenient Rome to sit in the Meeting House to their edification by reason of the disturbance the boys make in the Gallery."[39]

But if the church and the ministers of Roxbury influenced John Wise, so did its free school. The Roxbury School Charter of 1645 in its opening lines reveals what the nature of that influence may have been. Here it was stated that

Whereas the Inhabitantes of Roxburie out of theire relligious care of posteritie have taken into consideration how necessarie the Education of theire children in Literature wilbe, to fitt them for publicke service both in Church and Commonwealth in succeeding ages; They therefore unanimously have consented and agreed to erect a Free schoole in the said Towne of Roxburie.[40]

The Wise children must have attended the school the town of Roxbury provided. Joseph Wise was among those fifty-odd donors who signed the "Covenant" with schoolmaster John Prudden to pay him "ye full, & just summe of twenty-five pounds," three-quarters payable "in Indian=corne, or peas, & ye other fourth=part in barley, all good & merchandable, at price currant in ye countrey rate, at ye dayes of payment."[41] The donors were usually parents who had children in attendance, and Joseph Wise was at this time providing for the education of his children. But this particular provision very likely did not contribute to the education of his son John. The covenant with Master Prudden was for the school year 1669-1670, and John is supposed to have been graduated in 1669.[42]

Before a Roxbury boy attended the town grammar school, he had to gain the rudiments of knowledge, perhaps just reading, which he could have learned at home or at a dame school, because "all A b c darians" were excluded from instruction. The school was excellent and trained its pupils well.[43] In the agreement with the school authorities, John Prudden did "promise & engage to use his best skill, & endeavour, both by praecept, & example, to instruct in all scholasticall, morall, & theologicall discipline, the children, (soe far as they are or shall be capable) of those persons whose names are here underwritten"; and that he made good his promises seems certain, for the "covenantees," writing on the same agreement, pronounced themselves satisfied at the end of the year. The teachers preceding Prudden were probably engaged under similar terms.

It would be interesting to know what texts Prudden and his immediate predecessors used for his "scholasticall, morall, & theologicall discipline." In 1681 Comenius's *Janua,* a phrasebook of simple Latin and Greek words, was used;[44] and a copy of *Ethicae Ciceronianae, libri duo* (London, 1652), was once a possession of John Wise's schoolmate George Alcock and is now in the Prince Collection of the Boston Public Library. Cotton Mather, in his commemorative poem upon Ezekiel Cheever, said Cheever taught Latin grammar, prosody, and composition, Lily's grammar, *Sententiae pueriles;* the *Colloquies* of Corderius; Cato's *Distichs;* Ovid's *Metamorphoses* and *De tristibus;* Cicero's *Offices;* and Vergil. Mather also made allusions to Homer, but Mather's knowledge probably came from instruction outside the Boston grammar school. In addition, he called Cheever "a Christian Terence," an epithet which suggests the presence of that author in the school curriculum.[45]

Two teachers who kept Roxbury school when John Wise was grammar-school age were Thomas Mighill and Daniel Weld. Mighill's parents had lived in Roxbury, but he had been born and brought up at Rowley. He attended Harvard College, taking his M.A. degree in 1666. Before entering the ministry, he taught for two years at Roxbury.[46]

Mighill should have found the school building in tidy shape when he arrived, for it had been repaired in 1665. Nevertheless, in that first year of his teaching complaint was made of the sad state of the schoolhouse. But surely it was not then so much out of repair as it was in 1681, when a schoolmaster protested it was "not fitting for to reside in; the glass broken, and thereupon very raw and cold, the floor very much broken and torn up to kindle fires, the hearth spoiled, the seats, some burnt and others out of kilter, that one had as well nigh as goods [*sic*] keep school in a hog stie as in it."[47]

Roxbury school was not always so fortunate as to have a college graduate in charge. The master of Roxbury free school for fourteen years before Mighill's tour, Daniel Weld, seems not to have had a college degree.[48] Still, he was a man of experience, having taught the Braintree school for several years; and he gave such satisfaction to Roxbury that he was retained until his death in 1666 at the age of eighty.

Schoolmaster Weld, oldest brother of Thomas Weld who had been the first pastor of the church, had settled in Roxbury in the early part of 1652[49] and in the same year had entered into a contract with the feoffees, the seven school authorities designated to act for the town. By this contract, Weld was to "provide convenient benches and formes wth Tables, for ye schollers to sitt on and to write att, with a convenient seate for ye schoolemaster and a deske to putt ye Dictionarys on and shelves to lay up bookes and to keep ye house and windows and doore wth ye chimneye sufficient & proper . . ."[50] for which he would receive a stipend of about twenty-four pounds. In addition he was to collect his own salary, having the support of the feoffees if any donor proved refractory.

But if the church and school played their parts—and no slight ones—in the life of young John Wise, so must have the town and the surrounding countryside. Captain Edward Johnson, in his *Wonder-Working Providence* (1654), the first published history of Massachusetts, has left a description of the early Roxbury which Wise knew. The town, built on land "well watered" and fertile, possessed "dwellinge-houses neere upon 120." Though some of these dwellings were "fayre Houses," the "House for Church-assembly was desti-tute and unbeautified with other buildings."[51] Johnson wrote before the church had the benefit of any of its improvements.

An even earlier description was that of William Wood in *New Englands Prospect*. Wood, one of the founders of Lynn, had come as a young man with his father in 1629 for the ex-press purpose of gaining first-hand knowledge of the New England regions for the Puritans in England. The results of his observations he published in 1634. Wood's description was, like Johnson's, a favorable one. He described the nearby streams, spoke of how the town got its name,[52] and explained why the town had no harbor.[53] Those nearby streams, such as Smelt Brook and Stony River, were full of fish, and the pond across Jamaica Plain was good for both fishing and swimming. Surely, two such useful activities as fishing and swimming were not denied the Roxbury boy.

Earthquakes occurred in 1660 and 1663, and the people of Roxbury town talked forebodingly about them.[54] The towns-people tied Quakers to the end of a cart and whipped them through the streets.[55] The church subjected drunkards to public admonitions,[56] and Danforth described comets to give his sermons a minatory effect. Indians wandered into town now and then and aroused curiosity and dread. And nearby was Boston harbor with its ships to delight the eye.

There was no lack of interesting events in the Puritan town of Roxbury. It would have been an unusual boy whose active body and eager mind would not have sought them out. John Wise as a man had both an active body and an eager mind, and it is hardly too much to believe that, in his case the child was "the father of the man."

CHAPTER II

Years at Harvard

JOHN WISE was seventeen when he went up to Harvard.
In Puritan days the age of seventeen was not one of im-
maturity and irresponsibility. The Puritan young man of
that age was supposed to be directed by intelligent and pur-
poseful ambition. Indeed, a few young men had even finished
college by the time they were seventeen.[1]

The attendance of John Wise at Roxbury free school when
he could have been out in the world making his way, and his
perseverance in completing a grammar school education when
he had reached a rather mature age, would indicate that
something further was planned for his life. George Alcock,
who went from Roxbury to Harvard at the same time that
Wise did, was only fourteen, and Wise was older than the
other two members of his college class, though seventeen was
not an unusual age for entrance.[2]

The opportunity to go to Harvard may have fallen suddenly and fearfully upon John Wise.[3] If so, his first thoughts
about a college education may well have been vague. But he
must have known, before he had been at Harvard many
months, that for him an education led almost inevitably to
the ministry, as it did then, indeed, for most of those who received it.[4] The Cambridge Platform of 1648 stated that the
purpose of schools was "the trayning up of such in good Litra-
ture, of learning, as may afterwards be called forth unto office
of Pastor or Teacher in the church."[5] Indeed, Harvard College had been established in the dread of leaving "an illiterate

Ministery to the Churches."⁶

Yet the young college student Wise, however early he resigned himself to study for the ministry, could hardly have
realized what that ministry would require of him. He could
not have anticipated such hardships as his son-in-law
John White was long afterwards to describe as common to
ministers.

A *Sedentary* Life exposes Health; *Pastoral Visits* in time of Malignant and Mortal Distempers, expose Life. And their *Publick La-
bours* many times put them into such Ferments, as to expose them
to take cold; for which causes many are disinabled for their Work
while Young. And if they live to Old Age, they are wont to feel
a double portion of grief and pain. . . . Man is hard to please; If
God speak, immediately men fear, and tremble, and fly. If God
speaks to them by man, he is apt to despise what is said, for the
sake of the Speaker; one speaks too slow, another too fast; one
speaks too low, another in too general terms: One is too florid,
another too dull.⁷

The young aspirant Wise would have to wait for years of
experience before he could understand the difficulties which
his own son Jeremiah would one day describe.

*They are much in the wrong, who take the Ministry to be an easy
Employment; and the Work of a Minister to be an easy Task.*
Some People may think *Ministers*, above *all* Men, live a fine, easy
Life, who have a whole Town or Parish, *to take care* of them, of
their comfortable Support; as tho' they themselves had nothing to
do but to look about them & take their Pleasure. But alas! It's no
such thing; for the *Minister* has the most laborious, careful, tho't-
ful Life of any. He has the Souls, if not the Bodies, of a whole
place, to take care of and provide for; and they that will fulfil
their *Ministry* will find little leisure Time.⁸

But even if Wise, the young student, could have forseen
such penalties, he would surely have had no good reason to
hesitate. He had already experienced hardships enough, and

merely being a student was no easy achievement. The gap in
the social hierarchy that he had to span was greater than con-
fronted most collegians. So far as the records show, he was
the first son of an indentured servant ever to attend Harvard.[9] When Wise thought of the ministry, he must have
thought of it as a seat of eminence and a source of security
such as he had never known before. In later years, when the
ministerial cape had long lain heavy upon his shoulders, possibly he saw the pastoral office in the light of a steady realism,
but it would hardly have been so in the flush of his youth.

To enter college, John Wise had to pass an examination.
It was probably given by the president soon after commencement, which in these years was about the second week in
August.[10] The authority for the examination is found in the
laws of Harvard College that were promulgated in 1655 and
governed that institution for thirty years. There it is formally
stated.

When any Scholler is able to read and understand Tully Virgil or
any such ordinary Classical Authors, and can readily make &
speak or write true Latin in prose and hath Skill in making verse,
and is Competently grounded in the Greeke Language; so as to
be able to Construe & Gramatically to resolve ordinary Greeke,
as in the Greeke Testament, Isocrates, & the minor poets, or such
like, having withall meet Testimony of his towardlinesse, hee shall
be capabl[e] of his admission into the Colledge.[11]

Such a direction rendered exactly could have involved the
would-be freshman in an exhaustive examination; but if it
was brief and oral as evidence indicates it was at the end of
the seventeenth century, then it could have been passed
without great difficulty. After President Charles Chauncy
had examined Wise, he would have provided the boy with a
copy of the college laws—in Latin, of course—or required
him to copy them. Wise would have found the latter task no

small chore.

Some of these laws, as Wise read or copied them, must have struck dismay to his heart: "A Scholler shall not use the English tongue in the Colledge with other Schollers, unlesse hee be called thereunto in publique exercises of Oratory or the like."[12] Latin was always to be spoken. There is evidence, however, that the enforcement of this regulation was not always strictly insisted upon.[13]

A beginning student might well have been frightened as he read that "noe Student shall under any pretence whatsoever use the Company or familiar acquaintance of persons of ungirt or dissolute Life" and he may have nodded with righteous approval over the stipulations against the taking of tobacco and the conveyance into his chamber of inebriating drinks. The rule against taking tobacco was not stringently enforced either—in fact it was widely disobeyed[14]—and it may have been at this time, while Wise was in attendance at Harvard, that he first became fond of a pipe.[15]

But one law could not be overstepped and had even to be complied with before Wise's admission. It was stated that unless an applicant's "Parents or Freinds shall both lay downe one quarter expences, and also give the Colledge Steward security for the Future" he shall not be admitted.[16]

Only after Wise and "Parents or Freinds" had thus satisfied the requirements, would President Chauncy write *admittatur* across Wise's copy of the laws and send him off in the company of a senior scholar to be assigned to his study and have his name entered on the "buttery table." This last was a bulletin of prime importance that authorized him "commons and sizings" and defined the seniority by which he would receive them. "Commons" were dinner and supper, served at eleven in the morning and seven-thirty in the evening; "sizings" were the bread and beer that comprised the only food for breakfast and tea, commonly known as morning and afternoon "bever."[17]

The Harvard that John Wise had come to had been in active operation about thirty years and was now under the administration of its second president, or third, if the absconder Nathaniel Eaton is counted as the first. The main building, Old College,[18] was fast falling into disrepair, and subscriptions for its replacement would be taken during Wise's residence. On its right was the Indian College, built in 1655 to train Eliot's young Christian savages for Harvard, and about two hundred feet in front of these buildings and facing on Braintree Street were the President's Lodge and Goffe College, a dwelling converted to student use. The College Yard, on the other side of the main building, extended three hundred yards or so to the Charlestown road, and on the left of Old College beyond a couple of properties was the college orchard.[19] *New Englands First Fruits*, published in 1643, describes the early college, though not in detail.

The Edifice is very faire and comely within and without, having in it a spacious Hall; (Where they daily meet at Commons, Lectures, Exercises) and a large Library with some Bookes to it, the gifts of diverse of our friends, their Chambers and studies also fitted for, and possessed by the Students, and all other roomes of Office necessary and convenient, with all needfull Offices thereto belonging.[20]

A new student would probably be taken to a chamber in the Old College and there introduced to the room's two or three other occupants. One of these was presumably a student of several years' standing, who was supposed to keep order among his chambermates and for whom Wise as a freshman, despite college forbiddance,[21] would run errands and perform chores. Wise could rent, though the practice was not usually permitted until the sophomore year, one of the two or three little studies that blocked off the corners of the central chamber—if there happened to be one vacant.

Now Wise could settle down to the routine of student life, which, beginning with prayers at five or six in the morning, might last until eleven at night, although candles were usually blown out at nine o'clock. In this day came one or two lecture hours, an hour or so of recitation, evening prayers at five, and, after dinner and supper, an unsupervised recreation period of an hour or more. The rest of Wise's time was supposed to be given over to study.[22] This was his weekday schedule. Sabbaths he attended chapel and perhaps the town meeting house alongside Goffe College.

A vigorous athletic young man would participate in the recreation after meals—not to mention the meals themselves —with more than ordinary gusto, and Wise was growing into a man whose physical endowments were legendary. As a new student, he would quickly accustom himself to his lowly place in the dining hall, determined, it is said, by intellectual merit within the classes. He may even have waited table to help pay his school fees. Wearing his hat at mealtimes—for to sit uncovered was a punishment—doubtless did not detract from the palatability of the veal, beef, mutton, lamb, and pork, the wheat, rye, and cornbread, the cheese and eggs, the peas and apples, and beer which made up commons.[23]

Because Wise's father operated a malthouse and had made disbursements of malt to the college, payments in malt could have kept Wise at Harvard. Certainly malt, because of its use in brewing, proved very acceptable to the college authorities in payment of fees and, along with wheat, was the most often mentioned credit in the college records of the time.[24] While there is not any real evidence of how Wise met his expenses, the records are by no means complete.[25]

From *New Englands First Fruits* the subjects that John

Wise studied may be pretty well conjectured. In the first year there were logic and physics, Greek grammar, Hebrew grammar and readings, history, and the nature of plants; in the second there were ethics and politics, Greek grammar and poetry, and Chaldee, with readings in the books of Ezra and Daniel; and in the third there were arithmetic and geometry, astronomy, Greek composition in prose and verse, and Syriac with readings in the New Testament. Subjects common to all years were rhetoric, disputations, and divinity catechisms. Some subjects were more emphasized than others: rhetoric was studied all day once a week throughout the student's entire stay at the college, while the nature of plants was taught Saturday afternoons in the summer of the freshman year. Usually, however, the whole day was allotted to the study of one subject.[26] This schedule accounted for only three full years, and President Henry Dunster extended the three years of training to four. The fourth year, under President Chauncy, was spent in the study of metaphysics, mathematics, rhetoric, oratory, and divinity.[27]

John Wise, one of the thirty or so[28] undergraduates that made up the freshman, sophomore, junior, and senior sophister classes, absorbed this curriculum from the tutelage of the president and fellows. These latter were usually Masters of Arts who were awaiting with some eagerness a call to the pulpit, for tutorial pay was not large. The riches of the library, which included among its three hundred and fifty or four hundred books the works of Terence and St. Augustine,[29] were not for the undergraduate. The library was chiefly for the use of the faculty and the few graduates in residence.[30] Wise got his textbooks from booksellers or schoolmates, and for extra-curricular and light reading sought the books and sheets that were circulating among his friends.[31]

During most of Wise's stay at Harvard the president

was Charles Chauncy, who had taken over the college in 1654. At that time Henry Dunster had resigned in resentment over the General Court's interference and its disapproval of his determined stand against infant baptism. Chauncy, who as a fellow of Trinity College, Cambridge, had held a twin lectureship in Greek with George Herbert the poet, also harbored offensive views about infant baptism. But unlike Dunster, Chauncy believed in total immersion for infants. And not stopping there, he insisted on serving the Lord's Supper at night because it happened so in the New Testament. So great was the opposition in Plymouth Colony and among his colleagues to these practices that Chauncy, discouraged, was about to take ship for England when he was prevailed upon to take the Harvard presidency on condition that he keep his views to himself. There being no infants to baptize at Harvard, he settled comfortably into the 100-pounds-a-year job, and, though he found himself pinched for money at times while he was educating his six sons, he served well and long, teaching until his eighty-second year.[32]

President Chauncy was one of Wise's teachers, for not only would he take the place of an absent tutor, but he taught regularly Greek and his favorite subjects, Hebrew and the oriental languages. When he died, in February, 1672, the college was without a president until Leonard Hoar was formally installed the next December.[33] President Hoar could have been Wise's teacher only during a few months of 1673, when the controversy that unseated him was beginning.

Who Wise's tutors were cannot be determined with any nicety, for the fellows were a shifting group. Two tutors during Wise's college years stayed longer than most. Thomas Graves, alleged member of the Church of England, and Alexander Nowell, student of astronomy, were appointed in 1666 and stayed until 1672, Graves giving up his fellowship and Nowell dying at his post in July.[34] Solomon Stoddard was chosen a fellow with them, but remained only until 1669, when he left to begin his long ministry at Northampton.

The tutors heard recitations, assigned and aided in lessons, lectured in certain subjects, and saw to it that their charges performed all prescribed tasks. Each tutor was supposed to take over a class as its members enrolled and guide them through all their undergraduate years. The tutor having most to do with Wise, if any deductions can be drawn, may have been Alexander Nowell, who has been called "the most brilliant man of his college generation"[35] and was in charge of Harvard a short time after Chauncy's death.

John Wise did not always behave himself. Led by the promptings of a healthy appetite, he joined his classmate Edward Pelham and a sophomore named Jonathan Russell in feasting on a stolen turkey at the house of Samuel Gibson, a shrewd rascal who figured in most of the Harvard mischief of the time.[36] Pelham, who kept a gun in defiance of the academic authorities,[37] thrust it into the willing hands of two boys, Urian Oakes, fourteen-year-old son of the Cambridge minister, and Percival Green, a Harvard graduate in 1680, and directed these young fowlers in a hunt for fat turkeys. A bird belonging to Captain Daniel Gookin was eventually dropped, was roasted by Mrs. Gibson, and was eaten by Wise, Pelham, Russell, and the Gibsons.

The incident came to light as the Middlesex County Court Records show, and Samuel Gibson, having been "convicted of enterteyneing some of the Studts. contrary to Law," was "sentenced to be admonished, and to pay a fine of forty shillings in money."[38] What Wise and his fellow students suffered the records do not tell; but if college law was strictly enforced, they were publicly admonished, perhaps at commons, and a penalty was imposed, such as a public confession or eating commons uncovered.[39] This was no offense for expulsion, and the punishment had no blighting effect upon their college careers. All graduated in good standing.[40]

In the four years that Wise had attended Harvard, there had been spent on his education approximately fifty-five pounds, not counting the cost of clothing, laundry, books, and other incidentals.[41] The sum covered a greater time than that now spent in residence for the bachelor's degree, for then there were no vacations.[42]

The summer of commencement was a trying time to the candidate for a bachelor's degree. As a candidate, Wise would first have to fulfill the requirements set down in the college laws.

Every Scholer that upon proofe is able to read ex tempore the Pentateuch, and the New Testament into Latin out of the Originall Tongues, & being Skilled in Logicke, & competently principled in Naturall and Morall philosophy & the Mathematicks, & also of honest Life & Conversation, & at any publicke Act hath publicke approbation of the Overseers & President of the Colledge, he may be invested with the first degree.[43]

Then the candidate had to undergo a series of public examinations. Cotton Mather has thus described them.

Those who then stood *Candidates* to be *Graduates,* were to attend in the *Hall* for certain Hours, on *Mondays,* and on *Tuesdays,* Three Weeks together towards the Middle of *June,* which were called Weeks of *Visitation;* so that all Comers that pleased, might examine their Skill in the *Languages* and *Sciences,* which they now pretended unto; and usually, some or other of the *Overseers* of the *Colledge,* would on purpose *Visit* them, whilst they were thus doing what they called, *sitting of Solstices.*[44]

For the commencement feast in August, Wise, as well as all other senior sophisters, had to provide a fee of three pounds in addition to tips. Then, during the forenoon of commencement day, he joined with his fellows in a long-drawn-out exercise, which, since the class numbered only four students, probably required a lengthy oration or more than one speech by each of them. In the afternoon, which was given over to the performance of the Master of Arts candidates, the new bachelors would enjoy a respite.[45]

After graduation John Wise was ready for the world. He did not choose to read for a few months, as graduates often did, in the college library. The church at Branford, Connecticut, gave him a call and he accepted it. As his return to Harvard for the Master's degree would mean only a brief reappearance there, he was virtually ending his college days.

CHAPTER III

Unsettled Years

JOHN WISE remained at Branford almost four years, but he was interrupted in his ministerial duties at least once. Ever since the departure in 1667 of the Reverend Abraham Pierson for Newark, New Jersey, with parishioners drawn from Guilford, New Haven, Milford, and Branford, the latter town had found it hard to keep a pastor. When Pierson left, he engaged a John Bowers to serve out the year in his stead, and without formal installation Bowers served from time to time until 1678.[1] The church had sought his settlement just before Wise's coming, but had not obtained it. Except for Bowers, Wise was to be the first of several who supplied the church during the years following Pierson's departure, and the town was to have no settled pastor until 1687. In fact, formal permission from the Connecticut General Court to organize a church was not granted until that year.[2]

Nevertheless, in the preceding years the town had sought to make the Branford pulpit more attractive by increasing the preacher's salary. Bowers, for his first year, 1668, had received thirty pounds and "the cuting and Carting of thirty Lod of wood" besides tax-free and rent-free house and lands. This salary had been in addition to the twelve pounds that the town paid him for filling out Pierson's year. In the year before Wise came Bowers had received forty pounds and the usual privileges and exemptions.[3] Soon after Wise left, an agreement was drawn up that gave the minister fifty pounds "pr year for ye time he taryes with us and wood and candles";

and in 1679 arrangements were made to pay sixty pounds and "his winter's wood" to Samuel Mather, whom finally the governor and council of Connecticut would not allow to come but sent to Windsor instead.[4] It was during Wise's years— 1673 to 1677—that the jump in salary from forty to fifty pounds occurred, and his pay probably began at the lower sum and rose to the higher.

Of course, the salary was always "to be paid in provision at price currant with ye merchants." In the early years of his ministry Pierson was getting for his first half year's salary provision "in beefe or porke or Indean corne or wampham" up to the value of thirty pounds and for the second half year "wheate and pease good and merchantable according to the generall Currant price." In addition he received two pounds of butter per year for every milk cow owned by the members of the congregation.[5] His successors likewise received their salaries in kind.

The locality of Branford was attractive enough. Southeast of New Haven and fronting on Long Island Sound, the township covered an area that extended ten miles inland, by grant of General Court,[6] and was a favorite resort of the Indians for wild game and shellfish. For ten years or more Branford, which took its name from Brentford, suburb of London,[7] was called, by Indians and white men alike, Totoket, "place of the tidal river."[8] Attracted here by the "good hunting" of the region, Indian tribes came from some distance, a circumstance alarming to both the white settlers and the friendly Indians, who had sold the land to New Haven Colony in 1638. The Mohawks were especially feared, and at the six-foot palisades surrounding the church there was always a settler on watch for Indian marauders while his fellow townsmen attended the service.[9] By Wise's time, however, the vigilance had slackened. The town then believed its authority so feared that it could promulgate a law that no strange Indian could hunt or kill deer within its bounds. According to the law he could be challenged and his gun taken from him, but one wonders if it would not have been an unusually hardy, if not foolhardy, settler who would have attempted the seizure of an Indian's weapon.[10]

The Branford meetinghouse was probably primitive. When it was built, soon after the town's first settlement, in 1644, by a group of colonists from Wethersfield, Connecticut, it may not have been much more than a log shelter provided with a roof of sedge grasses and with log benches resting on an earthen floor.[11] Improvements, such as a board floor and ceiling, were doubtless added during Pierson's devoted ministry of twenty years; still, it is unlikely that Wise found such refinements as a steeple and pews.

Wise may have had an inkling of the disturbed state of the Branford church before he came, for the controversy in which its minister Abraham Pierson had been deeply involved was one that had shaken all Connecticut. Pierson had led several families to Branford from Southampton, Long Island, in order that they might live in a colony where only church members could become freemen. When the charter of 1662 included New Haven Colony within the limits and under the jurisdiction of Connecticut, a colony where the franchise was not limited to church members, Pierson, John Davenport, of New Haven, and others rose to do battle for their church-state. But to no avail. The charter that authorized the union of the two colonies could not now be changed, and Pierson determined to remove to a region where his church-state ideas might be practiced. He signed a "plantation covenant" with twenty-two members of his congregation to remove to Newark,[12] and these men and others from nearby towns made the journey in the fall of 1666 and spring of 1667.[13] After Pier-

son's removal, those interested in maintaining a church gathered and in an agreement signed by forty-odd pledged their
support to "Congregationall Principles." They agreed that
an orthodox minister should be called and maintained.[14] For
several years they sought to bestow a permanent settlement
upon John Bowers, but were unable to do so. When Bowers
was at last about to give up his temporary ministry, in the
winter of 1672, certain members were designated to consult
a Mr. Eliot to find a suitable candidate. If this was Mr. John
Eliot, of Roxbury, as it may well have been, he could have
recommended Wise, a boy who had grown up in his church.[15]

Wise had served the congregation at Branford for three
years when he was called into the army. On January 14, 1676,
he was assigned to a chaplaincy in the forces of Connecticut
colony, then engaged in the war with King Philip that had
broken out the previous spring.[16]

Since the outbreak the Indians had had things much their
own way, marauding and ambushing over a wide area. The
first important victory for the colonies had come in December
in the Great Swamp fight, forced upon the supposedly neutral
Narragansetts.[17] This tribe had been driven out of its winter
quarters in Rhode Island, and to prevent its reorganization
and alliance with other hostile tribes the January campaign,
in which Wise engaged, was undertaken.

The Council wrote a letter to Wise ordering him "to goe
forth minister to or army" and join Major Robert Treat, who
was then gathering the Connecticut forces at New London
for a march to Smith's Landing in the Rhode Island country
in order to meet the troops of the other colonies. Wise complied with this order, and left for Smith's Landing with Major
Treat on January 26.[18] The rendezvous was reached next
day, and the Connecticut contingent of three hundred
brought the assembled forces to a total of fourteen hundred.[19]

Then began a movement against the Indians, who were supposed to be seated eight or ten miles northwest of Providence,
about twenty-five miles from Smith's Landing. This was
known as the "hungry march." Inadequately provisioned in
the beginning, by the time the army reached Marlboro,
Massachusetts, where it was disbanded, the troops were re-
duced to eating ground nuts and even their horses. The Indians were in as bad a plight. At one spot twenty-five miles
from Warwick, Rhode Island, the troops came upon the
skeleton heads of sixty horses, which the Indians had slaugh-
tered for food.[20] The Narragansetts moved ahead of the
troops and only a few were captured. By the time Marlboro
was reached, on Tuesday, the third of February, the paucity
of supplies halted the pursuit. The various bodies of
troops were dismissed and went to the separate colonies,
Major Treat's forces reaching Hartford Saturday, February
7.[21] Riding horseback, Wise could have arrived in Branford
the following morning in time to hear the drummer summon-
ing the congregation to church.[22]

So far he had known only a short period of severe depriva-
tion and physical hardship, and of the hostile Indians he had
seen only a few worn-out old men, some squaws, and children.
There had been little loss among the troops themselves, and
he could not have seen much bloodshed.[23] This tour of military duty may have been all he wanted, for there is no record
of his going out again during the Indian troubles of those
years, but whatever his experience had been, he considered it
extensive enough to warrant his speaking with authority during a later war.[24]

If Wise had remained in the field against King Philip, it
seems that there would have been some hint. The Reverend
Gershom Bulkeley, who as surgeon also accompanied the
Connecticut troops on the march to Marlboro, is frequently

mentioned in the annals of the war.[25] But however long or
short his tour as chaplain, Wise resumed his duties as minister at Branford after it was over.

And he added to his dignity by accepting a new honor.
Three years having passed since he was graduated from Harvard, he made application for the Master's degree, and at the
commencement of 1676, along with his old classmate Samuel
Angier, he received it. He took part in the commencement
exercises by an affirmative argument on the question *An impossible sit Mundum fuisse ab aeterno*—whether it is impossible that the world has existed from all eternity.[26]

Not until late in 1677 did Wise take up another ministry,
and then only after obtaining permission to leave his Branford charge. Evidently he had promised to stay at Branford
throughout the winter, and the townspeople reminded him of
his promise. Wise, notwithstanding permission from the Hatfield church to stay through the winter at Branford, desired
to be in Hatfield and promised to come in November. Wise's
Branford congregation, perceiving his desire, did not stand
in his way, but "left him to his liberty as god should direct
him to go or stay."[27] Writing to Increase Mather on November 29 of that year, Solomon Stoddard, pastor at the neighboring town of Northampton, reported: "Mr. Wise is come
to Hatfield."[28]

Wise came to replace the town's first minister, Hope Atherton, who had died the previous June, weakened and half-
demented by the exposure and hardships of an expedition
against the Indians.[29] Even at this time, more than a year
after Philip's death, which had virtually ended the war, Wise
found Hatfield half in ruins and in the process of rebuilding.
For not only had the village suffered the loss of several lives
and the destruction of a number of its dwellings from attacks
of savages during the war, but on September 19, 1677, after

most hostilities had ceased, Indians had fallen upon a group of men outside the palisades, killed three of them and nine more persons inside the inclosure, set fire to seven houses, and carried off captive to Canada seventeen men, women, and children.[30] This was indeed a blow to a town that had had scarcely fifty houses before the war.[31] Probably in proportion to their population, no other towns in the Connecticut valley, except deserted Deerfield and Northfield, ever suffered so greatly.[32]

Notwithstanding its trials, Hatfield welcomed Wise and provided him with quarters. It is to be doubted that he stayed in the Atherton house, for by the terms of the settlement of Atherton, that was to go to his heirs if he died in office;[33] not until after Wise's departure did the Atherton family move away and the house revert to the ownership of the town.[34]

In addition to the house set upon a home-lot of eight acres and a portion of meadowland allotted to Atherton, there had been the allowance of his annual salary of sixty pounds, two thirds payable in wheat and one third in pork.[35] Wise's salary was probably comparable to Atherton's.

When the resources of the town and the small membership of the church are considered, the minister's salary seems no small item. Of the nine men who worked for the gathering of the Hatfield church, only six were members of any church,[36] and on the petition for a church separate from Hadley's, addressed to the General Court, May 3, 1667, there were only twenty-five names.[37] While the potential congregation of the westside group had increased from ninety in 1667 to a number between 300 and 350 in 1678, still there were only forty-eight tax payers in the latter year.[38] The church at Hadley fought the breaking away of the Hatfield parishioners, who felt inclement weather and an uncertain river crossing put their loyalty to too severe a test. There was no regular ferry between the towns until 1692,[39] and the settlers paddled back and forth in canoes and boats of their own making.

The westside proprietors not only cited the inconvenience and hardship of the often hazardous crossing but also objected that many, because of weakness and age, could not make the trip and that the departure to church across the river of all the able-bodied men left the settlement unguarded and open to attack. Indeed, they argued so sensibly that in spite of the opposition to the movement by John Russell and members of his congregation the General Court granted leave to form a church November 7, 1668.[40] Then the business of getting a minister, providing him with a home, and building a meetinghouse was taken care of.

The meetinghouse, built in the village street, was thirty feet square with a four-sided roof and a turret and a bell. It had galleries, and the pulpit was at the west end of the building with an aisle going to the doors in the east. By the time Wise arrived it may have had real glass in its windows and smoothed wooden pews for its seats.[41] Thus, for more than a year before the town was incorporated in May, 1670, and even before it had an official name—honoring one of the three Hatfields in England[42]—the settlement had a church and a regular preacher.[43]

When Wise came to Hatfield, the town was mourning its losses of the previous September and was in a state of anxiety over the fate of the captives. But Benjamin Waite and Stephen Jennings, whose wives and children were among the captives, made the trip to Canada in the dead of winter and, after negotiation with the French authorities, brought about the release of the whole group, except for three who had been murdered. This rescue engaged the interest of the whole colony. The two hundred pounds which the General Court

had promised to raise for ransom money the colony oversub-
scribed by one hundred and forty-five pounds.[44]

The fortunes of Hatfield were again bright. The townspeople besought Wise, who had presumably taken some part
in improving those fortunes, to settle among them perma-
nently and accommodated him in his desire for some of the
choice land of the town.[45] He signed the oath of allegiance—
an act to make him a freeman—in February, 1679.[46] Meantime, on December 5, 1678, he had married Abigail Gardner.[47]
Sixth in a family of ten children, Abigail was the daughter of
Thomas Gardner, of Muddy River, now Brookline, wealthy
suburban district of Boston.[48] Thomas Gardner, though not
a resident of the town, was a member of the Roxbury congregation, a not unusual circumstance, for the Muddy River
people, as well as those of West Roxbury and Jamaica Plain,
went to church at Roxbury.[49] Moreover, he was a generous
supporter of the church, a fact which bears some witness to
his worldly prosperity.[50] To the building of the new meetinghouse at Roxbury in 1672 Gardner gave more than any of
his fellow townsmen from Muddy River except one, and that
one only equalled, did not surpass, Gardner's gift of ten
pounds.[51] Probably John Wise had known his wife—just his
own age[52]—from childhood, and their love and marriage may
have been based upon years of association and knowledge of
each other.

But neither his marriage nor his acquisition of land and of
freemanship made him content to remain at Hatfield. Indeed,
he looked elsewhere for a permanent settlement, though he
was not to have the good luck to find a church that was more
firmly established than the first two he had served. The separation of the Chebacco branch from the mother church in
Ipswich was even more recent than the schism at either Branford or Hatfield. In fact, Wise found the struggle still going

on when he began to preach at Chebacco—now Essex, Massachusetts—in May, 1680.[53] There may be some significance in the fact that Wise was almost habitually drawn to recently separated parishes. Perhaps he was regarded as a peacemaker, or as a good fighter.

The desire for a church in the Chebacco River area south of Ipswich had been growing with each passing season. As the residents of this area made their four-, five-, six-, and even seven-mile journeys[54] to the Ipswich church, facing into the stormy winds of the north and the sleets and snows driven in from the ocean, their resolution to form a church more convenient to their homes must have been fired anew. At Ipswich they sat in a frosty meetinghouse, listening to the lengthy sermons of William Hubbard, member of the first graduating class of Harvard and historian of King Philip's War. Their only chance for warmth came when, between morning and afternoon service, they could go to the homes of friends or to the "nooning house"—a makeshift structure where fires could be built and man and beast sheltered and fed. Once afternoon service was over, then began the long, numbing trek homeward. And it was not the winter season alone that afflicted. Every season seemed to have its drawbacks. In addition to the cold of winter and the heat of summer, there was "ye excessive mieryness & Dirtynesse of . . . [the] waies in the Spring & fall." These ways led over "low & clay land, & partly Rockey," which made the journey "very tedious & uncomfortable both to . . . [them] & ye creatures."[55]

The Chebacco residents took the first step toward forming another church at a meeting held in William Cogswell's house in February, 1677. There they drew up a petition desiring liberty from the town of Ipswich to call a minister to preach among them, "but the Towne would not grant it neither did they seme to refuse it but would not vote conserning it." Besides the petition, several of the Chebacco inhabitants "had discours with most of the cheife of both towne and church." So cornered, "by themselves they would seem to be willing." Even William Hubbard, the teacher of the Ipswich church, had nothing against a minister preaching among them if the Chebacco people would continue to pay their rates at Ipswich. This conversation was later sworn to by Thomas Low and William Goodhue, two men of Chebacco.[56] Still there was no action taken by the town: "when the matter [was] in hand there woad be nothing done." In some impatience, then, Chebacco residents addressed the General Court in a petition dated May 23, 1677. The petitioners, forty-one of them, complained that the Ipswich people would call no town meeting to consider their grievances, and they cited a number of reasons why they wanted a church separate from the one at Ipswich. They spoke against the long toilsome ways, which caused them to spend a "great part of the Lord's holy Saboth . . . in servile labour . . ." and the inclement weather, which kept the children at home, away from the edifying Word, and the little meetinghouse, which could not accommodate all the parishioners.[57] While the Court made no decision on the matter and referred the petitioners to the town of Ipswich for settlement, still it stipulated that the town make responsible answer at the October sitting of the Court.[58]

On the first of October a petition was drawn up for Chebacco and sent to the town meeting of Ipswich. It requested leave to build a meetinghouse and to hire a minister, but on the condition that the Chebacco members be released from supporting the Ipswich ministry. If that proposal were unacceptable, then would not the Ipswich people join in building a meetinghouse more convenient to Chebacco, and the people of both communities support both ministries?[59]

Having received no answer from the town, Chebacco residents submitted this petition to show that the Court's order
had been fulfilled and requested a hearing of the case. But
the Ipswich people had answered the Court about the
Chebacco petition—on the same day that it was submitted.
The Ipswich document gave a list of reasons why the petition
should not be granted, arguing that the inconveniences were
not intolerable, but such as had been deliberately chosen,
that the proposal of another meetinghouse would "ease very
few," and that more room would be provided in the old
meetinghouse by additional construction. The General Court
then made answer that for the present the Chebacco petition
would not be granted, but that Ipswich should look to the
accommodation of the petitioners.[60]

In the interest of accommodation a town meeting was held
at Ipswich on the 19th of February, 1678. Chebacco representatives were present, but reported, "We could atain nothing but many impertinent alegations to while us of[f]." Some
seemed willing for Chebacco to call a minister, but it was
"only seemingly." The selectmen begged to be excused from
any decision until Mr. Hubbard, their teacher, returned from
England. While the Chebacco men replied—with some as-
perity—that the General Court had recommended the petition for consideration some time before Mr. Hubbard left,
still they would await his return and "not goe to the court for
any further order," if the town would grant them a minister
at that time.[61] Ipswich made answer in writing, and in April,
1678, supplied the General Court with a copy. It urged the
Chebacco people to forbear in their petitioning because of
the unsettled conditions arising from the Indian wars and the
attendant heavy expenses, because of the example that would
be set other distant parishioners, and because of the absence
of Mr. Hubbard.[62]

Petitioning went on nevertheless. A petition in this same month requested liberty to call Jeremiah Shepard to preach to the Chebacco group and avowed the willingness of the people there not only to bear the expenses of building a meetinghouse and the maintenance of a minister but also to continue their rates to the Ipswich ministers as long as Hubbard and Cobbet lived.[63] This petition seemed to meet with more favor than any previous one, for at a meeting in January, 1679, the selectmen of Ipswich did not deny Chebacco liberty to call a minister or disapprove of Jeremiah Shepard, whom the petitioners had "pitched upon" to preach to them. Before the end of the month Shepard was preaching in a private house, but the Chebacco residents were under some disadvantage to hear him. There could be found no room big enough to hold his listeners, who may have numbered as many as two hundred and fifty, so it was determined to build "a plain house" and seek permission from the town or General Court to put it to use as a meetinghouse.[64]

In the meantime, the Chebacco residents, finding the support of two ministries more than they could bear, reconsidered their previous commitment and requested either a release from supporting the Ipswich church or help in maintaining Shepard. It was further desired that "a few rods of ground by Goodm̄ Varneys" be granted "to Set a meeting house upon."[65] This request, submitted early in February, alarmed Ipswich. Here were substantial contributors slipping away. Steps had to be taken to bring them back. First, Shepard had to be scared off. Accordingly, "an honnorable brother of the church of ipswich" sent him a letter expressing the town's dissatisfaction with the irregularity of Chebacco's proceedings and urging an end to his preaching. Shepard read the letter at meeting on February 23 and presumably desisted from preaching thereafter. Chebacco representatives demanded that the Ipswich selectmen call a town meeting for a vote on allowing Shepard to preach, but this request was finally denied April 16, 1679.[66]

Ipswich had already put in a call for the General Court to exert its authority to stop Chebacco's separatist activities. The Ipswich petition declared that the Chebacco inhabitants "have fallen short of their wonted patience and respect to the body to which they belonged for neer thirty yeares [and under which] without any complaint they have borne what now they call insupportable." Indeed, they had been busy gathering materials to build a meetinghouse on land owned by William Cogswell "neare to Thomas Varney's," a site approved several months later at an Ipswich town meeting.[67] But at this time the Ipswich petition complained of these preparations for building, as well as of the choice of Shepard for preacher. The Governor's Council acted on the same day this petition was submitted. It ordered Chebacco residents to quit building until they obtained permission to build from the town and church of Ipswich or allowance from General Court. Jeremiah Shepard was to refuse the invitation of Chebacco in order not "to make any disturbance in the church & Towne of Ipswitch."[68] Ipswich laid further restraining orders on Chebacco. But by the time the Council's order was issued, timbers for the meetinghouse were in place ready to raise and the sills were laid.[69]

For a church that upheld the Cambridge Platform of 1648, wherein the gathering of a new church upon just cause was espoused,[70] the Ipswich body mightily opposed the efforts of the Chebacco group. The Ipswich church had denied any just cause for the formation of another parish, evidently believing its members not numerous enough for division, though Ipswich was thought at this time to be the second town in the colony.[71]

But the Chebacco cause had now enlisted the sympathies of the womenfolk; and since the Ipswich order forbade only the men from building the meetinghouse, Goodwives William Goodhue, Thomas Varney, and Abraham Martin undertook, with the aid of Goodman Martin and his hired man, John Chub, to raise the meetinghouse themselves. The women even recruited, unknown to their husbands, helpers from the nearby communities of Gloucester and Manchester, to whom the Ipswich order did not apply. The efforts of these workers proved so successful that the town constable soon came hurrying down from Ipswich with a warrant for the arrest of all the above-named persons.[72]

Resenting the effrontery of Chebacco in raising a meeting-house, the Ipswich church and town were now in the mood for apologies and, by remonstrances and by withholding the sacrament from the offenders, obtained them.[73] General Court also required an apology and prescribed the form that should be used. On May 28 those who were "delinquents in erecting a meetinghouse" were informed of their punishment, and a month later they appeared in the Salem Court to acknowl-edge: "we are conuinced that wee haue offended in being actiue to erect a meting hous contrary to the aduis and pro-hobession of the Counsell for which we are sory desier it may be forgiuen."[74]

Yet favorable ecclesiastical weather for Chebacco was about to set in. On May 29, 1679, "ye Inhabitants of Che-bacho" submitted another petition to General Court. This was a carefully drawn up document. It rehearsed briefly the fate of earlier petitions and announced the inducements that had led to this one. First was religion, "the main end of our Fathers Crossing the Vast Ocean, & pitching their Tents in this Western pt of the World." The inconveniences of dis-tance and weather were cited again, and the account of an aged woman dying from exposure on Sabbath day was given as a case in point. About the same time this petition was submitted, a declaration and vindication of the Chebacco proceedings was handed in. This paper summarized in detail the efforts of the past two years.[75]

A hearing was now granted the petitioners for the 6th of June, and the Ipswich selectmen were notified to be present or send delegates. But Ipswich relied on the defense of her representatives in the Court and sent no delegates. The day after the hearing, the Court granted the petition of Chebacco and gave permission to procure a minister, "provided he be Able, pious, & orthodox, wch ye law Desires." It declared itself satisfied with the humility of the Chebacco men for their offenses and ordered Ipswich to accommodate them. Furthermore, it appointed a committee of five, headed by Joseph Dudley, to look into Chebacco affairs and make report.[76] About this time fifty-one Ipswich townsmen chimed in with the finding of the Court and proclaimed themselves willing that their Chebacco neighbors "should inioye the preaching of the word of god."[77]

The report of the committee, submitted in July, recommended the establishment of Chebacco parish and the calling of some good preacher, but not Shepard until he joined a church. A second report, in October, underscored the recommendations of the first one.[78] Shepard still neglected to join a church, so Chebacco undertook to find another minister.

While a minister was being sought for, the parish went ahead with the building of its meetinghouse, the frame of which had been allowed to stand. So, when John Wise came, in May, 1680, after being unanimously agreed upon by the people for their minister and approved by General Court,[79] he found a plain, sturdy building. There was neither turret nor bell; these were to be added a year or so later, the turret "after the fashion and proportions of the territ at and-over."[80] Inside, a gallery was built at the same time as the turret. There were few pews; they would be built one or two at a time as the people could afford them.

But the affairs of the Chebacco people were not yet straightened out. They had to be released as members from the Ipswich church; otherwise, they were required by the ordinances of the church to continue their contributions for its support. In October, 1680, they petitioned General Court for release and obtained its approval.[81] Ipswich granted the release in February, 1681.[82]

The Chebacco residents, August 31, 1681, formally agreed to gather a church, and on September 6 invited the Ipswich church to join in its organization.[83] But the new church, for some reason, was not organized until two years later, and a formal call was not extended to John Wise until February, 1682, long after he had begun his ministry in it.

The formal organization of the church and the installation of Wise on August 12, 1683, doubtless waited upon the satisfaction of members and minister alike. As stated in the Cambridge platform: "It is meet, that before any be ordained or chosen officers, they should first be tryed & proved; because hands are not suddenly to be laid upon any, & both Elders & Deacons must be of honest & good report."[84] When there was no question about the approval of the people and the contentment of Wise, then the last triumphant measures might be taken. With the contentment of Wise in mind, the Chebacco residents offered a generous maintenance. On February 21, 1682, forty-three Chebacco men signed an agreement to provide Wise with "three-score pounds a year, forty pounds of it in pork, corn and mualt and twenty pounds of it in mony together with ye contrebution of strangers." They also engaged to bring yearly "to mr wises house so much wood in cord wood as shall be suffitient for his use" and to provide so much marsh every year as would yield him eight loads of hay. Further, they allowed him and his heirs forever ten acres of land if "it pleas god to continue him and incline his hart to take office amongst us." There was another proposition in the agreement; Wise could, if the terms already cited did not satisfy, take "twenty pound every year in corn together with a free contribution of all both inhabitants and strangers together with the land and wood and hay as before mentioned." According to the evidence of salary payment, Wise agreed to the first set of terms. In May ten more acres of land and a house "after the manner and forme of Samuell Giddinges" were promised.[85]

As the years went by, Wise's salary[86] was increased, at first by twenty pounds if he would find his own hay and wood and keep the parsonage in repair. Later there were other raises, and his acreage was enlarged.[87] All this was provided by approximately forty families, numbering scarcely more than two hundred and fifty men, women, and children.

Wise had finally got a permanent settlement. He could now adopt the quiet habits of a village pastor, acquire a library, and work his land. In the pleasant country alongside Chebacco River and near the sea, he could rear his children and give them a comfortable home. His family was rapidly growing. Jeremiah had been born in November, 1679,[88] and he was followed by Lucy, Joseph, Ammi Ruhamah,[89] Mary, Henry, and John. Wise must have rejoiced in the security that he could provide his family. Seemingly, peace was his, and serene years of fruitful ministry lay ahead. But in the quiet Chebacco country he was not to remain untouched by events in the colony. He lived in compelling days.

CHAPTER IV

For a Good God and a Good King

As WISE MERGED HIMSELF with the life of the community
and his congregation came to value him as friend and pastor,
the power of Massachusetts Bay Colony, despite the desperate grasp of many of its leaders, slipped from it. The Royal
Charter, granted as an encouragement to a trading company
and an infant settlement, was now deemed too generous, and
the growing and prospering colony must be "hauled up
short" to enrich the mother country. In 1676 came the agent
of the Lords of Trade, the odious Edward Randolph, with a
royal missive demanding that Governor Leverett and his
Assistants—the upper branch of General Court—send representatives to England. There they were to answer charges
against the colony for violation of the Navigation Acts.[1]
Randolph himself was to hand in a report on New England,
and that report later emboldened the King and councillors
to act against the colony.[2]

Representatives of course were sent to England, but their
efforts proved ineffectual. The charter was abrogated in 1684,
and Joseph Dudley, one of the chief representatives of the
colony in England, was blamed for its loss. This blame became surer and more abusive when Dudley assumed the reins
of the interim government until the problems of colonial administration could be threshed out. The Lords of Trade
recommended a council for the governor and even an elected
assembly whenever he thought it necessary, but the Duke of
York (later James II) and others of the party for the Crown,

jealous of the royal prerogative and suspicious of popular representation, overruled the latter suggestion and decreed that for levying taxes and like important matters the colony needed no assembly.[3] When Governor Edmund Andros arrived, late in 1686, and began, with soldierly impatience and tactless arrogance, to impose the royal will, the already existing dissatisfaction and resentment of the people grew apace.

Careless of religious prejudice, he asked the Boston ministers to let the Old South Meetinghouse, which was the meeting place of the Third Church, serve also as an Episcopal chapel. When the ministers refused, Andros, in high-handed manner, "borrowed" the building one Good Friday and authorized its use from that time on for Episcopal services.[4] Also, as a soldier performing the will of his sovereign, he insisted on enforcing the Navigation Acts, which required trade with England. The enforcement, because Massachusetts dealt in much the same exports as England, stifled the colony's sea trade.[5] In addition, the removal of all public records to Boston, the expensive administration of justice, and the invalidation of land titles were measures hateful to the people.

According to royal instructions, Andros at first tried to use the old tax laws, but, because of the loss of the charter, the colony had repealed the tax laws to embarrass the new government. So, March 3, 1687, Andros signed into law "An Act for the continuing and establishing of several Rates, Duties and Imposts," which required all male residents sixteen years old and upwards to pay a poll tax of twenty pence and a tax of a penny a pound on all property real or personal, "according to the rate of cattle hereafter mentioned."[6] The property tax has been estimated at the rate of four dollars a thousand.[7] It was not an exorbitant tax or dissimilar to some imposed upon the colony in the past, but it was not laid by the elected representatives of the people, and the rate was not to be decided by the town meetings, a practice the colonists had become thoroughly used to. Its passage would have been doubtful even under the Andros government, for the tax law was hotly debated and not voted on in council, but suddenly decreed by Andros to the surprise and disgust of some of the councillors.[8] The only choice left to the people of each town was the election of a town tax commissioner. The tax commissioner, working with the selectmen of the town, was every August to prepare a tax roll with a list of assessments. These findings were to be sent to the treasurer of the colony, after the commissioners had met in the county towns the first Wednesday in September for the purpose of correcting and perfecting their lists. The approved lists were then to be returned to the towns and put into the hands of the town constables for collection before the twentieth of November.[9]

Events like these did not leave Chebacco village unruffled. The pro-charter party was strong, especially in Essex County. All the towns in the county except three refused at first to obey the tax law of Andros.[10] And the most unbending in its opposition, not only in Essex County but in all New England, was Ipswich. Its protestation has been designated "one of the notable cases of resistance in colonial times,"[11] and the town seal bears today these words: "The Birthplace of American Independence, 1687."

In the forefront of town leadership marched John Wise. He was, as his funeral oration stated, ever "Zealously Affected towards his Country, and the Civil & Sacred Liberties and Priviledges of his Country: And was willing to Sacrifice any thing, but a good Conscience, to Secure and Defend them."[12] So, when the town, upon receipt of the Treasurer's warrant implementing the tax act, held meetings to determine its actions, Wise was there, and in dead earnest.

The first meeting was held at the house of the Ipswich

town clerk, John Appleton, Junior, on the night of August 22, 1687. Here the selectmen and other leading citizens of the town had assembled.[13] Those who bore subsequent trial with Wise were present: John Andrews, selectman and lieutenant of the town militia, who was to moderate the meeting; John Appleton, Junior, selectman and town clerk; Robert Kinsman, selectman and quartermaster of the militia; Constable Thomas French; and William Goodhue, Junior, deacon in the Chebacco church. The pastor of the Ipswich church, William Hubbard, was present, and other town and militia officers.[14]

John Andrews, the moderator of the meeting and a Chebacco parishioner, was in a position to invite his pastor and deacon to be present. Indeed, as leaders of Chebacco church, their presence could have been insisted upon. On such an errand a deacon and a minister whose properties adjoined could easily have made the five-mile journey to Ipswich together. There they would join the twelve or fourteen men of the town gathered at John Appleton's house.[15]

After the meeting was called to order by Moderator John Andrews, Constable French read the warrant that he had received from the colony's treasurer, John Usher. This warrant contained the provisions of the tax act and carried the instructions needed to put it to work. Whether to comply with the act or deny it was the question. The men assembled on this night ended by denying it. Wise said that they "did Discourse, & Conclude yt it was not ye townes Dutie any wayes to Assist yt ill Methode of Raising mony wtout a Generall Assembly, wch was apparently intended by abovesaid Sr Edmond & his Councill."[16]

Once a decision had been reached, plans could be made for the town meeting on the following day, and the group could adjourn. The band of leaders assembled at John Appleton's, aware of the feelings of the townspeople, knew that it could

count on their opposition to the tax measure. Still, to present
the issue clearly to the people and to direct them to an effective action, Wise and others may have been chosen to address
the town meeting. For Wise did speak the next day, August
23, 1687.

But he was not the only one who spoke. Constable French
testified that Moderator Andrews and Town Clerk Appleton,
as well as Wise, spoke at the meeting,[17] and the warrant for
Wise's arrest has suggested another speaker, William Howlett. Howlett attended the earlier meeting at John Appleton's
house, and the warrant that called for Wise's arrest called for
his, for they both "Did particularly Excite and Stur up his
Majesties subjects to Refractoryness and Disobedience—
contrary to and in high contempt of his Majties Laws and
Government here Established."[18]

Howlett, of course, joined in the vote against the election
of a tax commissioner for the town, but so did many townsmen who were not arrested. The activity for which Howlett
was arrested was similar to Wise's, but it took place in
another Essex county town. Howlett carried a "seditious
paper," the record of the Ipswich vote, to Topsfield in order
to promote a similar action in the town meeting there on
August 30. At this meeting, upon the urging of Howlett and
two others, one of whom was probably a relative, Selectman
Samuel Howlett,[19] nineteen of the prominent men of the
town voted down the election of a tax commissioner. So, it
would seem that Howlett's chief oppositional actions, while
by no means unworthy or timid, occurred outside his native
Ipswich. French did not mention him as a speaker at the
Ipswich town meeting, but he did mention the other two, who
probably acted only in an organizational capacity.

It would be the duty of John Andrews to take charge of
the meeting and lay the issue before the people and the duty

of John Appleton to read the treasurer's warrant. But for
John Wise, who held no office and did not even live in the
town, what purpose could there be in his speaking to the
people if he were not to exhort them to hold firmly to their
convictions and to direct them to a proper action? At any
rate, Wise's words were the ones that were remembered. Wise,
in his speech at this meeting, told the people that they "had
a good God, & a good King, and Should Do Well to Stand
for . . . [their] previledges."[20]

Or at any rate these words represented Wise's own version
of what he said, for they come from the complaint that he and
four others drew up in 1689 to help the colony substantiate
its charges against Andros.[21] But John Appleton, in his testimony before Andros, said that Wise "spoak agt. raising mony
without an Assembly." On the same occasion Appleton
pointed out his own part in the town meeting: that of drawing up the record of the town vote. After it was unanimously
decided not to comply with the treasurer's warrant, he withdrew from the meeting, under the direction of John Andrews,
to set down the action of the town. When he returned with
the written account, it was read and approved at the meeting,
and a copy sent to the Governor's Council.[22] This last was a
bold act, and the recipients must have been not a little
amazed at the temerity of Ipswich when they read:

At a Legall Town meeting Augst; 23 assembled by Vertue of an
order from Jno Usher Esqr Treasurr; for choosing a Comissionr; to Joyne wt ye Selectmen to Assesse ye Inhabitants, according to an act of His Excellie; ye Govrnr & Councill fr; Laying of
Rates; ye Towne yn considring yt ye Sd act doth Infringe yr
Libertie as free=borne English Subjects of his Majestie by Interfeiring wt ye Statute Lawes of ye Land, by wch it was Enacted
yt no taxes Should be Levyed on ye Subjects wtout Consent of
an Assembly Choasen by ye free=holders, for Assessing of ye
Same, they Do therfore Vote yt they are not willing to Choose a

Comissionr for Such an End wtout Sd Previledge; & more
over Consent not yt ye Selectmen do proceed to Lay any Such
Rate untill it be appointed by a Genll; Assembly Concurring wt
ye Govrnr & Councill.[23]

The publication of the Ipswich vote Andros and Council
found particularly reprehensible and no doubt thought the
transmission of a copy to the governing body of Massachusetts an act of impudent effrontery. But Ipswich did not take
its stand alone; other towns were following suit. Haverhill
refused to elect a tax commissioner. So did Andover.[24] Rowley and Topsfield, with the record of the Ipswich vote before
the town councils, would not honor the treasurer's warrant.[25]
If this disregard for governmental authority was to be
stopped, repressive measures had to be applied. And they
were. Within a month many arrests and commitments to
prison had been made, and Andros was besieged by letters of
the most humble apology from participants in the protestation.

The Governor and his Council especially directed their
authority against Ipswich. On September 14 an order to seize
the town book was issued. Herein was recorded the rebellious
action of the town meeting, and the book could thus be used
as important evidence against the people.[26] Joseph Dudley
and Peter Bulkeley of the Governor's Council, sitting as
magistrates at Ipswich, brought action against the town and
at the same time served formal notice upon some residents of
Ipswich and those of other towns to appear before the
Council.[27]

The warrant for Wise's arrest, however, came directly from
the Governor, at Boston. There were two copies drawn, one
dated the fifteenth and the other the sixteenth, but the latter
was doubtless the official one, for it was more legibly written
and the only one that was signed. It called for, as has been

stated, the apprehension of both Wise and William Howlett
and required their appearance before council.[28] On this same
day, the sixteenth, John Andrews, John Appleton, and
Thomas French, having been called before the Governor, told
in detail the events of the town meetings and implicated
Wise.[29] From this implication doubtless came the warrant for
his arrest.

Andros's Council had forty-two members, but at the
majority of the meetings not more than ten members were
usually present. Randolph, Dudley, Stoughton, and Usher
were the most regular in attendance.[30] On September 21,
these and eight others, counting Andros, sat in council.[31] Besides this group, there were present certain ones in secretarial
and clerical capacity. One of these was Deputy Secretary
John West, a New York merchant to whom Randolph farmed
out his office as secretary for 150 pounds a year and who had
served Andros as secretary when he was Governor of New
York.[32]

Wise and several of his townsmen were brought before this
group and examined. They were charged with "contempt &
High Misdemeanor" and directed to stand trial.[33] At this
hearing were spoken the most disturbing sentences of the
entire court proceedings against Wise and friends. Apologies
for repeating these statements give evidence of the time they
were spoken. One such apology, "the humble Petition of
Francis Wainwright," a resident of Ipswich, was drawn up
because the petitioner had "inconsiderately rehearsed & repeated some words or expressions proceeding from Mr. John
Wise which he declared to have passed from John West Esqr.
at the time of sd. Wise upon his Examination before yor. Excellency and Councill." This apology was dated September
24, and the trial was not held until October 3. Wainwright
went on to say what he had repeated: upon Wise's "asserting

the priviledges of Englishmen according to Magna Charta,
It was replyed to him that wee had no further priviledge reserved saveing to be exempted from being Sold for Slaves, or
to like Effect."[34] Wise's version of the statements, set down
in 1689 in the formal complaint against Andros, was not
much different, but is the familiar one: "Mr. Wise you have
no more previledges Left you yn not to be Sould for Slaves."[35]
These were words indeed, and it was no wonder that "when
the People heard this, they lookt upon themselves in a manner Lost."[36]

Wainwright's apology to the authorities did not keep
others from talking. On October 12 two petitioners, who stood
"bound by Recogniscance for appearance at the next Court
of Grand Assise for the County of Suffolke to answer for re-
hearsing and divulgeing some words reflecting upon John
West Esqr. said to be reported by mr. John Wise as proceeding from sd. mr. West at the time of sd. Wise his examination
before yor. Excellency and Councill," sued for the Governor's
pardon and "a Supersedeas to the said Recogniscances."
These petitioners, in their abjectness, even denied believing
the report that West spoke as he did.[37]

West's words have usually been ascribed to Joseph Dudley,[38] and the formal complaint of Wise and his fellow sufferers might lead one so to ascribe them. And of course Dudley could have echoed West then or later. But in an earlier
complaint, dated May 3, 1689, and subscribed to by Wise,
John Appleton, John Andrews, Robert Kinsman, William
Goodhue, and Thomas French, even West did not get the
credit for the hateful words. According to the report, they
came from Robert Mason, a member of the Council who was
present at the arraignment on September 21. However, West
spoke in similar vein. Also reported were some statements
of Andros, but whether they were spoken at the arraignment

or the trial cannot be discovered. It is likely, though, that they were spoken at the meeting of the Council, for Andros did not preside at the court of oyer and terminer on October 3. In this first complaint, then, briefer than the version written in December, 1689, it was stated:

And some of us can give in Testimonye yt prsons of ye. latter Governmt., declare us to be not much happyer yn Slaves, Viz: — Mr. Mason in Open Councill, sd: yt. we had no more Privilidge left us then not to be sold for Slaves, all ye. Councill manifested consent by their Silence.

Mr. D.[eputy] S:[ecretary] West Declared to some of us yt. we were a factious people and had no Privilidge left us.

The Governor Sr. Edmd. Andros sd: to some of us, By way of Ridicle [*sic*], whether we thought if Jac & Tom might tell the King what monyes he must have for the use of his Governmt. Implying that the people of the Country were but a pcill [parcel?] of ignerant Jacks & Tomes, and that he & his Crew had ye. immediat dispose of our Fortunes, and we were to be put to Bedlam for mad=men, as not knowing how to use an Estate wn we had gotten it though with never so much prudence pains & frugalitye.[39]

The charges later leveled at West and Andros support the account given above.[40] It would seem, then, that the reports that got abroad about the arraignment combined the statements of West and Mason, since they were similar, and gave sole authorship to West. Attributing the statements to Dudley probably derived in part from the account given in "A Memorial of the Present Deplorable State of New England," printed in 1707 by someone evilly disposed toward Dudley, and from the juxtaposition of Dudley's name to the statements made by "one of ye Judges" in the formal complaint of Wise and friends.[41] As Wise did not hesitate to credit Dudley with influencing the jury, why should he have hesitated to attribute other speeches to him? West and Mason, the latter one of the judges, were both present at the trial and could have repeated statements similar to those made at the examination on September 21.[42]

Wise and his townsmen now realized that their situation was hopeless. They could not look for justice from the Governor and his Council. The recent examination had sufficiently demonstrated the lack of it. They could no longer consider themselves Englishmen with rights and privileges hallowed by ancient and benign tradition. By the circumstances of history and in the isolation afforded by a broad ocean, they had made the mistake of thinking themselves Englishmen, but now they saw their error. They were English in descent truly, but they were Englishmen who lived outside England, and consequently without the rights and privileges of those who lived therein. Wise said: "We too bouldly Endaivred to perswade Orselves we were English men, & undr previledges."[43] Unless they were prepared for organized rebellion, with its attendant bloodshed, they had better submit. Wise and the rest of the New Englanders who had stood against a law springing from an unpopular and oppressive principle of government had hoped by their opposition to bring the authorities to the realization that they were dealing with a people long accorded a large measure of self-government. Their battle lost, Wise and his friends had now to give in to an arbitrary rule and to hope for better days.

To this end, a letter signed by Wise, the selectmen, and the constable of Ipswich was submitted on the day of Wise's arraignment. All of these men had been subjected to examination before Council, and out of their experience they wrote a letter of thorough acquiescence to the will of the government. They expressed their sorrow that they had fallen under Andros's displeasure and, praying for his and the Council's favor in overlooking their neglect of the treasurer's warrant, sued for him to put the law into effect.[44]

But no favor was granted. Wise and others were carried off
to the stone jail in Boston. The mittimus to the Suffolk
County sheriff concerning Wise and seven others bore the
date September 23,[45] and yet a letter written by Wise on that
same day gives evidence that he had already spent some time
in jail. Perhaps he was committed to jail immediately after
his examination before the Council, and the document au-
thorizing that commitment was not issued until a couple of
days later. At any rate, the favor Wise sought of the Governor and his Council was not granted when he wrote:

I Do Humbly Begg your Honours Licenc, that I may Bedd wt my
Relations at Roxburie Being very much Disadvantaged on the
account of my Naturall Rest Here wher I am, I have had But
Little Sleep Sinc I have Been your Prisoner, Here in towne, the
place Being so full of Company, I Dare not Be prolix at this time:
I shall be Ready In the Daytime to Attend the pleasure of the
Councell.[46]

Certainly Wise did have relatives in nearby Roxbury with
whom he could have stayed.[47] But the letter was not regarded. Nor was a third one submitted by Wise and eleven
others on September 27. In it they begged that bail might be
allowed and, as an argument for its allowance, feelingly
pleaded:

That it's no less afflictive than uncomfortable unto yor. Petrs. to
be confined, and deteined at so considerable distance from their
Familys and occasions, which they are very sensible must needs
deeply suffer by their long absence; most of yor. Petrs. Imploi-
ment & livelihood depending upon Husbandry, and the Season of
the year drawing on which will necessarily require their attendance and help in the gathering in their Indian Harvest &ca for the
support and provision for their Familys in the ensueing year.[48]

The abjectness of a petition and the enumeration of individual needs gained no sympathetic hearing for the petitioners. A selectman of Topsfield in his plea for pardon ex-

claimed: "I fall downe at your feet humbly baiging your marcy,"[49] and John Andrews, who had been moderator of the Ipswich town meeting, sought bail on the grounds that the "long confinement and the hardships of a Prison have [had] very sensible Effects upon his weake and crazey Body; which is attended with many Infirmities of old age, and his continuance there being likely greatly to impaire his health."[50] These pleas were disregarded. Andros and Council members were not touched and turned a deaf ear to all special pleaders.

Plans went ahead for Wise's trial, and a draft calling for the session of a court of oyer and terminer was drawn up September 28. Ten judges were named to the court, but three were to be a quorum, so all of those named to the court may not have been present.[51] Before this body on October 3 were brought the prisoners, Wise among them. They all answered not guilty to the charge of contempt and high misdemeanor; and

in Or, Defenc was pleaded ye Repeal of ye Law of Assesmts; upon ye place, also ye maga; Charta of England, & ye Statute Lawes yt Secure ye Subjects proprties, & Estate, &ca to wch was Replyed by one of ye Judges ye Rest by Silenc assenting; yt we must not think ye Lawes of England follow us to ye Ends of ye Earth, or whether we went.[52]

Most of the twelve jurors, Wise said it was reported, were nonfreeholders of any land and some of them strangers and foreigners "geathered up to Serve ye present turne."[53] A packed jury does not arrive at a verdict without instruction, nor did this one. Wise and those on trial with him have affirmed:

Mr Dudly aforesd; cheif Judge, to Close up ye Debate, & Tryall trimed up a Speech yt pleased himself (we suppose) more yn ye people; amongst many other Remarkable Passages to this purpose he bespeakes the Juryes Obedienc, who (we suppose) were very well preinclined. Viz I am glad (Sayes he) ther be so many worthie Gentlemen of ye Jury so Capable to do ye King Service, and we Expect a good verdict from you Seeing ye matter hath been so sufficiently proved against ye Criminalls.[54]

The evidence against the "Criminalls," according to report, seems to have been slight; none the less the jury returned them all guilty, and they were sent back to prison, there to languish for twenty-one days awaiting sentence.

Wise has attested that a writ of habeas corpus was sought and denied. Whether it was sought at that time or during the days before the trial is not known, but the letters of Wise and his fellow prisoners seeking release on bail were almost tantamount to a call for such a writ. At any rate, for denying him the privilege of habeas corpus Wise sued Dudley in 1689 for a thousand pounds and had Dudley's estate attached.[55]

The prisoners passed the time between verdict and sentence as best they could. Doubtless they were allowed visitors, for the relatives of the prisoners had to provide "necessary Succour, & Support." They did not lack for society, for the jail was somewhat crowded at the time, there being six of them and others coming and going. By October 24, three weeks after the trial, it was decided what should be done with them. They were called before the judges, and in the absence of Dudley, but with his approbation, Stoughton passed sentence upon them. Wise and Appleton were fined fifty pounds apiece and for their good behavior were put under bonds of a thousand pounds for one year. Andrews was fined thirty pounds, Kinsman and Goodhue twenty apiece, and French fifteen, and all four for their good behavior were put under bonds of five hundred pounds for one year. All were assessed court costs and restrained from holding public office, Wise being suspended from the ministry. The court costs were no small item; they amounted to over a hundred pounds. Court costs, fines, and other fees "of Messengers [,] prison Charges, & mony for Bonds, and transcripts of Records Exhausted by thos Ill=men one way, and another to ye value of three= or foure Schoar pounds, besides our Expenc of time & Imprisonmt, and cost to relatives," Wise and his friends estimated at not less than four hundred pounds.[56] Several years later the town reimbursed these men for their losses, generally by selling portions of the town common squatters had encroached upon.[57] According to the records, Wise, however, did not get much of a return. On thirty-five pounds that he paid for eight acres he received a discount of forty shillings for the service he did the town as representative.[58] But perhaps this award covered only his service in General Court, which was brief, and he received a larger sum for his losses under the Andros prosecution.

The ban against Wise's preaching was lifted a month after sentence was passed, upon his petition and the "Applycon of Several Worthy persons in his behalfe."[59] It is interesting to note that on the day the ban against Wise was lifted, constables of Ipswich obtained the receipt for turning in the town tax money.[60] This circumstance might have carried some weight in lifting the ban.

Wise and his fellow-sufferers, released after several weeks in jail,[61] went back home and quietly took up their interrupted work and old associations. The people of Ipswich, however, did not yield their spirit of independence. The struggle with the government continued. Major Samuel Appleton, justice of the peace and former Assistant (member of the Council) of the colony, was arrested and imprisoned on false information and kept in jail from October, 1687, until March of the following year, when he gave bond for a thousand pounds to appear at the next session of the Salem Superior Court.[62] This measure was no doubt designed as a threat to quell the rebellious spirit of the townspeople, inasmuch as Appleton was never brought to trial, nor was anything ever proved against him.

After having endured so much from the Andros government, Ipswich must have rejoiced when that government fell, on April 18, 1689. Reports of the success of the Glorious Revolution reached New England in March, and two weeks before the uprising in Boston a copy of the Prince of Orange's Declaration, which authorized the resumption of office by those magistrates unjustly turned out, had been brought into the town. This Declaration was excuse enough for the New Englanders to believe in the illegality of the Andros government. Broadsides of the Declaration were printed, and the ministers and other prominent men of Boston laid plans.[63] On April 18 the militia acted, under their direction, seizing the captain of the frigate in the harbor, jailing Randoph and others of the Governor's party, and besieging Andros in the harbor fort, whither he had fled for refuge. Eighty-six-year-old Simon Bradstreet, last governor under the Charter, various ministers and leaders of the colony, and certain disaffected councillors of the deposed Governor then marched forth from the Town House, where they had been conferring, and made a declaration to the people. This document, the author of which was very probably Cotton Mather,[64] described the grievances of the people under the late government and assigned to those grievances the reason for its overthrow. It cited the action against the Ipswich men and rehearsed some of the oppressive statements made at their trial and examination before the Council.[65]

People, aroused against Andros, began to pour in from the country. Jeremiah Shepard, who had first preached to the Chebacco congregation and was now pastor of the church at Lynn, led a considerable number of his townspeople into Bos-

ton to participate in the insurrection against Andros.[66] It was
midweek lecture day, and many people not usually in town
had assembled for meeting. They doubtless joined in the
popular uprising, since the lecture was "put by." In the next
two days the fort and frigate were surrendered. Andros was
first put under guard in the house of John Usher, but later
removed to the fort, from which he tried to escape in women's
clothing, and, after passing two guards, was detected by the
third, who noticed his shoes.[67] Dudley, returning from Long
Island, where he had been holding court, was discovered at
the house of a fellow-councillor in Rhode Island, escorted to
his own home in Roxbury, and there put under guard. Soon
he joined Andros, Randolph, West, and others in jail, where
all were held without bail.

A General Court assembled, to which Wise went on May
9 and again on the 23d as one of two elected deputies from
Ipswich.[68] The Court began action against Andros and his
officers by collecting evidence against them. Among the complaints submitted to the committee of Essex County were
French's account and that of Wise and those five who were
fined with him, in which it was charged that "the subscribers,
have under the Late Governmt. of Sr. Edmd. Andros been
damnifyed in Or. psons & estates severall Hundred, yea
Thousand Pounds, most Wickedly, yea, without & Contrary
to all Law, Reason & Equitye."[69] These complaints were submitted in May, 1689; another much more in detail was submitted and sworn to in December of that year and sent to
England.[70]

Thither Andros had been summoned to answer the charges
made against him, and evidence was gathered for and against
the late government. Favorable and unfavorable accounts of
the insurrection were written and circulated.[71] In some of
them the words of Wise and his oppressors figured. One of

these was "An Humble Memoriall of the present Condition of
the Dissenters of New-England" by Increase Mather, probably written about the middle of 1688.[72] In the margin opposite the paragraph "That they are under great Fears & Dis-
couragemts, being told by som in Governmt that they are no
better than Slaves, that they have no Title to Property or
English Priviledges, & they are treated accordingly" is the
sentence: "John Wise, John Nelson, & severall others in New-
England can attest to this."

Independently Wise took court action against Dudley for
denying him the privilege of habeas corpus. In October, 1689,
Dudley's estate at Roxbury was attached for a thousand
pounds.[73] Whether Wise was awarded damages is not known,
but if one considers the sympathies of the time, his cause
should have been the popular one.

With this action and the formal complaint drawn up in
December, Wise ended his opposition to the Andros party
and thought to devote himself to the spiritual needs of his
parish. But his part in the recent struggle had been a striking
one, and his contemporaries did not forget him. When the
expeditionary forces of Sir William Phips were being got up
for the movement against Quebec, Wise was thought of as a
likely man for a chaplain. On the last day of July, 1690, he
and three others were chosen to "carry on the worship of God
in that Expedition,"[74] and nine days later he embarked with
a force of twenty-five hundred soldiers and mariners and set
sail "from Massachusetts bay with great hopes and expecta-
tions to conquer New France."[75]

CHAPTER V

Chaplain against Quebec

THE EXPEDITION that Wise was now engaged upon was the most costly and elaborate that New England had ever launched against the French and the Indians. The English colonists had long harbored enmity to the French because they believed the French were instigators of Indian unrest and hostility. To the Puritans the French were particularly repugnant because of their "popish" religion; and now that war was proclaimed between England and France, the colonies of New York and New England, out of desire to serve their Majesties William and Mary and to save themselves, joined forces in 1690 to make a land and sea attack upon French Canada.

Major General Wait Winthrop was to lead overland a thousand English and fifteen hundred Indians against Montreal, and Sir William Phips was to sail with a fleet for Quebec, the chief settlement of Canada. The Indians, weakened by an outbreak of smallpox among them and dissuaded from the alliance by Jacobite sympathizers, made no very great showing at the rendezvous with the English. Winthrop would not proceed without the Indians and disbanded his troops.[1] This mistake allowed the French to concentrate all their strength at Quebec, for assuredly they knew from a number of sources—Indians, traders, and others—of the approach of Phips's fleet and of the disintegration of the forces for Montreal.

Phips sailed with thirty-two ships of varying sizes. Aboard

were two thousand soldiers and five hundred sailors. Phips's flagship had an armament of forty-four guns and carried a complement of two hundred sailors to man them.[2] Since only three hundred sailors then remained to man the other thirty-one, in comparison to Phips's vessel these ships must have been small and lightly armed.

The fleet, divided into three squadrons, sailed without mishap, but in rather disorderly fashion,[3] until it came to the "Canada River"—the St. Lawrence—and then moved up the river. It stopped at a few small islands for water and provisions. These islands were scouted for inhabitants, and on one prisoners were taken. Several fishing boats and light vessels were captured and burned, their occupants providing Phips and his council of war with information.

Quebec was reached October 5, and the next day, under a flag of truce, a summons to surrender was dispatched ashore. Count Frontenac refused to surrender and sent back the reply "yt no other answer was to bee Expected from Him but what should bee from ye mouth of his Cannon."[4] Phips made ready to land his forces, but the following day was too windy to effect a landing. However, on this day a captured French bark ran aground with about sixty English aboard who, without loss, beat off two hundred attackers until full tide could take the vessel off into deep water again.

The English, because of the successful defense of the bark, considered the episode an encouraging event, and on October 8 Lieutenant General John Walley landed with all his effective fighting force. That amounted, however, to only fourteen hundred men,[5] smallpox having got into the fleet. The English ran almost at once into an ambush and a few of their men were slain, but the French did not pursue their advantage and withdrew after a short engagement. That evening the field pieces of the English were brought ashore, "desirous to befriend" the soldiers,[6] but no plans were laid to employ them. The next day the land forces saw no action. Phips, however, having begun his siege in the evening of the previous day, battered the city ramparts with his guns and received in turn a damaging fire. Friday, the third day[7] after the landing, it was proposed that the men reëmbark and land in another place. While this plan was being studied, another brief encounter with the enemy occurred,[8] and forces were discovered large enough to verify the report of a French deserter that the Governor of Montreal had joined Frontenac in the defense of Quebec, swelling the number of defenders to three thousand. Saturday there were a few brushes with the enemy, but in the evening the army reëmbarked, leaving behind on the beach, by order of General Walley, five of the six field pieces, which by morning the high tide had completely submerged. It was thought to land and make an attack in another place, but, as an anonymous chronicler of the expedition recounted, "a storm arose wch separated or fleet; & a great Snow fell & ye Cold was So Extreme yt wee could not wth Safety continue Longer in ye River."[9] All but six of the ships arrived in Boston November 19, and of these six several were lost.[10] Besides losses from shipwreck, there were slain about thirty soldiers "by ye Sword," and a hundred and fifty died from "Small Pox & a malignant feaver."

Wise, if we are to credit his own account, played no small part in the undertaking. There is some evidence besides his own testimony to speak for the importance of his role. First, the very position of chaplain lent him some distinction. The instructions to Sir William Phips from Governor Bradstreet and the General Court thoroughly described the chaplain's station. Phips was "to take especial care and command that the holy Worship of God be constantly celebrated & attended in daily reading of Gods Word and Prayers and that the Sabbath be duly sanctified that so you may obtaine the presence and blessing of God upon yor undertaking to Crowne it with Successe you have the Company and Assistance of some Revd and worthy Divines to further that worke, unto whom you are to show all due respect & kindness." Moreover, the "Revd Divines" were to join in the councils of war.[11] There is evidence to show that they participated in both activities.[12]

Wise, one of the two ministers ordered ashore,[13] entered into the military movements of the troops with enthusiasm and showed himself always ready with advice and busy with plans for the army's advance. A funeral eulogy, appended to John White's oration, called attention to Wise's service in this expedition, "where not only the Pious Discharge of his Sacred Office, but his Heroick Spirit and Martial Skill and Wisdom, did greatly distinguish him."[14] An account compiled from the diary of one who presumably had been a member of the expedition stated that "one of ye Chaplains (mr John Wise) Encoraged Them [the troops] very much."[15] Wise's own narrative tells enough about his efforts to urge upon General Walley a more aggressive conduct of the attack. Wise's earnest proposals were sometimes followed, and once, doubtless in recognition of his sound judgment and undaunted spirit, he was called on board ship, along with General Walley, for a conference with Phips.[16]

Wise wrote his narrative, dated the 23d of December, 1690, in response to a request for "the full account" of the expedition and the reasons for its failure. Wise deemed "the full account" impossible for him to render, but he would accord to his correspondent—thought to have been Increase Mather[17]—an enumeration of the reasons for failure "according to . . . [his] Apprehensions." These reasons included a shortness in provisions and ammunition, want of a seasonable time to complete the action, the mischance of landing at an inconvenient spot,[18] and cowardice. Defending the troops from the charge of extravagance in the use of ammunition, he avowed:

Souldiers of all men may be indulged in a Prodigality whilst they without sparing spend up the Stores of Warr upon the Walls heads and Hearts of their Enemies and whilst they have Courage to do it Pity 'tis any should blame their Martial Zeale for being over prodigal but rather blame they had not a more lasting Store for it's hard to confine Martial men when their blood is up to all the Niceties of good husbandry.[19]

Cowardice Wise laid unequivocally and wholly upon the head of the commander of the land forces, Lieutenant General John Walley. The anonymous chronicle which was found together with Wise's narrative supports this allegation: "But what is an army of Lyons wn They must not go on Except a frighted Hart shall lead Them."[20] It was made clear who the "frighted Hart" was. Walley's own exposition of the reasons for failure included some identical with Wise's: "The land army's failing, the enemy's too timely intelligence, lyeing 3 weeks within 3 days sail of the place, by reason whereof they had opportunity to bring in the whole strength of their country, the shortness of our ammunition, our late setting out, our long passidge, and many sick in the army." Walley defended himself against the charges of cowardice and described his unaggressive leadership of the army as emanating from the decisions of the council of war.[21] The depositions by gunners and officers concerning the loss of the five field pieces, however, are damaging to Walley's defense.[22] Walley supposedly feared that the loading of the field pieces would jeopardize lives and was reported saying that "he had rather loose all ye field pieces then one mans life."[23] But Wise would not "pardon & Discharge" the general because of "good affection to his mens lives." He conceded that

Were field pieces and mens lives to be bought & Sold over a Dish
of Coffee by an Inch of Candle then indeed let any man be Rec-
coned inhumane and Cruel that will not bid more to save a mans
life then he will bid for five field pieces.

But the expedition against Quebec, he thought, was no such
petty affair. He declared:

We must know what all the banners & Ensignes of honor in Warr
which are the Glory of a Crown, of a Nation, of an Army ought
Stoutly to be defended with the Peril & loss of mens Lives rather
then basely to be betrayed or Surrendred into the hands of the
Enemy.

Five field pieces, which made "between two Able Armies . . .
the Odds & Difference of 500 if not a 1000 men," ought especially to have been secured, the more so in this instance since
"to have taken them of[f] with us had cost our men at the
most but a little more Sweat and or Lieut Genll but a little
more fear if he would have been so valiant as to have stayed
the Doing of it."[24]

Of course, from the time that he came ashore, Wise had
been dissatisfied with General Walley's leadership, and by
the time of the reëmbarkation he was thoroughly critical.
When Wise, landing soon after the troops had had their first
encounter with the French, found "the Army brought by this
Scout of the Enemy to an Ill-convenient Stop," he marched
up "to a party of or Army then at a Stand" and exclaimed:
"Gentlemen you are out of yor Witts we did not come hither
to drive a parcel of Cowardly Frenchmen from Swamp to
Swamp but to attaque Kebeque thither Gentlemen is or buis-
ness Why Dont we march away for the Towne of Kebeque[?]" He inquired after General Walley, but no one
knew his whereabouts, so Wise went from company to company until he found him. Then Wise poured forth a steady
stream of advice to the general, and it was probably too over-

whelming to be entirely acceptable. Wise had described in detail this meeting and of course with no discredit to himself.

I was affected when I first saw him for to me he seemed very much downe in his Spirit to say no worse I saluted him with the Ordinary Complement and said Sr what doe you meane by these kind of methods? Saith he I cannot rule them To whom I replyed Sr you must not expect when men are let loose upon an Enemie that they should attend all the Ceremonies martial and that are in fashion in a field of Peace But Sr said I what do you intend to doe he replyed I think they intend to lodge here all Night.
Good Sr said I by no meanes but let us march away for the Towne as fast as we can or men are now Warme by to Morrow they will Stiffen and Coole therefore Good Sr Give ye Word to march & send away to those companies in the rear to march away.[25]

Wise's advice was followed, and the troops marched to within a half mile of Quebec before they halted for the night. But still, to Wise, "things went on wth Unsufferable Dulness enough to Discourage any men." To right matters as far as he could, Wise entered into all the military activities of the day. He persuaded the sailors who brought the field pieces in boats to the shore to unload them as a favor to the soldiers because they had "had an Ill Afternoone" in standing off the ambush of the French. Then he sought out the lieutenant general, whom he deemed "by the Index of a certain reserved Gravity & a Lonesome walk from place to place" to be under "the Invincible Arrest of fear." Wise advised that the rear companies be brought up, and by the opportune arrival of messengers from those companies, this advice was put into effect. But no plans were made for the morrow; rather "the night was spent in little else but padling and fooling." Wise, completely at odds with Walley's uninspiring conduct, declared that

had we had a man that would have ventured his Life, his way had

been to have stilled all noyse got himself and army into a few
hours Sleep sent on board and had ready one bisquet cake pr
man and a good round Dram and have put these into their bellys
the next morning & in the heat of it marcht up to Towne the
Army would I am satisfied by their Valour have payd him his
Kindnesse in good Roast meat for Supper by the next night and
a good feather bed to have layn on instead of Boards or Straw.[26]

The days passed; and as opportunity afforded, Wise offered
further plans for the troops' employment. He urged an attack
upon the town more than once; and when these suggestions
were unavailing, proposed an orderly plan of reëmbarcation,
which was likewise disregarded. He even went over Walley's
head when, on an errand to procure "some comfort" for the
troops, who had been moved in the middle of the night from
comfortable lodgings to lie "30 or 40 in a heap like hoggs in
a Stye" upon a cold beach, he gave Sir William an account of
the irretrievable situation of the army. Wise had tried to
rouse the men the night before by challenging them "to get
up and run for a Dram of the bottle a Temptacon fit for
Souldiers that they might be kept in accon," and had en-
treated the lieutenant general to put the men upon a march
for the town, if only to keep them moving, "else many of
them [would] be Spoyled this Desperate cold Night."[27] The
men, however, had not only to endure the exposure of the
night but to remain on the beach until "about two hours before Sunset" the next day, awaiting embarkation, which Wise
and others have reported a confused and ill-managed affair.[28]
After embarkation came the tempestuous return voyage to
Boston, and Wise took up his ministry again at Chebacco.

The failure of the expedition disappointed and saddened
many, and explanations were sought for the poor performance of the army. Wise, in his narrative, gave an explanation.
Whether it was accurate on all points cannot now be deter-

mined. It was doubtless not an impartial and carefully weighed statement. He spoke as honestly as he could of events in which he had been caught up and thoroughly immersed. Perhaps he blamed Lieutenant General John Walley too much, but on the basis of present evidence it would be difficult to absolve Walley completely. And perhaps Wise was too firmly optimistic about the chances of the attacking troops. Certainly they faced no easily surmounted defenses.[29] Governor Bradstreet, in his letter of November 29 to the colony's agents in London, attributed the failure to "the awfull Frowne of God."[30]

Wise was not unaware of deficiencies in the narrative and asked his correspondent to "Pardon Some Expressions of Immodesty or Such as Carry Self Arrogance with them for they are the very Native dress of matter of fact &c Therefore I use them rather than dress a Discourse in another Skin then it was born in."[31] Still, in leaving this narrative behind him, Wise has done himself no disservice.

Other, more material rewards were forthcoming. For Wise's participation in the Canadian expedition his heirs were to receive, by order of the General Court, "three hundred Acres of the Unappropriated Lands of the Province." This acreage had later to be petitioned for, but it was obtained.[32]

CHAPTER VI

"Storms of Witchcrafts"

WHEN THE WITCHCRAFT MADNESS spread through Essex County, in 1692, it drew the attention of all Massachusetts Bay Colony. The sufferings and accusations of the afflicted children were from the first hidden under no bushel. On the contrary, they were observed, listened to, and talked about with morbid and growing interest. As belief and horror mounted, responsible people viewed the demonstrations of the increasing number of the afflicted as evidence of a desperate Satanic attack upon New England. Several of the Essex County ministers hurried forward to repel the minions of the Evil One. In the forefront, of course, there was Samuel Parris, Salem Village minister, upon whose household the curse of baleful witchcraft had first been laid. He was duly attentive to the incriminations of the distraught children and assiduous in writing up the examinations of the accused. Deeply involved also were Nicholas Noyes, of Salem, and a John Hale, of Beverly, who had been one of the chaplains designated to serve in the Canadian expedition. They were diligent in exhorting the accused to confess to a witch's horrid crimes.

But John Wise, so far as any record shows, did not go near the witchcraft trials. That he may have been present at various times is, of course, possible, especially since he was very much interested in John and Elizabeth Procter,[1] two of the accused. They had been parishioners of his; and though they had moved to a farm near Danvers, which was then called Salem Village, they renewed old friendships from time to time by occasional visits to the Procter farm near Ipswich.[2] At any rate, Wise and thirty-one members of his congregation thought enough of the Procters to sign a letter in their behalf and send it to the Court of Assistants sitting in Boston. Wise himself probably wrote the letter, since his name led the list and stood to the side, separate from the other signatures, as an author's name usually did on such documents.[3] Interested as Wise was in petitioning court for his former parishioners, it would have seemed out of character for him to have remained silent at their trials, had he been present.

The letter written for the Procters was no ordinary document. It showed an enlightenment that was not possessed certainly by the judges of the trials, and perhaps not by many others. It definitely sponsored the belief that the devil could, with God's permissive powers, impersonate innocent and Christian men and women—a view not widely held until the witchcraft trials were over. From the beginning of the examinations, conducted before Justices Hathorn and Corwin, to the end of session of the special court of oyer and terminer in October, 1692, administered by Stoughton, Sewall, Corwin, and others, the principle was consistently expounded and applied that the devil could not take upon himself the forms of innocent persons, that they had to enter into league with him—namely, become witches—before he could gain this power. Therefore, when the afflicted complained of suffering at the hands of any person, there was the evidence, so far as the judges were concerned, that the one cried out upon was a witch and must be apprehended and tried. This unquestioning dependence upon what was known as "spectral evidence" and what Thomas Brattle called "the devil's information"[4] was warned against early and importantly in the letter of the

Boston ministers to Governor Phips in June, 1692.[5] Wise, of course, did not sign this letter, but he did sign, with thirteen other ministers, a commendatory preface for Increase Mather's *Cases of Conscience*, dated October 3 of this year, wherein Mather sought to show the inadequacy of spectral evidence and "trial by the sight and touch."[6]

The undated petition for the Procters was probably submitted in June, though it has been reported as being submitted in August soon after John Procter's condemnation.[7] But the heading of the petition would seem to offer evidence favoring the earlier submission in the words "now in Trouble & undr suspition of Witchcraft."[8] Moreover, the Court of Assistants sat in May and June.

The passage arguing the extended powers of the devil came at the beginning of the letter and put the matter unequivocally when it stated:

we do at present, suppose that it may be a Method wthin the Seveerer But Just Transactions of the Infinite Majestie of God yt he sometimes may permitt Sathan to prsonate, Dissemble & therby abuse innocents, & such as Do in the Fear of God Defie the Devill and all his works. The Great Rage he is prmitted to attempt holy Job wth. The abuse he does the famous Samuel in Disquieting his silent Dust, by Shaddowing his venerable prson in answer to the charms of Witchcraft & other instances from Good hands, may be Argd. Besides, the unsearcheable footstepps of God's Judgments, yt Astonish or weaker Reasons, to teach us Adoration Trembling & Dependence &c.

The letter went on to ascribe its genesis to the operation of the Golden Rule and a desire to testify to the good repute that the Procters had always known.

we Reccon it wthin the Duties of or Charitie, that Teacheth us to do as we would be done by; to offer thus much for the Clearing of or Neighbrs. Inocencie. viz. That we never had the least knowledge of such a Nefarious wickedness, in or said Neighbours, since they have been wthin or acquaintance. Neither doe we remember any such thoughts in us concerning them or any action by them or either of them, Directly tending that way no more than might be in the lives of any other prsons of the Reputation as to any such Evills. What God may have left them to, we cannot go into Gods pavilions Cloathed wth Cloudes of Darkness Round About. But as to what we have ever seen or heard of them upon or consciences we Judge them Innocent of the crime objected.⁹

The neighbors of the Procters in the Salem Farms country also made a declaration of their good name, stating that "they lived christian-like in their family and were ever ready to helpe such as stood in need of their helpe."¹⁰ This paper was submitted presumably to the justices of the special court of oyer and terminer. And John Procter himself sought to enlist the sympathies and offices of the Boston ministers by a letter he addressed late in July to Increase Mather, James Allen, Joshua Moody, Samuel Willard, and John Bailey.¹¹ But all these addresses did not save the Procters. On August 5 they were condemned, and on the nineteenth John Procter was hanged, his wife escaping only by a plea of pregnancy.¹²

Possibly on the basis of John Wise's efforts to rescue the Procters, it has been suggested that he "was perhaps the only minister in the neighborhood or country, who was discerning enough to see the erroneousness of the proceedings [of the witchcraft trials] from the beginning."¹³ This, of course, was not true. Wise's fellow minister at the Ipswich church, William Hubbard, wrote on June 20 a testimonial letter to the good character of one of his former parishioners, and two other ministers added substantiating statements.¹⁴ Such letters, however, as this one of Hubbard's and the petitions for the Procters were few enough. Had there been more such letters and petitions besieging the authorities, the witchcraft madness might have ended sooner. The concern Wise felt for the witchcraft victims doubtless did not end with Procter's death. As time passed, not only the injustices done to the victims themselves but the hardships visited upon their families would be more evident to the community.

The Procter family had been particularly stricken. Along with the parents three of the children were charged with witchcraft and jailed.[15] In the latter part of May, 1692, complaints were filed against Benjamin Procter, aged thirty-three, William, aged seventeen, and Sarah, aged fifteen. The extreme youth of the other children then at home probably saved them from like treatment, the oldest being under seven. A confession was dragged from William, and his father in the letter to the Boston ministers told how the admission was extracted: "they tied him neck and heels till the blood gushed out at his nose."[16] Even the relatives of Procter's wife in Lynn were not safe from the charge of witchcraft and imprisonment.[17]

Procter's estate suffered as well. Calef has painted a black picture of the descent of the sheriff upon Procter's farm. While the owners were in prison, the sheriff "seized all the goods provisions and cattle that he could come at, and sold some of the cattle at half price, and killed others, and put them up for the West-Indies." Making a clean sweep, he emptied a barrel of beer and a pot of broth, even carrying off the pot. No food was left in the house for the livelihood of the children.[18]

Along with Procter were hanged three men and one woman, one of the men being a minister of God's word. Samuel Sewall, having witnessed this hanging, made an entry in his diary descriptive of the event, and opposite the entry he wrote in the margin "Dolefull Witchcraft!"[19]

Sewall might indeed lament "Dolefule Witchcraft." When the special court of oyer and terminer ended its session in October, nineteen persons had been hanged and one pressed to death, eight more had been condemned, fifty or so had confessed themselves witches, a hundred and fifty were in prison, and two hundred more had been accused.[20] "Storms of witchcrafts," Cotton Mather averred, had broken upon the people of New England.[21]

At Procter's death, his wife did not inherit. Because he knew almost for certain his wife would be condemned a witch and her share in his property forfeited, Procter designated that his lands, a total of seventy-five acres of salt marsh, tillage, pasture, and upland with a valuation of 208 pounds, be divided equally among the children of his three marriages. His two eldest sons, Benjamin and John Junior, he appointed executors.[22] By a petition to the General Court in 1696 in an effort to recover her dower right, Elizabeth Procter appealed the justice of a will that excluded the widow from sharing in her husband's estate;[23] and on April 19, 1697, she received a full pardon from the crime of witchcraft and became "alive in law" and eligible for her dower right.[24]

As the conscience of New England pricked itself more and more fiercely over the witchcraft affair, restitution to the witchcraft victims and their families for loss of property and reputation was finally sought. Wise and eleven other Essex County ministers hurried restitution along by an address to the General Court, which was read to both the House and the Council in July, 1703. They recommended that the case of those who had recently petitioned the Court for lifting the infamy of witchcraft from their names be "duely considered."[25] A petition to this effect had been submitted in 1700,[26] but the document referred to in the address of the ministers had been sent to General Court the previous March. Among the twenty-one signatures were two belonging to the Procter children.[27]

The ministers were moved to draw up the address because,

they said, "it is apparent and hath been Acknowledged, that there were Errors and mistakes" in the witchcraft trials, that "notwithstanding the care and conscientious endeavour of the Honorable Judges to do the thing that is right: yet there is great reason to fear that Innocent persons then suffered, and that God may have a controversy with the Land upon that account." The ministers therefore humbly queried whether something might not and ought not "to be publickly done to clear the good name and reputation of some . . . for whom there are good grounds of charity."[28] A few days after the address was ready, action was taken to remove the infamy of witchcraft from the victims' families.[29] Petitions for payment of damages were sent in several years later and acceded to in 1711, Procter's heirs receiving the largest amount, a hundred and fifty pounds.[30]

CHAPTER VII

Life at Chebacco

THE LIMITS of Chebacco parish were no more definitely fixed than "from Goodman Chotes up to Nicolas Marbles." All within those bounds—probably a hundred families or so in the 1690's,[1] some of which were scattered along the creek that gave the community its name—paid their rates to the Chebacco ministry.[2] The original deed of land sold by Maskonomett, Sagamore of Agawam, to John Winthrop, Junior, founder of Ipswich,[3] included the area of Chebacco parish; but at the recommendation of the General Court, that area had been set apart from Ipswich parish and allowed a church of its own.

The parish had few, if any, community enterprises. Its center was marked by a meetinghouse, but by little else. There was probably not even a cluster of houses near the meetinghouse to denote a hamlet—at least in the early years —for the residents of the parish lived and worked on their farms. John Wise himself farmed sixty acres, and his new house, built in 1703, stood at least a quarter of a mile distant from the meetinghouse. Only gradually did a town grow up about the meetinghouse.

For a number of years Ipswich continued to be the center of life for Wise and parishioners. Until 1695, when a school was set up in Chebacco, Wise sent his children to Ipswich for instruction. He took his grain to the Appleton mill in Ipswich and picked up his malt at the Appleton malthouse.[4] Doubtless Wise could brew very satisfactory ale and beer, since he could have learned and practiced the proper recipes in his father's malthouse.

The people of Chebacco had to obey the laws of the town of Ipswich, for though Chebacco was a separate parish, it did not become a separate town, with the name of Essex, until 1819. What ordinances the Ipswich town meeting declared against sooty chimneys, undisposed carrion, "whereby wolves may be drawn or people annoyed," or unringed hogs traversing the streets or common, Chebacco people observed. And the men of Chebacco doubtless claimed now and again the generous bounty Ipswich paid on wolves and foxes.[5]

The church at Chebacco, too, probably functioned in much the same way that the one at Ipswich did. Chebacco's congregation must have gathered in all weathers in an unheated meetinghouse to hear lengthy prayers and longer sermons, to join in not very accomplished singing of awkward psalms unaccompanied by any instrument, to be edified by public confession or testimony, to bring tithes and offerings for the support of God's kingdom. In churchly conclave it would duly elect elders, deacons, tithingmen, and sextons and receive half and full communicants into its midst and excommunicate others. It would accept baptized children, according to the Halfway Covenant adopted by the Synod of 1662, and by admonition and corporal discipline solemnly endeavor to nurture them in the Christian life.

The town of Ipswich, of which Chebacco parish was a part, submitted to ordinances like this one.

It is ordered that from henceforth whosoever shall suffer any of his Dogs to come into the meeting house (wherby disturbance may be made) upon any Sabbath days or Lecture days between 12 of the clock and three he shall forfeit 6d for every such Dog so coming and being there.[6]

As the dogs in winter proved themselves very agreeable footwarmers, a ruling against their presence at meeting could hardly be enforced without the threat of a fine.

Wise and his congregation had no irremediable disagreement during his whole pastorate. Though funeral orations are not always to be trusted for their accuracy, Wise's son-in-law probably did not exaggerate the veneration in which Wise was held.[7]

Differences were settled in friendly fashion. In a ministry as long as forty-five years adjustments had of necessity to be sought, and the records show both the minister and his congregation ready to make concessions. In 1701 it was voted to grant Wise fifty pounds if he would "forgive" his parish certain commitments. Wise accepted the fifty pounds and the condition.[8] Late in life, he found it necessary, because of the depreciation of paper money, to ask for an increase in salary. While he had finally to sue for redress at "ye Genll Sessions of ye Peace held at Newberry for ye County of Essex" September 25, 1722, he seems to have been motivated by no ill will or to have incurred any by his court action. Wise was still allowed the rents of the old parsonage after he had built himself a new house, in 1703, and a new meetinghouse was donated for his ministry in 1717 and erected the following year. Wise contributed his share to the spiritual improvement of Chebacco by converting more than a hundred persons, if one judges from the names that were added to the church rolls during his ministry.[9]

Certain legends grew up about Wise. That they were current during his lifetime is highly probable, for they identify him both as a man of athletic prowess and as a minister potent in prayer.

Tradition has described Wise as a formidable wrestler. Notice of his skill got about to nearby communities and excited, probably, no little curiosity, wonder, and envy. Captain John Chandler, of Andover, who fancied himself an expert wrestler, found his pride piqued by reports which praised a scholarly preacher and resolved to challenge the parson. Over to Chebacco he rode, and leading his horse into the courtyard past the low stone wall surrounding the parsonage he called for Wise to come out and try his skill.

Wise was at first reluctant to enter into a contest; perhaps he thought that by participating in what might be deemed common brawling, he would put his ministerial position in a bad light. Nevertheless, he let himself be persuaded and engaged in two bouts. Not only did he win both bouts, but in the second flung his opponent over the stone wall. When the surprised Captain Chandler got to his feet, he vowed good-humoredly that if the parson would throw his horse over the wall, too, he would be on his way.[10]

A New England antiquarian a hundred and thirty years ago said that in prayer Wise was "solemn, fervent, and impressive."[11] He may well have been. Legend had him resorting to public prayer for some of his parishioners who, while fishing off the coast, had been captured by pirates. At Sabbath morning service he prayed from the pulpit for his abducted people, climaxing his address to heaven by the exhortation: "Great God! if there is no other way, may they rise, and butcher their enemies!" The next day the prayed-for ones returned and recounted their adventures, declaring that on Sabbath morning they had overcome and slain their captors. Common talk would not be slow to associate the prayer with deliverance, and the relationship would hardly be looked upon as coincidental.[12]

Almost any youngster takes pride in the stories of his father's strength, except at those times when corporal punishment is his lot, and Wise's children would not likely be exceptions. There were seven of them: Jeremiah, Lucy,

Joseph, Ammi Ruhamah, Mary, Henry, and John. Three of Wise's sons—Jeremiah, Henry, and Joseph—were graduates of Harvard. Jeremiah (A.B. 1700), who during two years at college drew the scholar's annual stipend of four pounds, taught the Braintree grammar school for a year after graduation; then he took up the ministry, having been bred to learning by his father,[13] and, like his father, served as chaplain to forces fighting the Indians. For at least a year he was chaplain to the garrison at Fort Mary, Saco, Maine. In 1706 he accepted a call from the church at Berwick, Maine, a frontier community, where he remained until his death in 1756.[14] Lucy, the next oldest child, married the Reverend John White of Gloucester (A.B. 1698), who in preaching his father-in-law's funeral paid Wise eloquent tribute. Joseph, the second son (A.B. 1728), became a physician and merchant of Boston. His attendance at Harvard when he was a man past forty probably arose from a desire to back up his professional reputation with a formal college education. His father contributed fifty pounds to "his setling at Boston."[15] From his shop in Anne Street,[16] Joseph may also have watched over the shipping interests of his father, who was part owner of two merchant vessels, the sloop *Dolphin* and the bark *Good Intent*.[17] This son died of dropsy in Boston in 1745.[18] His brother Ammi Ruhamah rose to the rank of major in the colonial militia and served honorably in several campaigns. He also became a merchant, reputedly wealthy, to which position he may have been helped by his father, for by 1717, according to Wise's will, he had received one hundred and thirty pounds. He served as a justice of sessions court and a representative of Ipswich to General Court in 1739-40, dying suddenly in Boston in 1749.[19] Mary probably ended life an old maid, for at the time Wise drew up his will, August 28, 1717, she was still unmarried, and in the account we have of

the death in 1736 of a fifty-four-year-old spinster, Mrs. Mary
Wise of Chebacco, she is very likely referred to.[20]

In the year Wise's will was drawn up his son Henry graduated from Harvard. The following year he taught the Roxbury Latin School, and after that kept shop in Boston for a
while. He received the degree of M.A. in 1720 and began in
that year a tenure of eight years as schoolmaster of the Ipswich grammar school.[21] Then he resumed shopkeeping and,
along with his brother Ammi Ruhamah, joined the group
withdrawing from the Chebacco church, which set up the
Fourth Church of Ipswich in 1747. He died in 1775, the
longest lived of all John Wise's children, having had the
pleasure, in 1772, of seeing two new editions of his father's
writings issue from the press.[22] To Jeremiah and Henry their
father left his library, perhaps because he reckoned they
would make the most use of his books, since they both held
degrees from Harvard College. He did, however, reserve three
volumes from his library for his youngest child, John.[23] This
son was the executor of his father's will and inherited the
estate. Since he, by his father's will, became the owner of
more than sixty acres of land, he probably engaged in farm-
ing until his death in 1762.

Because there was no school in Chebacco, Wise's children
had to make almost daily the five-mile trudge to Ipswich and
back for their schooling. This arrangement was hardly convenient, not to mention the blizzards, thunderstorms, and
other hazards of weather and road that must have made Wise
and his wife anxious over their children's safety. So, when a
school for Chebacco was being considered, Wise, according to
tradition, was quick to speak up for its establishment. At a
session of the freeholders, convened in the meetinghouse for
the purpose of acting upon a proposal to found a grammar
school, he urged his parishioners to take a favorable action

that they might "save their children from ignorance, infidelity, and vice." To implement the enthusiasm aroused by this meeting a committee was appointed to find a teacher and provide a schoolhouse. Nathaniel Rust, Junior, was chosen teacher and opened the first grammar school in his own house in June, 1695. The steps undertaken to provide a school at Chebacco were officially approved a year later upon petition to the town meeting in Ipswich, and land was granted on which to build a schoolhouse. But it was not until 1702 that the first schoolhouse was erected.[24]

Toward the end of the seventeenth century the inhabitants of Chebacco, or Essex, as it was then beginning to be called, were led to believe that they could have a happier life in the colony of South Carolina. A friend and former neighbor of the Chebacco parishioners, Benjamin Singleterry by name, had settled on land about "the Read-Banks," South Carolina, and had found life pleasant and prosperous there. He sent back such glowing accounts of Carolina to his old friends and neighbors that they, too, were drawn to remove to this "Rich and Plentifull Countrie." Wise shared his parishioners' longing and readily joined his hopes to theirs. A company was formed to sponsor the emigration, plans were carefully laid, and a common purse was collected to help finance the scheme. Six men, styled "adventurers," were to board ship for South Carolina and, as an advance group in the hire of the newly formed company, particularly scout out the region about "the Read-Banks"[25] and make report as to the adequacy of the land for the support of a hundred families. They were to draw funds from the common purse and be guided by a set of some quite thorough instructions formulated by Wise.[26]

The proposed emigration of such a large number of well-established families must have aroused a good deal of comment and curiosity. To the parishioners of Chebacco, their relatives, and friends must have come many a disquieting thought. Wise showed his concern over the enterprise in a letter written to Judge Sewall, March 21, 1698. Though the letter was penned chiefly to thank Sewall for his gift of a "crazie fining Pot" to the Chebacco church—whatever that was— and presented remarks upon Wise's reading, Wise also took the opportunity to seek Sewall's advice on the move to Carolina. In his reply of April 12 Sewall rejoiced that Christ was carrying his trenches so near sin's stronghold, but, Sewall sensibly thought, those fellow-ministers of Wise who were acquainted with the circumstances and conditions of the Chebacco church could best advise him.[27]

The plan of removal fell through. The would-be emigrants stayed at Chebacco. Whether their hopes were dashed by the unfavorable report of the six adventurers, whether the governor of the country would grant no "Good and Sufficient Tract" for settlement, or whether they themselves turned back from the project because of the advice of friends and relatives and because of their own doubts cannot be discovered. Whatever the discouragement, it was thorough and widespread. The plan was dropped, and no further mention of it is found. The Chebacco people, as they adjusted to the project's failure, must have evaluated their life anew and doubtless decided that their own New England fields were greener and more comforting than those of the Carolinian regions far away.

CHAPTER VIII

The "Popish Plot" in New England

WISE, who had stood stanchly for democratic practices in civil government, could be expected to uphold the self-rule of the individual church. Independence (though the reverend elders did not like the word)[1] had been a characteristic of the churches of Massachusetts Bay Colony ever since its founding. The confinement of the people of each community by weather, distance, and convenience contributed to the development of congregational autonomy, but so did the purpose that fathered the New England settlements. The Saybrook platform in 1708 stated "that the Colonies there were Originally formed, not for the advantage of *Trade and a Worldly Interest*: But upon the most noble Foundation, even of *Religion, and the liberty of . . . Consciences.*"[2] This was only a slight exaggeration of the truth.

There was of course a mold in which Puritan churches should be cast, albeit some learned it with difficulty. Perhaps to advertise this mold, certainly for "the maintenance of the faith" and "the holding forth of Unity & Harmony," among both their own churches and "reformed churches throughout the world,"[3] the New England elders met in 1648 and set forth a plan of church discipline and government that has become known as the "Cambridge platform." Here the power, duties, and offices of the single congregational church were largely dealt with. Despite admissions of synodical power and the authority of civil magistrates, the government of a Puritan church in New England was demonstrated to be pretty much within the individual church, administered jointly by the elders and the membership. As the platform stated, "there is no greater Church then a *Congregation*, which may ordinarily meet in one place."[4] And the Synod of 1662 approved the following proposition:

Every church, or particular congregation of visible saints, in gospel order, being furnished with a presbytery, at least with a teaching elder, and walking together in truth and peace, hath received from the Lord Jesus full power and authority, ecclesiastical within itself regularly to administer all the ordinances of Christ, and is not under any other ecclesiastical jurisdiction whatsoever.[5]

But the years would bring their changes, and along with them would creep tiny encroachments upon established authority. Little by little new ideas had their way in the world. The loss of the old charter, the struggle with the Andros government, and the dissatisfaction with the new charter proved that the colony could be touched and influenced by outside forces. And if the political weather was inclement, the witchcraft tempest ridden by more than a few of the ministers had quite frayed their vestments of unchallenged authority. The rise of a merchant class which was discovering its own authority, the Act of Uniformity, which by its elevation of the Church of England caused a crumbling of strictly Puritan rule, and the influx of people who were indifferent to the interests of religion—all tended to subtract from ministerial authority and the church-state that had flourished in the past and was now beginning to fail.

In Boston, a busy port, these changes would be first perceptible, and in Boston, of course, the ministry would be first alarmed at the waning of church power. They would take measures, form associations, issue resolutions, and even propose that all the churches come under an ecclesiastical government in order to present a more united front to worldliness. This last step—in the form of sixteen proposals—was going too fast for the conservatism that yet held a great part of the colony in its sway. In championing that conservatism, John Wise championed something else—a mode of thought that was to rule the century. Little did Wise know when he crushed the 1705 proposals in the name of democracy that he was giving impetus and *élan* to a form of government that was to enamor men's minds for years to come and to nurse hopes and dreams for an improved civilization.

Since in Wise's *Churches Quarrel Espoused* the proposals called forth an argument of some consequence and a satire of some skill, the genesis of these sixteen rules for ministerial association and consociation deserves telling. The proposals did not derive alone from tight-lipped opposition to the Brattle Street Church. One persuasive argument against such a supposition is that Benjamin Colman, its pastor, was one of the signatory ministers. Also, the ministerial associations formed in the last fifteen years—by this date there were five[6]—had their influence. Delegates from the associations met and drew up the proposals in September, 1705, and two months later the Cambridge association sent them out to the ministers.

Still, the 1705 proposals owed something in their formulation to the controversy over the Brattle Street Church; how much, it would be difficult to say. But since the swarming of Boston's fourth church—not to count a languishing King's Chapel, an outcast Quaker meeting, and a First Baptist society— caused an unusual disturbance, the direction the controversy gave churchmen's thoughts may have led straight to the proposals.

Chronologically, however, the ministerial association came first. Writing in 1710 or so, Wise stated: "About Thirty years ago, more or less, there was no Appearance of the Associations of Pastors in these Colonies, and in some Parts and Places there is none yet."[7] Wise was either not cognizant of the earliest founding date or not interested in being exact. The first association in New England was organized in 1690 among the ministers in and about Boston and was patterned after a similar body that had existed in England during the Commonwealth.[8] The members agreed to associate themselves *"for the promoting of the Gospel"* and for their *"mutual Assistance and Furtherance in that great Work."* To accomplish this purpose, they met every six weeks at Harvard College on Monday morning at nine or ten o'clock and proposed to do the following "Work":

1. To Debate any Matter referring to *our selves.*
2. To Hear and Consider any *Cases* that shall be proposed unto us, from *Churches* or private Persons.
3. To Answer any *Letters* directed unto us, from any other *Associations* or Persons.
4. To Discourse of any *Questions* proposed at the former meeting.[9]

At these meetings such topics as *"the Power of* Synods" and *"the Power of* Elders" were discoursed upon, and the final opinion was reported. Once even the question *"Whether it be Lawful to* Eat Blood and Things Strangled" was considered.[10]

Doubtless this body was alarmed at the divergences from the old way that were being talked about at the end of the seventeenth century. Not only did the ministers have to put up with the manifestations of Quakers, Baptists, Anglicans, and other sects beyond the pale of Puritan orthodoxy, because of the Act of Uniformity, but also in orthodoxy itself they had to bear with peculiar behavior. Increase Mather stated that in May, 1697,

no less then Thirty Ministers in this *Province,* did declare and

subscribe it with their hands, *That they were made sensible of
the tendencies amongst us towards Deviations from the good Order wherein our Churches have according to the Word of the Lord
Jesus Christ, been happily established and continued.*[11]

Perhaps these ministers so declared and subscribed, for one
thing, because of the deviations William Brattle of the
wealthy Boston family had introduced in his ordination at
the Cambridge church the previous November. There he had
preached his own ordination sermon and had forbidden a
layman elder to put his hand upon his head in the ancient
ceremony of "the laying on of hands."[12] However, there was
a general defection that was far more disturbing in its vague-
ness and ubiquity than William Brattle's unusual behavior.
The elder Mather lamented "a great decay of the Power of
Religion throughout all New-England."[13]

It was no wonder, then, that the forming of the Brattle
Street Church, since it intended to institute practices hitherto
shunned by New England orthodoxy and to dispense with
the sanction of sister churches, met with heavy criticism and
set off a lengthy controversy. The church had its beginnings
in a disaffection among some of the prosperous Boston merchants who disliked the exacting road to church membership
and had become weary of the barrenness of the order of
service. The press of people at meeting, too, may have seemed
to warrant the building of another meetinghouse, but this
was an excuse easily found. Nevertheless, Oliver Noyes, one
of the undertakers of the church, used it in describing the
causes for the formation of the new church when he invited
Benjamin Colman to become its pastor.

The Occasions or at least some occasional Causes of their Proceedings [those of the Gentlemen Undertakers] at this Time have bin
These the want of convenient Seats in other Meeting houses being
full; the Need of another House, Some Trouble that Many have

Conceived (perhaps not Unjustly) against Relations a Custom
You know, a Particular Church Covinant exclusive of Universal
Communions & the Like.[14]

And another letter to Colman cited the excuse of "want of
roome in the meeting houses" and went on to urge the un-
adorned reading of the Scriptures to the people, a practice
which Colman was supposed to have liked in the past.[15] Colman himself reported that the undertakers, in their letter of
invitation, proposed "that the Holy Scriptures might be
publicly read every Sabbath in ye Worship of GOD, and that
they might lay aside the Relation[s] of Experience: which
were imposed in the other Churches in the Town, in order to
ye Admission of Persons to ye Lords Table."[16] Reading the
Scriptures without expounding the text, called by Increase
Mather "dumb reading,"[17] smacked too much of the prayer-
book to the orthodox; and dispensing with public recital of
personal religious experience as a requirement for full church
membership seemed to many to put the Lord's table within
too easy reach of impious and hypocritical hands. The undertakers further aroused criticism when they proposed not to
"confine the right of chusing a Minister to the Male Communicants alone" but avowed that "every Baptized Adult
Person who contributes to Maintenance, should have a Vote
in Electing."[18] But these differences were not widely known
when the initial steps for the church were taken, and disapproval only gradually built up.

Thomas Brattle, treasurer of Harvard, brother of William,
and only a "half-way" member of the Third Church (he had
not been admitted to the communion table because he had
not related in meeting an experience of religious conversion),
took the lead in the formation of the Brattle Street Church.
He offered to sell some land, known as Brattle Close, as a site
for the new church. Twenty interested persons, the under-

takers of the church, bought the land in January, 1699, and the erection of the meetinghouse in Brattle Square was begun. It was completed in November.

How the "men of repute and figure" happened to hit upon Colman in choosing a pastor can probably be explained by the influence of the Brattle family again. Colman, as an admiring student of William Brattle, had sufficiently impressed his Harvard tutor to deserve a recommendation to the sponsors of the new society. Brattle, adding his solicitation to that of the undertakers, declared in a letter to Colman: "As for my own part, I shall account it a smile from heaven upon ye good design of these Gentlemen, if you can send them an answer of peace; & I would hope that you[r] so doing will result in your mutual rejoycing."[19] And one of Colman's solicitors reminded him of sentiments expressed in a letter (perhaps to William Brattle) whereby he professed a preference to spend his days in New England rather than England, were there "a Prospect of an honourable Maintanance."[20]

Two tutors of Harvard, John Leverett and Ebenezer Pemberton, the one to be its president and the other soon to join Samuel Willard in the ministry of the Third Church, were among those who urged Colman's coming. Leverett honored the inception of the Brattle Street Church, for it "had it's rise from a zeal that is not Common and the progress of it is Orderly and Steady."[21]

But despite some approval, a tide of opposition to the new church was rising. The last-named men were in a camp hostile to the Mathers, Pemberton especially nursing a dislike to them over the years.[22] Their very presence on the side of the Brattle Street Church told something of the forces gathering against it. It was recommended to Colman, then, that, in order to bypass any trouble the Boston churches might make, he be ordained in England.[23]

Colman received these letters in July, 1699, found the invitation acceptable, "for his Heart was always very much in his native Country,"[24] speedily procured ordination, and set sail for New England the twentieth of August.

What sort of man was young Colman? What were his origins? How had he prepared himself for his present ministry? For one thing, he had been baptized by Increase Mather and was a member of the Second Church. For another, two years after graduation from Harvard in 1693, he had gone to England, where for four years he had been "imploy'd as a Candidate for the Evangelical Ministry, to wch," he said, "my Parents & my own Choice devoted me," preaching in a number of places before accepting the ministry of "ye Dissenting Congregation in the City of Bath."[25] For the rest, Colman's biographer and admiring son-in-law, Ebenezer Turell, can best speak. When Colman went to England, he was on a ship a French privateer attacked and boarded. For awhile the English ship returned the fire of the French vessel, and Colman entered into the fight. Turell in contrasting the bravery of the sensible man and the bravado of the foolhardy one, has left us an attractive portrait of his subject.

God graciously preserved Mr. *Colman* in the Fight, exposed all the while on the Quarter-Deck, where four out of seven were wounded, and one mortally. He was much praised for his Courage when the Fight was over; but though he charged and discharged like the rest, yet he declared he was sensible of no Courage but of a great deal of Fear; and when they had received two or three Broadsides he wondered when his Courage would come, as he had heard others talk. In short, he fought like a Philosopher and a Christian. He looked Death in the Face and prayed all the while he charged and fired,-----while the Boatswain and others made a Frolick and Sport of it.[26]

In another episode Colman revealed his power in preaching.

One Afternoon as he came from Oxford . . . he saw a Number of
People before him on the *Downe,* and was soon told that a Robber
was just taken and carried to the next Village. He had the Curiosity to go into the Tavern and see him. He was a young Fellow
of nineteen Years old, and one of the Company was telling after a
boorish Manner, how he rode after him, came up with and took
him.—But said the miserable Wretch, "I yielded honourably.
"Yes, yes, said the other, that you did.—Well, 'tis but a *Swing,*
cryed the Robber very impudently. This turned Mr. Colman's
compassion into Indignation, and he said,----"But vile Wretch consider, whither that *Swing* is? Is it not into Eternity? And an Eternity of Misery if you die without Repentance; as you seem willing
and likely to do? Do you like and can you bear to think of *A
Swing into Hell,* into unquenchable Fire and everlasting Burnings?
A Shivering Horror fell upon the Villain, and all the Room turned
and stared on the Preacher; as if they had never heard a Serious
Discourse before. This animated Mr. *Colman* to go on, and he
found himself helped to speak very much to his own Satisfaction,
on the Occasion for a Quarter of an Hour.[27]

Colman arrived in Boston the first of November, and the
next day the undertakers of the Brattle Street Church visited
him. A few days later Thomas Brattle presented him with
fifty pounds in money in the name of the undertakers, and
soon after they kept a day of thanksgiving in private.[28] The
relationship between pastor and undertakers thus firmly
established, plans went forward for the church's organization.
To clarify the church's position and to prevent "all Misappre-
hensions and Jealousies,"[29] there was issued a Manifesto
which though avowing loyalty to the Westminster Confession of Faith of 1680 and expressing a desire for fellowship
with other churches, nevertheless plainly stated the practices
to which the church would adhere.

In this publication were set forth sixteen articles of profession and practice. Among them, of course, were those practices which made this church different from the others,

namely, the reading of Scripture without explication in public worship, the admission to membership without public relation of religious experience, and the extension of the vote in choosing a minister to all baptized adult contributors.

This document was viewed somewhat sourly by the adherents of orthodoxy and earned for the new church the nickname of the Manifesto church. Conservatives John Higginson and Nicholas Noyes, of the Salem church, set themselves to defeat it, point by point, after objecting to the use of "Manifesto" as an "imperial" word and chiding the undertakers: "how could you forsake the dear churches some of you belong to, whose breasts you had sucked, and on whose knees you had been dandled, without dropping one tear for in your declaration?"[30]

On December 12 a church of fourteen members was organized, and on the twenty-fourth held its first meeting, attended by a numerous congregation, for Sewall reported that the Third Church meeting "was pretty much thin'd by it."[31]

Sewall had earlier conversed with Colman about the "Manifesto," and they had parted amicably.[32] But not so easily reconciled was Cotton Mather. In his diary he hailed the Brattle Street Church as bringing a "Day of Temptation" upon the town and the "Manifesto" as subverting the churches. He wrote "a large monitory Letter, to these *Innovators,* which, tho' most lovingly penn'd, yett enrage[d] their violent and impetuous Lusts, to carry on the *Apostasy.*"[33] Mather accounted himself and his father as chief sufferers in this apostasy and averred they had preparing in the press "a faithful *Antidote*" when he decided to make "one Attempt more, for the bringing of this People to Reason." Mather reported his efforts successful and wrote of "much Relenting in some of their Spirits."[34]

But the Brattle Street Church had made the first overture

of peace. It "voted that Mr. Colman present the Desires of the Society to the Ministers of the Town to keep a day of Prayer" with it.[35] To this request James Allen of the First Church and Increase Mather of the Second would agree only if the new society would "lay aside" its "Manifesto" and "keep to the *Heads of Agreement,* upon which the *United Brethren* in *London* made their union." But these things the society had "altogether Declined and Neglected to do"; therefore, they could not join in an action that would be "Interpreted as an Approbation, of the miscarriage, which both before and since the publication of the said *Manifesto,*" it seemed to them, the society had fallen into.[36]

But others besides Cotton Mather had been laboring for peace. Turell listed the peacemakers, among whom were Lieutenant Governor Stoughton, the Reverend William Brattle, and two other ministers not of Boston.[37] And the moderation of Colman himself was having its effect. Stanchly conservative Sewall wished Colman's church well after expostulating with him over some part of the *Manifesto.* The efforts of the peacemakers prevailed to the extent that on January 31, 1700, all the congregational churches of Boston joined in a fast with the Brattle Street Church, and their ministers participated in an all-day service.

On this "close dark day" Increase Mather preached on the text "following Peace with Holiness,"[38] and "Mr. Willard and C. Mather pray'd excellently and pathetically for Mr. Colman and his Flock."[39] The Brattle Street Church, thus publicly recognized and prayed over, found itself grown popular. People flocked to get pews. In nine months' time the communicants increased from fourteen to twenty-seven, and fifty-three persons were baptized in the first year of Colman's ministry.[40]

But the controversy was not at an end. The Mathers con-

tinued to look upon the establishment of the Brattle Street
Church as an affront to themselves and orthodoxy. Cotton
Mather, even after fast day, complained of "the Venome of
that malignant Company, who have lately built a *new
Church* in *Boston"* which disposed them to "add unto the
Storm of my present Persecution." He evidently sought protection in prayer from that "Venome," for he received "an
Assurance from Heaven" that something would befall "the
disorderly Society of Innovators (now causing much Temptation and Inequity in the Place) ."[41] Despite their admittedly generous resolution for peace, the smell of printer's ink
was too strong for the Mathers, and Increase let issue forth
in March, 1700, his *Order of the Gospel,* which criticized the
new practices, but left unmentioned the Brattle Street
Church. It was plain, of course, even in the preface, at whom
he was directing his criticism. There he proclaimed:

If we Espouse such principals as these, Namely, *That Churches
are not to Enquire into the Regeneration of those whom they
admit unto their Communion. That Admission to Sac[r]aments
is to be left wholy to the prudence and Conscience of the Minister. . . .That Persons not Qualified for Communion in special
Ordinances shall Elect Pastors of Churches. . . .That Persons may
be Established in the Pastoral Office without the Approbation of
Neighboring Churches or Elders;* We then give away *the whole
Congregational cause* at once, and a great part of the *Presbyterian Discipline* also. To begin a change in one of these Particulars
without *Decision* of the *Synod,* would in other Churches of the
Reformed be counted *Persumptious,* but to design all or most of
these *Innovations* at once, is certainly a bold *Attempt.*[42]

The object of his criticism became even plainer as he gave
short shrift to the innovations introduced by the Brattle
Street Church. Eight of the seventeen questions he discussed
dealt in some degree with those innovations. No contemporary would have needed briefing to know what church was

now honoring a superstition (so called by Mather) when it practiced as a duty the reading of the Scriptures without explication.

Certainly the partisans of the Brattle Street Church were under no difficulty to identify the object of Mather's animadversions. Soon after Mather's book appeared, they countered with one of their own called *The Gospel Order Revived*. This work held suspect the disinterestedness of Mather. The very heat with which he argued would seem to set down all those who did not share his views as "not on the Lords side, [but] Enemies to the cause of Christ, and the Churches of New-England." The authors suggested that the contest on Mather's part was "more for Lordship and *Dominion* than for *Truth*" and remarked the strangeness of trying to burden men with impositions such as those the founders of the colony had fled.[43] Then one by one Mather's opinions on the seventeen questions he considered were opposed. Mather's avowal that one chapter of the Bible read with explication "will Edify the Congregation more than the bare reading of Twenty Chapters"[44] did not, the partisans declared, "savour of modesty," and they assured "the Reverend Author": "Alas! Sir, the Scripture wants nothing of ours to make it Perfect."

In the light of what Wise later said against the consociation of churches sponsored by the 1705 proposals, it is interesting to note the unfavorable reaction at this time by the partisans of the Brattle Street Church to consociation. They considered inexpedient the consociation, or agreement, of churches over "matters of more than ordinary Importance, such as the gathering of a new Church, the Ordination, Deposition, or Translation of a Pastor." The Cambridge platform, after all, made provision enough.[45]

The partisans found more to assail than the opinions of Increase Mather. They swore that they could not obtain the

printing of their book because the Boston printer stood too
much in awe of this "reverend scribbler." The printer made
depositions denying the charge, and the partisans made coun-
ter depositions.[46] It is difficult now to say where truth lay. It
is true that *The Gospel Order Revived* was first printed in
New York, and the excuses the printer gave for not accepting
the work may have been real ones, but still such as he found
easy to make when he reflected upon the good business the
Mathers brought him.

Cotton Mather, of course, could not let pass unrebuked
The Gospel Order Revived. He considered it an attack upon
his father, himself, and the New England churches. "All the
Rage of Satan, against the Holy Churches of the Lord, falls,"
he declared, "upon us [his father and himself]. First Calf's
[Calef's] Book, and then Coleman's,[47] do sett the People in a
Ferment." He thought the work of the partisans "a most
odious Mocking of the Religion of the Country" and proposed, by a bare recital from the book's pages, a refutation of
the "vile Things" written against his father and himself and
what he saw as a plot against the churches.[48] But his answer,
A Collection of Some of the Many Offensive Matters, did
more than recite. The twelve points that he made into the
plot of the partisans against the New England churches were,
on the whole, strained, corrupted, and imperfect renderings
of the arguments in *The Gospel Order Revived.* Mather took
affront at all disagreement. Seemingly he could not look upon
satirical constructions with any degree of calmness, but must,
maddened, twist and pull the whole discourse of the partisans
into a monstrous piece of impudence. Doubtless, he saw it "a
Considerable Dunghil."[49]

For *A Collection's* more ready reception, his father ham-
mered out a red-hot preface, in which he declared the proper
title for the late work of the partisans should have been "The

Order of the Gospel *Reviled*," that its chief author (Colman
is obviously meant) was "a Raw & an Unstudied Youth, but
also of a very Unsanctified Temper and Spirit," and for
Thomas Brattle, who called him "a Reverend Scribler"—
well, he took the roof off. Charging that "a *Moral Heathen*
would not have done as he has done," he called for church
discipline of this offender, saying: "If the Church to which he
does belong, will not *Exercise Discipline* towards so *Scandalous a Scoffer*, it is Time for Neighbour Churches to Consider
what their Duty is, with respect to a Soceity, that shall allow
of such *gross Immoralities*."[50]

The Mather party had many adherents, and there were
others who resented *The Gospel Order Revived*. Sewall saw
a copy of it and found the following interesting doggerel inscribed by one obviously not in sympathy with the partisans.

*A Simple Poem on the Authors and
Designs of this Booke.*

Begging Manifesto proves but a great Pesto.
Blackman[51] is Synodalian.
Pray stay there and stop, lest next hap & hop
Ben't Peters chair Italian

The old strait Gate is now out of Date,
The Street it must be broad;[52]
And the Bridge must be wood,[53] tho not half so good
As firm Stone in the Road.

Relations are Rattle with Brattle & Brattle;
Lord Brother mayn't command:
But Mather and Mather had rather & rather
The good old way should stand.

Saints Cotton & Hooker, o look down, & look here
Where's Platform, Way, & the Keys?
O Torey what story of Brattle Church Twattle,
To have things as they please

Our Merchants cum Mico do stand Sacro Vico;
Our Churches turn genteel:
Parsons grow trim and trigg with wealth wine & wigg
And their crowns are coverd with meal.[54]

The opposition of the Mathers did not stop with publications. Under Increase's leadership, "a General Convention"
of ministers at Boston on May 30, 1700, directed its disapproval toward the Brattle Street Church when it voted to
republish the decision of the Synod of 1662 against unadvised
gatherings of people into new churches.[55]

But the Brattle Street Church[56] was soon to have a respite.
The vexing problems of Harvard's charter and presidency
would absorb the opposition more and more, and the new
church would quietly assume an accepted position in the
town. By the time the Harvard presidency had been wrested
from the grasp of the Mathers and the government of Dudley
had begun to disappoint them, they had let the earlier struggle drop and were uncritical of allies in their associational
work, for meanwhile Benjamin Colman had become a member of the Boston-Cambridge association.

The 1705 proposals had several earlier and slighter forms.
At almost every annual convention of ministers for several
years before their formulation, there were proposed anticipa-
tory measures. One June, Cotton Mather drew up and laid
before a convention of nearly thirty ministers *Proposals for
the Preservation of Religion in the Churches, by a Due Trial
of Them That Stand Candidates of the Ministry.* He then had
copies published so that the paper might be "dispersed into
all parts of the Countrey, for the Concurrence and the Direction of all concerned."[57] At the convention in June, 1704,
pastors of twenty churches signed a circular letter, recom-
mending greater pastoral activity and cooperation in each
church and between churches. Samuel Willard, moderator of

the convention, head-officer of Harvard, and senior minister of Boston's Third Church, sent forth another letter in November, urging communication among the associations in order to watch over the interests of religion. The following September the 1705 proposals came full-fledged from a meeting where they were approved by nine delegates representing the five associations of Massachusetts. The proposals were emitted in answer to a question probably propounded at the earlier ministerial convention: "What further steps are to be taken, that the councils may have due constitution and efficacy in supporting, preserving and well ordering the interests of the churches in the country?"

Cotton Mather busied himself in finding the answer to this question. In his Diary he wrote:

In the Beginning of *September,* pretty much of my Time was taken up in preparing of Matters, for the Service of the Churches: The Ministers of the several Associations in the Province, having ordered their Delegates, to meet at *Boston,* that so they might there make Proposals, for the more convenient Management of many Things, in the Churches throughout the Land; especially, when their Necessities Call for *Councils* to be convened.[58]

Of course, Mather's time was not completely taken up in fostering the proposals. He was absorbed in many duties and activities. Especially charmed by do-good societies, he helped organize and belonged to fourteen or fifteen of them—such as those for the Suppression of Disorders and the Propagation of Religion.[59] While the proposals had the backing of the Mathers—and naturally wholehearted and excessive that support would be—nevertheless, a sustained and carefully planned campaign to institute them as instruments of authority over the churches of New England was probably never undertaken.

The proposals were again assented to at an associational

meeting in Cambridge on November 5, and copies were sent
to ministers. They were received with some dubiety, however.
The proposals[60] were meant to crystallize orthodoxy by
means of supervisory power, but they went too far. The first
eight dealt with the powers of the individual ministerial association, and the remainder with the powers of a larger body,
composed of lay and clerical delegates from the associations.
It was too much formalism. The burden of government was
too great, and participation was too limited to recommend
the plan to individual churches. Many ministers, of course,
approved the plan, and more ministerial associations were
formed, but their powers were not so sweeping as those the
proposals recommended. Not until 1790 was any one of the
proposals ever adopted, and then only that providing for
examination of ministerial candidates.[61]

Congregations were far too circumspect to yield themselves
to a strangling formalism administered by corruptible men.
It was better to have the present flexible organization, each
congregation adjusting to the passing times. The Cambridge
platform in allowing to each church large liberty for action
did not err, after all. So many laymen thought, and ministers,
too. John Wise was one of those who stood stubbornly on the
old platform. In *Ratio Disciplinae Fratrum Nov-Anglorum*,
an account of church discipline published in 1726, Cotton
Mather himself confessed that "there were some very considerable Persons among the *Ministers,* as well as of the
Brethren, who thought the *Liberties* of *particular Churches*
to be in danger of being too much *limited* and *infringed* in
them. And in Deference to these Good Men, the *Proposals*
were never prosecuted, beyond the Bounds of *meer Proposals.*"[62]

Probably another cause of defeat was the indifference of
the Massachusetts government. The Saybrook platform, a

body of measures similar to the proposals and adopted in 1708 by the Connecticut churches, was enforced by that colony's government. Connecticut still ran under its old charter and elected its upper house and governor, who in 1708 was a minister. In contrast, Massachusetts had received a new charter in 1692 and now submitted to a royal governor, in the person of Joseph Dudley, who exercised veto power over the upper house. Dudley, though a member of Roxbury church, attended King's Chapel and looked with a cold eye upon ecclesiastical enlargement. To him the church-state was a dead, dead letter. He was deeply imbued, from both his service under Governor Andros and his experience in various offices in England, with the principles of English civil rule. From him could come no support for the proposals.

There was one other cause working for the ultimate defeat of the proposals—John Wise's writings. The proposals were not liberal, for all their newness. They were cramping and restrictive. They sought to saddle on the churches a government under which all that was narrow, all that was illiberal in the Puritan religion could have full sway. Wise discovered to friend and foe alike the democracy which had operated in congregational churches for many years, first by his specific attack upon the proposals, *The Churches Quarrel Espoused,* and secondly by his general defense of church democracy, *A Vindication of the Government of New England Churches.* His first book was, according to Allibone's frequently repeated assertion, printed in Boston in 1710;[63] certainly it was printed in New York in 1713[64] and found a reception warm enough to warrant its reprinting in Boston two years later. No one ventured a reply to it until two years after the publication of both of Wise's books, in 1772,[65] and by that time the proposals were well off the stage. In fact, they were probably on their way off when John Wise's book gave them the final boot.

CHAPTER IX

The Churches Quarrel Espoused

THE 1705 PROPOSALS had been circulating in New England for almost five years before John Wise wrote his answer. Unless Chebacco were one of the most out-of-the-way places in the world, he must have seen a copy of the proposals soon after the Boston association broadcast them in November. After all, representatives of the Salem association had helped to formulate "Question and Proposals" two months earlier, and word of this activity, it seems, would have trickled back to the church of Chebacco, not many miles away. If Wise read the proposals in 1705, he may have thought them no effectual threat to the established government of New England churches, for he seems to have written nothing against them then.

And if, as seems probable, he did not object to them at that time, what caused him later to change his mind? Did he fear, as it has been suggested,[1] because of Connecticut's submission in 1708 to the Saybrook platform—a system of controls similar to that projected by the proposals—the future subjection of the Massachusetts churches? Certainly he professed to see in the scheme of the proposals "the *Spectre Ghost of Presbiterianism,* or the Government of the Church by Classes."[2] Or did the movement to institute the proposals grow with the years, and was he, therefore, alarmed and finally driven to refutation? The sponsors of the proposals were doubtless not idle. The indefatigable Cotton Mather was continually getting up a question for the annual considera-

tion of the ministers, the answer to which might have brought
in its train subversion of the autonomy enjoyed by congregational churches. In May, 1711, he wrote down the following
"good device" in his *Diary*.

The Ministers of the Province in their anniversary Meeting at
the Time for the Election of our Counsellors, ought to have a
Quæstion gott read for them to discourse upon. The Quæstion
which I would prepare and propose for them is this:
*What may we perceive arising in any Part of the Countrey, which
may injure or threaten the Interests of Piety: and what may we
propose, for the preventing of such Evils, and the preserving of
our best interests?*[3]

Such activities, by a gradual impact, could have stirred
Wise to a serious consideration of the proposals and led him
to seize them as the most palpable example of what seemed to
him a dangerous trend. For, according to his own admission,
Wise viewed the proposals as a plan to curtail freedom and
wrote *The Churches Quarrel Espoused* in answer. Because of
the proposals, he told laymen, "ye have been called unto
Liberty."[4]

But whether the drift of events roused Wise to reconsider
the proposals and to discover them a threat to church freedom or whether, by some strange retarding, he just now, in
1710, saw them for the first time and immediately began his
answer is not clear. At this time, anyway, he was writing *The
Churches Quarrel Espoused*, for at the end of "The Epistle
Dedicatory" he inscribed the date "May 31, 1710." Perhaps
this inscription has led to the citation of 1710 as the date of
publication. No extant copy of such an edition is known. Indeed, there was no contemporary comment—at least, none
that has come down to the present day—until after the
second edition was published in Boston in 1715.

At the beginning of *The Churches Quarrel Espoused*, Wise

set down the "Question"⁵ and the 1705 proposals, even to the final paragraph giving their origin and direction for distribution. Then by an "Epistle Dedicatory," a number of queries, and a detailed consideration of each proposal, he proceeded to discredit and refute the plan of the associated ministers. He wrote in satire and apologized for doing so. Some might think, he said, that because of the satirical form of his discourse, he assumed a superiority over the sponsors of the proposals, but he begged readers to ascribe his efforts rather to "my love and veneration for so great an Interest as I appear for, and not to any base intent of sinking the honour, or darkening the Luster of better Men." He vowed: "*I* Solely aim at ERROR, that is the But *I* Level for."⁶

In "The Epistle Dedicatory," addressed to the fraternity of New England churches, he gave his reasons for writing, urged the acceptance of several petitions, and prayed for God's blessings upon the royal and colonial governments of England.

He addressed the fraternity, or brethren, rather than the pastors, because the privileges of the fraternity were "so peculiarly the Theam and subject" of his discourse and because he wrote "in Defence of their sacred Liberties." Intimating that their church liberties were threatened, Wise exhorted the brethren (echoing *Galatians* v:1): "Stand fast therefore in the *Liberties*, wherewith Christ has made us free, and be not Intangled again with the Yoke of Bondage." For his belief "that the Constitution and Way of *New-England* Churches . . . [could not] be mended by Exchange," he offered two reasons: The present church government had only a mild interest in the streams of revenue, so leaving them undepleted to civil power for the maintenance of the subjects' liberties; and the present church government, in emulating the English civil system, considered "the best God of a whole

People." He declared:

By the suffrage of our Nation, that Government which sensibly
Clogs Tyranny, and Preserves the Subject free from slavery, under the ambition of men of great Fortune and Trust, is the only
gover[n]ment in the *state*, to advance mens temporal Happiness;
and we in the Country Honour the Resolve in Civil Affairs, and
also affirm (upon great Experience) that such a Constitution in
Church Government is (also) the only way to advance Grace
and Mans Eternal Happiness.[7]

After exhorting the brethren again to be concerned for the
rich cargo of their churchly vessels, he encouraged, in the
form of petitions, the acceptance of six considerations. In the
first petition he urged the brethren to know who and what
they were, to set a proper valuation upon themselves.
"Imagine your selves to be something more than Ordinary,"
he wrote, "for Really you be so." They were not to be discouraged because of the presence of the unworthy in the same
group with the noble nor to infer "the Insufficiency of the
great and wise, because of the mean and base mingled in the
same Communities."

Having weighed their own importance and worth, the
brethren were, according to the second petition, "to put such
an Estimation and value on . . . [their] Church Liberties as
the English . . . [did] on their Civil," remembering the sacri-
fices by which those liberties had been obtained.

In the third petition, where he urged the brethren to
"Honour and Oblige" their pastors, Wise took occasion to
warn against "Currupt and Prejudiced" ministers. Wise
would be "very loath to share in their [the bad ministers']
tryumphs, tho' their gains should be seemingly great, and
their signals and shouts equal with the Cesars of the World
in their going off."

Wise next petitioned the brethren, in order to preserve better their liberties, to appoint a ruling elder in each of their churches, notwithstanding "Complaints of great Poverty, and of a Dearth and Scarcity of suitable men." Wise was concerned over the lapse from the old way in respect to this office, for he admitted that the ruling elder had become *"rara Avis in Terra,* like a blak Swan in the Meadow," and he set himself to find out the cause of the office's neglect. He suggested that the blame might be laid to brethren who distrusted their own abilities, to ordained officers who acted from motives of jealousy, misunderstanding, or custom, and to churches that were indifferent and irresponsible.

From the consideration of the ruling elder, Wise went on, in his fifth petition, to another neglect. He feared that a copy of the Cambridge platform was "scarce to be found in the hands of one in a Thousand" and called for "a New impression," crying to the brethren:

Don't you hear from the top of yonder Proud and Lofty Mountain, the Enemies Trumpets, and their Drums Beating a Preparative? Therefore, let all the good Souldiers of Christ be Compleat in this and all other parts of their Armour, and at an hours warning, unless you reckon your Treasure not worth Defending.⁸

Another aid to the churches would be a general synod. In his last petition Wise promoted such a gathering so that any emendation to church government or measure "necessary for the Advance of Religion . . . [might] be fairly decided for the service of the whole." Such a meeting was especially to be desired in order to prevent

small Juncto's of Men, or particular Persons, Member or Members of the Churches (let their Character and Capacity be what it may be) . . . from being so hardy and bold as to Divulge their Pernicious Doctrines, and seditious Sentiments, with such Presumption, and such hopes of Impunity, as some of late have done.

He had no further hope to add to "The Epistle Dedica-

tory" than the one that his discourse, "tho' it be but as a little
Goats Hair, or a Badgers hide, or two Skins (not well drest),"
would be "some way useful for the Tabernacle." He concluded by suing for God's blessings upon Queen Anne, the
provincial government, and the New England churches,
and in praying for Christ's preservation of those churches'
liberties.[9]

"The Epistle Dedicatory" was skillful writing. It provided
the readers with a subject of almost universal interest as a
rallying point, church liberties, and it underscored the defense
of those liberties. The danger that occasioned their defense
Wise did not here explicitly describe, but he hinted at its
nature a number of times. And if his hints went unperceived,
there were the "Question and Proposals," printed without
comment in the opening pages, to guide the readers to the
author's meaning. It would be an undiscerning reader who
could get through "The Epistle Dedicatory" without feeling
that his church liberties were threatened somehow, some-
where. The petitions of the epistle directed him to a better
defense.

Wise adopted a humble attitude, but it was a humility that
could not be scorned, for he made clear that for him to keep
silent was to harbor cowardice, and he would not be a coward.
In one petition he said too much: when writing about ruling
elders, probably a favorite topic, he drew near prolixity, a
fault he admitted wanting to avoid. But he had also been
eloquent: he had shown laymen their present good fortune
in church government and made acceptable the duty of defense. Now he would not only reveal plainly the reason for
the call to arms, but deal the first blow. And he chose to improve the effectiveness of his blow by the use of satire.

Wise proposed to let his satire take the form of a mock
trial, but after a beginning, which he said he borrowed from

the arraignment of Sir Walter Raleigh and in which he summoned to "the Bar of Common Reason" "the Criminal Proposals," he made no extended use of this form, other than to recall the language of the courts by employing such words and phrases as "evidence," "writ of ejectment," "trial," "prosecution," "claimer," and "case," and to enclose his remarks in the frame of a mock trial again at the end. Having so arraigned "the Criminal Proposals," he first presented evidence against them by "a few Præliminary Queries" and then by "a more Critical *Examination* of the Proposals themselves."

In the first query he stressed again the many years of satisfaction the present church government had given and questioned whether any power but one superior to the churches or a voluntary act of the churches themselves could dispossess them of that government. During the sixty years that the plan of church discipline (the Cambridge platform) had been in effect, he pointed out in his second query, no "essential error" had been discovered, and the proposals did not now discover one. To fortify his own position and to damage that of his opponents, Wise selected quotations from the election sermon of Nicholas Noyes, of Salem, and from Cotton Mather's *Theopolis Americana*, wherein they preached a faithful adherence to the platform. Quoting these men against themselves, ministers whom Wise and others doubtless knew to be sponsors of the proposals, served not only to reveal the awkward and inconsistent behavior of those who sought to bring in the new, while still supporting the old, but also to damage the acceptability of those measures.

Once more quoting, in his third query, from Mather's unrestrained praise of the platform, even to giving the page number in *Theopolis*, Wise scored the impudence of "any particular Gentlemen" who would "invade, null, Alter or

Weaken" the government of the churches. While here defending church government, Wise set down some memorable sentences on government in general when he wrote:

Government is the greatest Blessing in the World, of a worldly Nature; it is Felony, cheaper by far to the Loosers, to plunder men of their Estate and wealth, nay, and of their Lives too, then to dispoyl them of Government; for by the latter, you harass and worry them in the world, with Plagues and miseries worse than death it self, that the basest is far better, then no Government; a churlish Tyranny, is better then an Insolent Anarchy, where men are without Law, and all *hail Fellows,* not well but badly met. And for men to alter or warp Government, without all Interested parties are agreed, is a very bold Intrusion.[10]

In the fourth query it was the turn of "the famous and Learned *Increase Mather,* D.D." to be quoted. In *The Order of the Gospel,* Wise noted the lament of "that worthy" over "Plots conspiring the Dissolution" of the congregational churches. Doubtless Wise took mischievous pleasure in his pompous references to I. Mather.

In emphasizing the basic disagreement of the proposals with the platform, Wise used satire to good effect. He pictured the sponsors of the proposals coming forward with trowel in hand

to plaister over a chink or two, where the Old work by length of time, is somewhat Weather-beaten, to pacify the Jealousies of the inhabitants, that they may think these Builders (surely) are mending, and not Maring their old Comfortable Habitation. But in Reality [Wise wrote] they have in the other hand a formidable *Maul* . . . to break Down the Building; for they are *all hands at work Banging the Platform in Pieces, upon which the old Fabrick is Built.*

Wise questioned, in his last query, the authority of these masons and their tool.[11]

Now Wise was ready for a general and particular examination of the proposals themselves. First came the general examination, and it had to do with the origin and nature of the proposals. "Unless they can derive their Pedigree," Wise averred, from God's "Immediate Inspiration," from ancient revelation, from right reason, or from the platform, "they forfeit their Essence." First, the proposals did not come directly from God; the sponsors dared not "put, a *Thus said the* LORD upon them." Second, from the Bible, "the saints Library, and the Clergy-mans Pandects,"[12] the proposals did not draw "the least tincture of Scripture to gaurd [*sic*] them from Contempt." Third, right reason, that "Ray of Divine Wisdom, instampt upon Humane nature," could not, Wise believed, reconcile the proposals with the present constitution of the churches. And finally, the platform, according to Wise, disclaimed any fatherhood. So he begged, using again the figure of the mock trial, "that Zeal and Conscience, those two Solicitors for the Crown . . . [would] at this Grand Court of *Oyer* and *Terminer* Implead and Prosecute . . . [the proposals] as Traytors to the Prince of Peace, and Fellons to these Churches, Christs Loyal Subjects."[13]

Nor in the nature of the proposals did Wise see anything to commend. Their composition was conglomerate, being a "Conjunction of almost all the Church Governments in the World," the least part of which was congregational. Not only was Presbyterianism there, but also "Considerable of *Prelacy*, . . . only the distinct Courts of Bishop[s,] with the *Steeples* of the *Churches, Tythes, Surplice,* and other Ornaments . . . [did] not shew themselves so visible, as to be discerned at the first look; yet with a Microscope" they might easily be discerned. "To Assume the Power of making Rules, to Ingross all Principles of Process, The Right of Election, the last Appeal, The Negative Vote, and all Super-Intending Power in Matters Ecclesiastick, as the Prerogatives of Clergy-men,

Distinct from all other Estates, and Ministers in Government," Wise's nose testified, smelled *"very strong of the Infallible Chair,"* that seat of "universal Pestilence." Should the ministers be invested with the powers of the proposals, Wise foresaw that their bulls would "upon any affront, Bellow and Thunder out a Thousand terrible Curses, and the poor affrighted and Invassal'd Layity, both Princes and Subjects . . . must forfeit their Salvation, if they . . . [did not] tamely submit, and obediently become their Executioners."

In the make-up of the proposals Wise saw the damning blemishes of disorder, usurpation, riot, sacrilege, rebellion, unfaithfulness, ingratitude, and impolicy.[14] He endeavored to prove the possession of these qualities by defining riot and by discoursing on the laws of England and New England and the rights of posterity; and in doing so he showed an understanding of and admiration for the democratic elements of English law. His approval is quite apparent in these sentences.

Under the Prosecutions of Law, no *English Subjects,* in Life, Limb or Estate, must be past upon, but by the Judgment of his PEERS; Yea, in all Pleas of the Crown, such Confidence has the Government put in the Loyalty and Discretion of the Commons, that our English Juries are stated Arbitrators, and Umpires between our Prince and his Subjects. Yea, such a dependance has the whole Nation in Keeping these Liberties in their own hands, that they Reckon the *Commons in Parliament,* and Juries in the *Common Wealth,* to be the great Pillars of English Honour and Liberties, and they esteem them as Ramparts built by the Wisdom of our Ancestors to Defend us from Tyranny and Slavery.[15]

His admiration for order found worthy utterance, too.

Order is both the Beauty and safety of [the] Universe; take aside the decorum whereby the whole hangs together the great Frame of nature is unpin'd and drops piece from piece; and out of a Beautiful structure we have a Chaos.[16]

At this point it would seem that the proposals should have been disintegrating before Wise, but he went on. And he would not only now, in *The Churches Quarrel Espoused,* exhaustively indict the proposals, but, using his first book as a springboard, plunge on, in his next one, to a notable treatment of democracy in church and civil government.

The first proposal, "That the Ministers of the Country form themselves into Associations, that may meet at Proper times to consider such things as may properly lie before them," Wise, in *The Churches Quarrel Espoused,* agreed with only in small part. That ministers could meet together he did not deny, but the plan "to meet at certain times and places, as Political Incorporate Bodies, or in the form of Classes, for the Exercise and Management of Government," he believed had to be approved by some "legislative Power," that is, the General Court or a synod called by the Court. Those who took into their own hands unauthorized power and called up representatives were "very Dispotick and Arbitrary"; and those who would be called up were "Servile in their Submission." The platform denied "the Classical State of the Church."

To the second part of this proposal, "That each of these Associations have a Moderator for a certain time, who shall continue till another be chosen, who may call them together upon Emergencies," Wise made several objections. Not only were the limits of each association undefined, he criticized, but the business of notification—involving messengers, expense, and way-stations—went unmentioned. This might seem a quibbling objection and one that could be easily answered when the associations were organized, but doubtless Wise felt that no thought, or not enough, had been given to practical considerations in the initial formulation of the proposals. Wise also looked askance upon the uncurbed power of the moderator to call or deny meetings, for the moderator could change his mind once he had got the delegates on the road, or ignore emergencies that touched his friends embarrassingly, or out of pique overlook a need for meetings altogether. Wise believed that such a careless plan would make "Fools of men." "For my own part," he declared, "I would slight such Methods in Government."

The second proposal, "That Questions and Cases of Importance, either provided by themselves, or by others presented unto them, should be upon due deliberation Answered," provoked Wise to wonder what questions had been going unanswered. He recommended the study of a couple of church fathers for the solution of difficulties rather than the dubious practice of consulting an associational conclave. Indeed, he professed not to understand the proposal and wondered if it might not be a strategical device to dazzle and ensnare the churches.

The third proposal also—at least the second section of it—Wise found difficult to understand. The first section, though, was easy enough. It stated "That Advice be taken by the Associated Pastors, from time to time, ere they proceed to any Action in their particular Churches, which may be likely to Produce any Imbroylments." Wise pointed out that this section was in violation of the platform and believed it chiefly constructed for the protection of timorous, weak-kneed pastors. He scorned it as "a Covering of Figg-Leaves," "a Harbour to Cowards and Fools," and a procedure useless to "men of spirit and Conduct." He warned, in language having a strangely modern application:

The Dream of an Imbroylment, can never Counter-Poyze Duty; If men are Trusted with Duty, they must consult that, and not Events. If men are plac'd at Helm, to steer in all weather which Blows, they must not be afraid of the Waves, or a wet Coat.[17]

The second section, proposing "That the Associated Pastors do carefully and lovingly treat each other with that Watchfulness which may be of Universal advantage," Wise was even more critical of than the first. He thought that he saw here the unworthy practice of spying, either urged upon the ministers themselves or to be indulged in by a higher order of clergy, created for the purpose. The first possibility he considered impractical, for the ministers did not bed and sup together as monks in a monastery, and the second possibility was inimical to congregational practices. Perhaps, he conjectured, the ministers were to go to the expense and trouble of keeping spies in each other's parishes. Surely such spying upon one another the few days the association met was not enough. Anyone could behave that short a time. Wise finally gave up trying to understand the measure and confessed: "a Riddle I found it, and a Riddle *I leave it.*"

The third section of the proposal Wise thought usurpation indeed. By it he believed the brethren would be divested of the chief power granted them by the platform, for it was stated in this section of the proposal

That if any Minister be accused to the Association where he belongs, of Scandal or Heresy, the matter shall be there Examined, and if the Associated Ministers find just occasion for it, they shall direct a Calling of the Council, by which such an Offender is to be proceeded against.

Wise held that according to the congregational way all "Delinquent private Members and Publick Officers are Tryable only" in their congregations and "there they must Receive the Definitive Sentence, and abide the Execution of it." In this privilege, he declared, lay the strength of the churches or

the Pick-Lock of their *Treasure;* for by this Key stolen, or wrinched out of their Hands, the Churches of Christ in the *World,* have been *Exposed* and *Plundred,* for more than a Thousand

Years, and many of them have nothing at this day left them, comparitively, but a poor, starved shabbid implicit *Faith,* and a dull, saturnal, blunt and blind Obedience, that a man would scarcely give a Groat for both of them.

The fourth proposal,

That the Candidates of the Ministry undergo a due Tryal by some or other of the Association, concerning their Qualification for the Evangelical Ministry; And that no perticular Pastor or Congregation, Imploy any one in occasional Preaching, who has not been Recommended by a Testimonial, under the hands of some Association,

would give the associations, Wise thought, an intolerable monopoly. It would be an inefficient one as well. The ministers making up the associations were too rusty in their learning to pass on the knowledge of a recently schooled candidate. They would have to be wary, "least when they became Posers of others, they should be posed themselves." The Harvard authorities were in a much better position to examine the qualifications of a candidate than any association. They did not form their judgment on a single sermon. To allow one sermon delivered before the association to stand as the candidate's bid for a ministerial license was unjust and inconclusive. After all, Wise said, calling upon an old proverb, "One Swallow makes not the Spring; so in this Tryal, one good or mean Sermon cannot Determine the man, or *umpire* his Case." The Harvard tutors, pastors, good men, and churches that had had to do with the candidate should be his recommendation. Nor should the youth of a candidate be against him. With lively examples and answers Wise dispensed with the objections usually brought against youth and showed that the proper test was, not years, but wisdom. Neither could Wise believe that the times now required a new method of examination. He asked for the naming of one minister whose unworthiness would warrant the installation of this method that he feared would be too soon abused by a body too easily corrupted.

Against the fifth proposal Wise arraigned the platform again. Not only did the proposal,

That they [the associated pastors] together be Consulted by Bereaved Churches, to Recommend to them such Persons as may be fit to be imployed amongst them, for present supply, from whom they may in due time proceed to choose a Pastor,

invade the rights of the brethren but assumed them incapable of exercising a right. Not only would the association decide on the ministers, a business that chiefly affected the well-being of the particular church concerned, but would imply in the process that the brethren were intellectually bankrupt. Such a measure reminded Wise very much of the decision made against the laity many years ago when they

were described by the Learned to be without the Knowledge of the Original Languages, and other parts of Polite Learning, and so no ways fit to Interpret Scripture; therefore it is very Rationally Enacted, That the BIBLE be taken from them, lest they should study Heresie and not Holiness out of that Divine Book.

Wise considered the sixth proposal another encroachment upon the rights of the church. He hoped that the gentlemen of the association did not "reckon the Churches to be making their last Will, and design them for their Heirs." He would inform those gentlemen, so far as the sixth proposal was concerned, that the New England churches had always been possessed of the right to convene councils for their welfare and had not had to consult an association for directions.

The designs of the next proposal Wise did not condemn as nefarious. Nevertheless, he censured them as expensive, luxurious, and ambiguous. The requirement, "That the several Associations in the Country maintain a due Correspondence with one another," would be, he thought, too expensive unless the associations were prepared to operate by carrier pigeon or by "the Platonick Notion concerning the Universal Soul of the World or Spirit of Nature (whereby one Body is affected by the Operations of another at some considerable distance)." Correspondence was, the proposal would have it, to make better known and to secure the state of religion in the churches. Such a purpose was in the interests of vanity, Wise declared in a passage noteworthy for its praise of religion, and served only to gild the lily. He doubted the feasibility of the last section, too, "That all the Associations in the Country meet together, by their Respective Delegates, once in a year," since "country," being undefined, might include much of America and the astronomical expense of meeting at far distant places be involved. Wise proposed setting aside the income from "some good stout Gold Mine in *Peru*" to bear the expense of assembling.

The last proposal of the group dealing with the individual association introduced the stipulation

That Ministers disposed to Associate, endeavour in the Most Efficacious Manner they Can, to Prevail with such Ministers, as Unreasonably neglect such Meetings with their Brethren in their Proper Associations, that they would not expose themselves to the Inconveniencies that such Neglects cannot but be attended withal.

The cocksureness with which the association was presented as the save-all plan for the churches caused Wise to accuse the proposers' presumption. The plan reminded him of the one that Epicurus had offered to explain the origin of the world: the chance coalescence of atoms. Both plans seemed to disregard the Creator. To demonstrate the completely mortal beginnings of associations, Wise unfolded their brief history in New England. In these associations ministers had been

led on by vanity to assume the possession of power that was
not theirs. He recommended a return to their former more
humble positions and a disavowal of these proposals, which
might be compared not only to Aaron's golden calf but to a
more natural sort of calf. Wise admonished "that tho' it be
But a Calf now, yet in time it may grow (being of a Thirsty
Nature) to *become a sturdy Ox, that will know no Whoa*, and
it may be past the Churches skill then to subdue it." There
was, of course, in Europe just such a monster, Wise claimed,
bellowing and trampling through the lands.

Before Wise began on the next eight proposals, he had a
little fun. He wondered at the obtuseness or audacity that
had permitted the issuance of the proposals on November 5,
a day notorious because of the Catholic conspiracy of Guy
Fawkes to blow up parliament. Since this was "the day of
the *Gun-Powder-Treason*, and a fatal day to Traytors,"
would it not denote as well the failure of the proposals? Wise,
for one, was sure of it. A conspiracy so inauspiciously begun
he would not join.[18]

The first one of the second group of proposals Wise gave
prolonged attention in order that the remaining ones could
be passed over more quickly. This proposal recommended:

That these Associated Pastors with a proper Number of Dela-
gates from their several Churches be formed into a standing and
Stated Council, which shall Consult, Advice and Determine all
Affairs that shall be proper matter for the Consideration of an
Ecclesiastical Council within their respective Limits, Except al-
ways the Cases are such as the Associated Pastors judge more
Convenient to fall under the Cognizance of other Council.

Wise suspected "the seeming Favour" with which the
brethren were treated in this proposal. Having noted the dependence of the proposed standing council upon the will of
the associated ministry, he considered the proposal only "a

Specious shew" that would ravish the brethren and leave them, like drones, without authority. The only recourse for the brethren, once the proposal had been adopted, would be to lament their slavish state. Wise warned:

And here we may dig a Grave to bury all our Ancient Priviledges in, and Hang our Harps upon the Willows, and when we are thus wasted, should you call us in once more to sing one of the Songs of *Sion,* all our Notes must be *Elegie & De tristibus,* yet the Broken Accents, and lowly Murmours of our Sorrow will *serve* for *Elahs* and Sweet Diapasans, in the Counquerours Song of Triumph.[19]

Wise then touched briefly on the expense of the plan and its lack of respectable origin, for it came neither from Scripture, civil law, governmental practice, church authority, nor imperial patent. In fact, Wise ventured to show in the light of a few great principles of English government the council and whole scheme stood condemned. Not only did the proposals violate established law and the jurisdiction of parliament, which alone bound the English subject; but the presumption and arbitrariness of the proposal aroused the hostility of the subject himself, for, Wise pointed out: "All Englishmen live and dye by Laws of their own making . . . they are never pleased with upstart Lawmakers. . . English men hate an Arbitrary Power (Politically Considered) as they hate the Devil."[20]

As Wise revolved the subject of arbitrary government in his mind, he reflected on how much the reign of absolute monarchy, a form of rule "contrary to the temper of the Nation, and the Ancient Constitution of the Government," had lost for England. Then, perhaps thinking of his own part in the rebellious action against the government of King James II, he wrote:

The very name of an Arbitrary Government is ready to put an

English man's Blood into a Fermentation; but when it really comes, and shakes its whip over their Ears, and tells them [Englishmen] it is their Master, it makes them stark Mad; and being of a Mimical *Genius*, and Inclined to follow the Court Mode, They turn Arbitrary too.[21]

As for the proposals, in their disregard for established law, Wise concluded: "They have out King'd all Kings on Earth .... They have out Bishop't all Bishops of *Great Britain*.... They have out Pope't the Pope himself."

Wise next questioned the need of all that the proposals would institute. He confessed to their sponsors, not without a view to humorous exaggeration:

Upon the first view of this stupenduous Business, I was ready to Phancy, whether or no you had Dream'd of or seen King *Henry* the Eighth a coming with his old Case and Question which involved the Pope, his Conclave and all the Accademies in *Europe*, and whether you were getting a Mighty Casuist ready, to take the Kings Conscience into Consideration? or whether you had news of the Old *Arian* War, its Breaking out again, that you should in such haste, (without Citing other Estates for the Defence of the Kingdom, but only by vertue of your Prerogative) Run up such a formidable and Costly Redoubt?[22]

After all, Wise queried, wasn't everything being done that should be done? Was not civil authority abroad engaged in upholding justice and piety and in crushing immorality and vice? Were not the New England churches tending the land with a marvelous husbandry? Was not the college at Cambridge a proper nursery of learning? And were not the God-fearing families of the country "so many little Sanctuaries?" What need of more, Wise wondered.

Since a standing council was superfluous in Christian New England, provision having been made in the platform "for the Convening of occasional and needful Councils," Wise called the measure a waste of time. Also, the assembly of a large number of ministers and brethren was liable to make civil authority suspicious and hostile.

With a few more objections, chiefly directed at the ambiguity of the proposal, Wise ended his critique and, probably believing that he had answered the rest of the proposals in earlier paragraphs, as indeed he had, wound up the discussion of the remaining seven in short order.

Wise censured the fifth proposal of this group for leaning toward Catholicism. It stated

That the Association shall Direct, when there is occasion, for this Council to convene, on any Emergency, and shall Direct whether the Whole, or only a certain Number of these Consociated Pastors and Churches shall convene on such occasions.

Wise saw a privileged ministerial hierarchy emerging from this proposal, and he objected thus:

The Beg'd Prerogatives of Clergy-men come so thick in this place, and smell so strong of the POPES Cooks and Kitchen, where his Broaths and Restoratives are prepared, That they are enough to strangle a *Free-born-English-man,* and much more these Churches, that have lived in such a clear air, and under such enlargements so long a time.[23]

The sixth proposal further made clear to Wise the ambition of the ministers who approved the proposals. The statement that

It appears agreeable with the present Condition of our Churches, and from our Beginning acknowledged, that no Act of the Council is to be reckoned, concluded and Desicive; for which there has not been the Concurrence of the Major part of the Pastors therein concerned,

set an undue importance, according to Wise, upon the word or vote of a minister and directly opposed the principle of equality in representative votes, as established in English parliamentary practice. Wise told the ministers of the association: "Your Challenge plainly Defines your Intention, that is to Null the Power of the Churches, and set up your selves, as the *Subject* or Fountain of a superintending Power."

The last two proposals dished up much of the material that was set down in the fifteenth and sixteenth chapters of the Cambridge platform, but that tardy dependence, Wise judged, could not atone for expressed intentions of supplanting. When England should see the ministers of the associations ready to raze the platform upon which the churches were built, she, who in the past had been quick to call the Puritans madmen or "Phanatics," would, Wise concluded, have the more reason now to do so, especially since the business of destruction was offered without any warrant from authority.

Wise, at the end of his discourse, rounded out the form of his satire. "The Criminal Proposals" had to be judged guilty or not guilty, all the evidence being in. Should the jury, "The Impartial Reason of the Churches," render them guilty, Wise petitioned the crown for the following judgment: "that the Proposals be *Sentenc'd to Dye the Death of Heriticks,* and their Ashes be Exposed to the four Winds; that the whole Scheme may, beyond all hope of Retrieve, be lost in Oblivion." As for the ministers who fostered the proposals, though he would leave their names to "repose under a mantle of honourable Piety and forgetfulness," yet he would advise them,

hereafter, when Temptation makes its Signal, let them rather Trespass upon *Gravity,* following the Hounds in the Forrest, or by a more submissive and moderate *Way* (to Baffle the Enemy, and wear off the Impression) let them write on the ground, or with [the] famous *Domitian,* spend the time in *Catching flies,* rather than Contrive how to subvert or alter the Government in the Churches, by such Dispotick Measures especially in an Empire and Province so Charmed with such *Inchanting Liberties* as ours are.[24]

The Churches Quarrel Espoused was published in New York in 1713 by the famous printer William Bradford, but perhaps few copies got back to the Boston area, for no comment has come down to posterity. Still, Wise's partiality to the Cambridge platform was known before the second edition came out in Boston in 1715, for Sewall recorded in his Diary in October, 1714, that, at the ordination of a pastor at Ipswich Farms, "Mr. Wise [gave] the Right Hand of Fellowship, much aplauding the N. English venerable Constitution."[25] And the first printing must have had some circulation in New England, for John White, of Gloucester, Wise's son-in-law, and the Reverend Samuel Moody, of York (the famous Father Moody), read it, for they wrote an introductory letter to the second edition. They commended the book, for it had opened their eyes to see "the Value and Glory of . . . [their] Invaded Priviledges," and they believed it could do as much for others. It would certainly be "a Testimony that all our Watchmen were not asleep, nor the Camp of Christ surprized and taken, before they had Warning."[26]

The second edition, issued early in 1715, attracted some notice. The Reverend Joseph Green, of Salem Village, wrote in his diary under the date of June 17: "I at study; read Mr. Wises mad book."[27] Of course, Cotton Mather rose up in wrath. On August 2 Sewall expressed his approval of Mather's reaction in his *Diary*. "Dr. Cotton Mather preach'd . . . Excellently; censur'd him that had reproach'd the Ministry, called the Proposals Modalities of little consequence, and made in the Keys; call'd it a Satanick insult, twice over, and it found a kind Reception."[28] Mather set down his own words September 17 in a letter.

No remarkable Disturbance is offered unto them; [the churches of New England] only that a furious Man, called John Wise, of whom, I could wish he had, *Cor bonum,* while we are all sensible, he wants, *Caput bene regulatum,* has lately published a foolish Libel against some of us, for presbyterianizing too much in our Care to repair some Deficiencies in our Churches. And some of our People, who are not only tenacious of their Liberties, but also more suspicious than they have cause to be of a Design in their pastors to make abridgments of them; are too much led into Temptation, by such Invectives. But the Impression is not so great, as our grand Adversary doubtless hoped for. And his Devices are disappointed.²⁹

Eleven years later he had a few more words to say.

There was indeed a Satyr, Printed against these *written Proposals,* and against the Servants of GOD that made them. Nevertheless, those *Followers of the Lamb,* remembering the Maxim of, *Not Answering,* used the Conduct which the University of Helmstadt lately prescribed under some Abuses put upon them; *Visum est non alio remedio quam generoso Silentio et pio Contemptu, utendum nobis esse.*³⁰

Perhaps it is needless to point out that Mather demonstrated here, in his reluctance to fall into print, a reaction quite out of character with his usual hot-to-publish self. Could it have been that he had no answer? Mather, it has been suggested,³¹ might have been moved to these last remarks because of the resounding defeat a petition of his met with in 1725, wherein he asked the General Court to call a synod to consider a proposal for the betterment of the churches. The disappointment could have brought to mind Wise's bitter pill that he had swallowed long ago.

Perhaps Increase Mather did make answer to Wise's book —though indirectly. One wonders whether he could have published his *Disquisition concerning Ecclesiastical Councils* in 1716 to offset the bad picture Wise gave of the ministers of the associations. If so, it was something of a whitewash, for

Mather expressed views here inconsistent with the proposals, which he had once approved with his signature.

Wise did a thorough job in answering the proposals, maybe too thorough. In his efforts to comment disparagingly upon every point, perhaps he fell over backward. But on the other hand, his arguments, since he dealt with ideas on a high and noble level, often transcended their subject. He might be further criticized for raising the same objection against many of the proposals: violation of the rights accorded the brethren by the Cambridge platform. Still, that was the objection he meant to emphasize, and he knew how to present his criticism in a variety of interesting ways. He applied learning with aptness and facility. Eloquence added seriousness to his argument, and humor provided him with a powerful weapon of ridicule. Of course, he went out of his way now and then to make quibbling remarks, but that practice is within the realm of satire. Wise had written a good book, but he was to write a better one. The one led to the other.

CHAPTER X

Wise's "Small Treatise"

A Vindication of the Government of New England Churches was "printed by *J. Allen,* for *N. Boone* [bookseller] at the Sign of the BIBLE in *Cornhill*," Boston, in the early part of the year 1717.[1]It was only 105 pages long—not so long as *The Churches Quarrel Espoused*—but those pages were full of sense. Wise, moved now to formal argument, proposed to defend the constitution of the churches by "solid truth."[2] Satire had done its work. "Question and Proposals" had been dealt with sufficiently, and there remained no other object to treat satirically. In his first book, Wise had, of course, written passages of "high seriousness" in addition to satiric passages. His second, though it was not without light touches, he wrote with an eye to sober argument and reasoned judgment.

Wise drew his weapons of defense from several arsenals—five in number, according to the title page. They were "Antiquity," the writings of the ancient church fathers and saints; "the Light of Nature," man's natural endowments and liberties as allowed by his Creator; the Scriptures; the "Noble Nature" of New England church government as "settled" by the Cambridge platform; and the "Dignity" God had "put upon" that government. From these Wise drew demonstrations[3] that justified the constitution of the New England churches.

The first two demonstrations were divided into chapters, which in turn, after the manner of writing in those days, endured an almost endless partition. The rest of the demonstra-

tions were not broken up into chapters but bore a considerable amount of division nevertheless.

The first demonstration called chiefly upon the Christian
writers of the first three hundred years of Christendom for
justification. Wise chose these centuries because in them, he
believed, the church was closest to the form Christ had designed for it. After them came the great apostacy, and the
church did not again attain to any purity of form until after
the Reformation.

The first chapter Wise devised as a brief essay on the three
periods of the Christian era. It was his belief that during the
first period the perils of espousing Christianity had a purging
effect upon its followers. It was "most Apparent," said he,
"that the Churches in those Ages, were under too good an
Influence Internally, and the Eye of too direful a guard, ex-
ternally to prevaricate with God, in the known Principles of
their Order."[4] Toward the end of this period there was some
falling away from the true worship of God and the proper
government of the churches. During the next twelve hundred
years the trend continued. In the beginning, Wise cited
authority to show, the pride and ambition of "Doctors of the
Church" had introduced the trend. One ambitious bishop
after another rose up to extend his sway over large areas of
the earth until at length the bishop of Rome rode "Admiral
of all the *Sees*," "and so *Rome* obtained the second Conquest
of the World." Wise then asked a rhetorical question. "What
can't wakeful Ambition, Learning and Fraud do, if Joyntly
agreed, at rifling the greatest Treasures bequeathed to Mankind; especially when the World is generally gotten into a
sleepy fit."[5]

The next age asked itself such questions as this one and
made militant responses. Various "Christian Heroes," some
of whom Wise singled out for praise, "went forward with the

Reformation." But they achieved a very imperfect one, the credit for which observation Wise respectfully gave to Dr. Increase Mather. Still, New England had gone the furthest toward a return to the practices of the primitive church; and "under the head of Discipline," it seemed to Wise, "Christ the Captain of Salvation" had issued to New England churches, "as to his Troops coming up in the Reer of Time," the following order.

As you were;[6] make good the Old front; or place your selves in that Regimental Order, which the Primitive Churches were in, whilst they march't under my Banners, & encountred the Devil in their heathen Persecutors for the first Three hundred years.[7]

Wise would now show how the government of these churches in the American wilderness was, in all essentials, parallel to church government among the early Christians.

But first he admitted that he did not go directly to the ancient writings themselves. He had a bridge to cross to them. He chiefly depended, as he said, upon "the Guidance of one who . . . [had] concealed his Name."[8] Wise was assured, however, of the fidelity of this "impartial hand" in transcribing the ancients and believed his study entitled *An Enquiry into the Constitution, Discipline, Unity & Worship of the Primitive Church*, extensive enough for dependence. Wise can be excused for relying on an intermediary. The editions of the early churchmen were doubtless none too numerous anywhere, and in New England probably even fewer than elsewhere.[9]

The library of Harvard, according to the lists of 1655,[10] had the works of Justin Martyr, Origen, and Cyprian, and when Wise wrote, may have had more; but Harvard was not convenient to Chebacco parish. So Wise, for the purpose of drawing a parallel between his own age and an earlier one, may have been fortunate in having the text he did. He depended upon it for help in organization and often transposed, un-acknowledged, portions of its text into his own book.[11] Some of Wise's references to the early authors, often with a tran-scription of the title, chapter, and page number of the sup-porting work— in abbreviated form—demonstrated knowl-edge that was not derived from his source, but for the most part he relied upon the authority of the intermediate work.

For a definition of the early church Wise translated from the Latin descriptions of Tertullian[12] and Irenaeus,[13] even setting down the Latin versions in part or in full. Then he quoted from the platform to show that the description of the congregational church was in basic agreement with those earlier ones. As the congregational church was divided into the brethren and the elders, even as the primitive church, Wise would continue his parallel by a discussion of the indi-vidual and joint duties of both groups.

First he took up "the Peculiar Acts" of the elders or clergy, who in early times were described as bishops, presbyters, and deacons. Bishop and presbyter, Wise concluded, were, in general, terms descriptive of the same office and signified no more than an elder or pastor of a church. He founded his con-clusions on the authority of the Bible and the writings of early church fathers (in the case of the latter *via* his sec-ondary source, of course). He then went on to ascertain the bishop's duty and the dimensions of his diocese. It was plain, Wise said, that among the ancients only one church com-prised a bishopric. In Asia, in those days, the bishopric was even called a parish, a word which in its original form sus-tained a meaning favorable to the idea that a bishop served only one congregation. He gave examples of the early churches acting independently in their congregations under the direction of a single officer and decided their practices were "plainly agreeable with the Sense, Custome & Platform of *New-England* Churches."

The prerogatives of the brethren in choosing, approving, and unseating their own officers and in censuring and admitting members, prerogatives that the New England churches knew, Wise disclosed, were also respected in the churches during the first three centuries of the Christian era. Wise could not refrain from lamenting the lapse from this good state and showing how the clergy, "thinking that the dignity which they had obtained, was not ample enough, if the People had any share with them in Elections," at length snatched or took "the whole Business into their own hands; The People through their supine negligence not much opposing of them." But this was not the subject to be considered, and Wise turned from it after remarking that "the plundering of the Churches" fell within the next twelve hundred years.

Again drawing examples from the procedures of the ancient churches, Wise demonstrated their similarity to the government of the New England churches, this time in the joint acts of the clergy and the laity. Wise found that in the first centuries both the elders and the brethren "made up that Supreame Court which was in every Parish, where all Church Offenders were tryed, and when found Guilty, were Sentenced and Condemned." Such, also, was the practice in New England as prescribed by the platform.

The last parallel that Wise drew concerned "the Fellowship and Communion that Distinct Churches had & held one with another." He believed that the ancient churches were independent in the sense that Thomas Hooker defined the term: "That is, every Particular Church had a sufficient Right and Power, without the Concurrence and Authority of any other Church, to carry on the Worship of God, and Exercise of Discipline in their distinct Society,[14] but that they did meet in synods and submit themselves to synodical decrees.

Wise seemingly had another fling here at the sponsors of the proposals, for Hooker—and Wise—deplored the possibility that

some small set of Wise Men should hold themselves wiser than whole Synods; and afterward should of their own heads in their more private Apartments set forward new Schemes, which in itself is disorderly, and a way to keep the Churches constantly fluctuating, and restless, like the unstable Ocean.[15]

To meet in synods with elders and brethren drawn from each church, as the ancient and New England churches did, was, Wise avowed, the better way.

Wise ended his first demonstration by quoting from Urian Oakes's election sermon a testimony to the purity of reformation in the congregational churches and by directing his reader to the next demonstration, which should "Inquire into the Natural Reason" for the constitution of the churches. In these prefatory remarks, although he begged the indulgence of the reader for any mistakes he might make along "an unusual and unbeaten Path," his realization of the importance of his argument was such that he seemed almost to exercise clairvoyance when he stated:

I have a great presumption that I may open a Road to Men of greater Learning, and a deeper Search, that will lead to a rich Treasure of Knowledge, and Wisdom, for Ease and Relief under those many Questions and crabbed Debates concerning Church-Government in the Christian World; for to me it seems most apparent, that under Christ the reason of the Constitution of these and the Primitive Churches, is really and truly owing to the Original State and Liberty of Mankind, and founded peculiarly in the Light of Nature.[16]

In making his second demonstration Wise first set down his assertions and beliefs, then gave his reasons for adherence to them. He began by declaring that "Wise and Provident Nature by the Dictates of Right Reason excited by the mov-

ing Suggestions of Humanity; and awed with the just de-
mands of Natural Libertie, Equity, Equality, and Principles
of Self-Preservation, Originally drew up the Scheme" of the
Cambridge platform. Next he associated "the Light of
Reason as a Law and Rule of Right" with the "Effect of
Christ's goodness, care and creating Power." The first assertion was something of an overstatement. He made too awe-
some the inspiration of the little group of ministers who
gathered at Cambridge in 1648 to write the platform. But the
next statement was an unusual one for a Puritan minister to
make, because the New England divine was likely to believe
that man's nature was depraved and that the "light of reason" operative in a person beyond grace was a mischievous
light and an untrustworthy guide. But Wise saw the light of
reason, as well as that of revelation, which he aptly designated "Natures Law in a fairer and brighter Edition," as the
"admirable Effect of Christs Creating Power in hanging out
so many Lights to guide man through a dark World."[*]

To show that the platform and the New England churches
were "fairly Established in their present Order by the Law
of Nature," he proposed to "disclose several Principles of
Natural Knowledge . . . with Respect to Mans Being and
Government" and to point out their operation in church
affairs.

It was now that Wise took, as he said, Baron Samuel
Pufendorf for his "Chief Guide and Spokes-man." Though he
quoted little from Pufendorf—at least in acknowledged
debt[17]—still this author furnished him with a number of ideas
and may have pointed him to others. Scholars are generally
agreed that it was Pufendorf's *De jure naturae et gentium*,
first published in 1672, that mainly influenced Wise. The
edition Wise depended upon was probably an English translation. Pufendorf, of course, wrote in Latin, and there were at

least ten Latin editions in Wise's lifetime. Wise doubtless knew enough Latin to read the original, but he probably used a translation, found at this time in two editions, the first issued in 1703 and the second in 1710. Probably Wise did not resort to the library of Harvard for a copy of the work,[18] but very likely possessed one of his own or obtained a long-term loan of a copy from the library of a fellow minister.

Pufendorf, a German jurist who spent most of his life in universities as a professor or in the courts of European rulers applying himself to various tasks of writing, assigned and otherwise, was admittedly one of the greatest thinkers of the seventeenth century. For many years he had meditated upon his readings in Grotius and Hobbes, and *De jure naturae et gentium*, the title of which came from the name of the chair that had been established for him at the University of Heidelberg, was the result of these reflections.

De jure, so far as Wise used it, influenced only the second demonstration of *A Vindication*, but this section contained the most advanced of Wise's thinking and makes the most interesting reading today. More than once Wise quoted directly from Pufendorf, sometimes prefacing the quotation by the Latin abbreviation "Scil.,"[19] and at other times giving no hint at all of indebtedness.[20] The passages are so nearly identical with the rendering of the translator in the edition of 1710 that one is led to believe Wise used that edition. The text of the 1710 edition largely followed the earlier one of 1703, but, in a section that Wise quoted, some lines from Boethius were translated differently. Wise, except for a word or two, kept to the 1710 version of the Boethius translation.[21]

Sometimes the differences between Wise's quotations and the text of the 1710 edition, besides those resulting from changes made, perhaps, by the printer in punctuation, spelling, and capitalization, lay only in the use of a preposition or a pronoun. It may be seen from the length and difficulty of the passage quoted below that it is highly unlikely that Wise could have made by accident a translation so nearly identical with the 1710 rendering.

The Word Man, says my Author, is thought to carry somewhat of Dignity in its sound; and we commonly make use of this as the most proper and prevailing Argument against a rude Insulter, *viz. I am not a Beast or a Dog: But am a Man as well as your self.* Since then Human Nature agrees equally with all persons; and since no one can live a Sociable Life with another that does not own or Respect him as a Man; It follows as a Command of the Law of Nature, that every Man Esteem and treat another as one who is naturally his Equal, or who is a Man as well as he.[22]

Indeed, the differences between this passage and that of the 1710 translation seem to have been introduced by design. From a comparison of the two passages, it may possibly be deduced that Wise, for purposes of his own, substituted "proper" for "last."[23]

The next two pages in *A Vindication* following the above quotation were largely drawn from the English text of *De jure,* and Wise, doubtless aware of his debt, at one point inserted "Scil." In most of this passage he seemed to have selected whole phrases and sentences that pleased him and combined them into a brief version of several pages of *De jure.*[24] Wise made two other acknowledgments of dependence on Pufendorf, but the passages in question were not quotations, but paraphrases.[25]

Certain books of *De jure* Wise leaned upon more heavily than others. These were books two, three, and seven. Book seven, because of its topics devoted to civil power, figured more largely than any other in the second demonstration of *A Vindication.* The ideas Wise used that recognizably originated in Pufendorf will be indicated as they appear. The organization and the style of the section, however, were Wise's own. And even as Grotius and Hobbes were provocative to Pufendorf's thinking and their ideas points of departure for his own, so may Pufendorf have been propulsive to Wise's thought and driven him to embrace ideas beyond his time. Certainly Wise, in his championship of democracy as the best government for church and state, advanced beyond his mentor.

The first idea that concerned Wise was the distinction between the natural and the civil being of man. He saw the one emerging from the other, but "Man in a state of Natural Being" he considered "a Free-Born Subject under the Crown of Heaven, and Owing Homage to none but God himself." Civil government was "the Effect of Humane Free-Compacts," "the Produce of Mans Reason, of Humane and Rational Combinations," and did not come direct from God. In all the Scriptures God prescribed no particular form of government, and Wise remarked that the Jews changed their government five times. Nor did Nature foster any particular form; otherwise it would have been the same in all parts of the world. Hence, it followed that monarchy could not claim nature for a parent.

Man, of course, as a natural being Wise viewed as "the Subject of the Law of Nature." If the law of nature were "the dictate of Right Reason," then he believed man's understanding was "Endowed with such a power, as to be able, from the Contemplation of humane Condition to discover a necessity of Living agreeably with this Law." Certain qualities in man —earlier pointed out by Pufendorf[26]—led Wise to acknowledge nature's sovereignty. One such quality was man's desire to preserve himself. But man found that desire most nearly satisfied by associating coöperatively with other men, by developing a sociable disposition. Then by means of sociability man entered into a civil state where he was "not so Wedded to his own Interest" that he could not "make the Common good the mark of his Aim." Where was God in man's natural state? To Wise, God was the author of the law of nature, and for man to listen to reason was for him to listen to God. This relationship was "Illustrable," Wise averred, "from the Peace and Guilt of Conscience in them that either obey, or violate the Law of Nature."

By the law of nature man had "an Original Liberty Instampt" upon him. Waiving "the Consideration of Mans Moral Turpitude"—a condition that many New England Puritans would have found hard to dismiss—Wise bound himself to view man as

a Creature which God has made and furnished essentially with many Enobling Immunities, which render him the most August Animal in the World . . . whatever has happened since his Creation, he remains at the upper-end of Nature, and as such is a Creature of a very Noble Character.[27]

For his dominion, man had "the whole frame of the Lower Part of the Universe . . . devoted to his use, and at his Command," and in this natural state he exercised a liberty that was "equal with his trust."[28]

Liberty was of two sorts: internal and external. The first implied "a faculty of Doing or Omitting things according to the Direction of his Judgment" and did not consist in "an unbounded Licence of Acting." The lower animals were restrained from a harmful and unlawful excess by their instincts. Man, to keep his place above them, had to obey reason; only then could he be "accounted free." It was Plutarch who said, and Wise quoted: "They alone live as they Will, who have Learnt what they ought to Will." Man's external liberty, so far as his natural state was concerned, consisted in being subject to no control or authority but his own. By this endowment every man stood equal with every other, and each could consider what was "most for his Behoof, Happiness and Well-being."

This equality Wise emphasized. Man, by his very nature and not from pride, set a high value upon himself, and if he would be considered the equal of others, he must, to lead a sociable life, consider them, Wise thought, the equal of himself. Man's physical existence, Wise could see, sustained the idea of equality. Were not the bodies of all men "Composed of matter, frail, brittle, and lyable to be destroyed by [a] thousand accidents?" Did not all men owe their "Existence to the same Method of propagation?" Wise quoted from *De jure*:

The Noblest Mortal in his Entrance on to the Stage of Life, is not distinguished by any pomp or of passage from the lowest of Mankind; and our Life hastens to the same General Mark: Death observes no Ceremony, but Knocks as loud at the Barriers of the Court, as at the Door of the Cottage.[29]

Such equality, once admitted, Wise thought, was "a very great force in maintaining Peace and Friendship amongst Men." Man, of course, transgressed the principle of equality when he, through pride and "without sufficient reason," preferred himself to others. No man, no matter how wise or seemingly fitted for government, had naturally the obedience and subjection of others. Though it might be more "natural" for such a man to rule if there was to be a government, still that man had not the right by nature to force others into subjection. Only "Voluntary Compliance" on the part of his equal fellowmen could grant him that right and subject them to a state of inequality. Pufendorf also looked upon government as originating in the consent of the governed.[30] Of course, usurpation and force could bring about a civil state, too, but to the degree that man's natural equality was abridged, to that degree was nature annulled.

The chief reason why man ever voluntarily gave up a portion of his liberty and equality to form a civil state was to
secure himself against injuries from his own kind, "for none
so Good to Man, as Man, and yet none a greater Enemy."[31]
Indeed, Wise stated, "if every Man could secure himself
singly; It would be great folly for him, to Renounce his
Natural Liberty," wherein he was "his own King and Protector." To that government, then, man surrendered the
power of life and death over himself, together with authority
to "injoyn" and "prohibit," so that he might often, "under
this Authority, [be] obliged to Sacrifice his Private, for the
Public Good." But the origin of this government, Wise was
keen to point out, was man himself—or man in mass, the
people. The people, of course, must first agree to the need for
a government. They must have found their state of natural
being unsatisfactory, their personal right too easily encroached upon by others. In an Eastern country, Wise gave
as an example, it was the custom after the death of an absolute monarch to allow a certain number of days to pass with
no ruler at all; the purpose of this practice was to "indear"
tyranny to the people, for during this time their tribulations
were so great that they were glad to "return under the Covert
of a new Monarch." So there must be a desire for government
before there can be government. Then the people must have
agreed to acquiesce in the decision of a majority vote for a
certain type of government. Once the type of government is
chosen, a covenant can be drawn up by which sovereignty
may be conferred and the obedience of the people yielded. In
this government there should be such a "Union of Wills" that
the state may be, according to Wise's—and Pufendorf's—
idea of its proper definition, "a Compound Moral Person."
The state's resemblance to a person Wise set forth in several

statements such as the following. "Equity and Laws are the Reason [of the state]." "Concord amongst the Members, and all Estates, is the Health."[32]

Sovereignty in government, Wise went on to say, involved certain powers—legislative, judiciary, protective, appointive —and he observed that as these powers resided "in some One Person, or in a Council (consisting of some Select Persons, or of all the Members of a Community) ," so the different forms of commonwealths were produced.

Wise stated first the conditions for the existence of a democracy, since he believed it to be the oldest[33] and most appealing form of government in the world. It existed when sovereignty devolved on a council made up of all the members of the society, each of whom had an equal vote. Certain conditions, of course, Wise projected, had to be met for it to function. The time and place of assembly must be agreed upon, and the vote of the majority must be accepted as binding by all the members. Also, since all the members could not be conveniently assembled for every affair, it was necessary to appoint magistrates to act for them and make report at regular assemblies.

Wise next defined an aristocracy and monarchy. For Wise —and for Pufendorf[34]—the difference between a democracy and an aristocracy lay in the council. In the council of an aristocracy were only a select few of the members of a society. A monarchy, of course, conferred sovereignty on a single person.

Then there were various kinds of mixed governments, Wise added, and he accounted "possibly the fairest in the World . . . that which . . . [had] a Regular Monarchy . . . settled upon a Noble Democracy as its Basis." Wise was setting out here to praise England. He designated its constitution "an *Elisium*" and declared that its government afforded "the main Advantages of an Aristocracy, and of a Democracy, and yet [was] free from the Disadvantages and Evils of either."[35]

Wise now made in his discourse on the civil state some application to church government. And his point of view could be expected when he stated:

it must needs be altogether repugnant, to think he [God] should fore-cast the State of this World by no better a Scheme, than to Order two Sovereign Powers, in the same Grand Community, which would be like placing two Suns in the Firmament, which would be to set the Universe into a Flame.

Wise seemed to have had in mind the rules of church and state in the Catholic countries and their frequent wrangles.

But before Wise came "to humour the several great Claimers of Government in the Church of Christ," he examined briefly the subject of "Rebellion against Government." He was thinking, to some degree at least, of Kings Charles II and James II, as he wrote his condemnation of rebels—who to him were tyrants robbing the people of their natural rights. Perhaps, he was also thinking of the ministers who sponsored the proposals. If the latter were included, they shared a harsh description, for Wise wrote:

Such Rebels [those who "break in upon Regular Communities duly Established"] in States, and Usurpers in Churches affront the World, with a presumption that the Best of the Brotherhood are a Company of Fools, and that themselves have fairly Monopolized all the reason of Humane Nature. Yea, they take upon them the Boldness to assume a Prerogative of trampling under foot the natural original Equality & Liberty of their Fellows; for to push the Proprietors of Settlements out of possession of their old, and impose new Schemes upon them, is vertually to declare them in a state of Vassalage, or that they were Born so; and therefore will the Usurper be so gracious as to insure them they shall not be Sold at the next Market: They must esteem it a favour, for by this time all the Original Prerogatives of Man's Nature are intentionally a Victim, smoaking to satiate the Usurpers Ambition.[36]

Another circumstance doubtless influenced Wise's remarks. He must have recalled here the encroachments of the Andros government upon the rights of New Englanders. His language echoes the judge's retort addressed to him and his friends: "Mr. Wise you have no more previledges Left you yn not to be Sould for Slaves."[37]

Wise characteristically saw the acts of the recent rulers which were disagreeable to New England as violations of the ancient English constitution. He considered the rulers then as rebels and the people in protest against these acts as honorable defenders. Similarly, in the government of the churches he viewed the "Popish" religion as a subverter of the ancient constitution established in the New Testament and believed that the congregationalists were its restorers.

One thing Wise cautioned against before he went on to a discussion of church government: the power of churches had only "a faint Resemblance" to civil power; the latter was "Coercive," and the former "perswasive"; civil power was sovereign in worldly affairs, while the power of the churches was delegated from Christ and was ministerial.

Of course, the church government to be compared to a monarchy was easily discovered. Wise did not call it by name, but no one could mistake his references. He questioned whether the government of the ecclesiastical monarch who claimed "absolute Sovereignty over the Christian world" had not "plainly subverted the Design of the Gospel, and the end for which Christ's Government was Ordained, *viz.* the Moral, Spiritual, and Eternal Happiness of Men," and decided that it had. He looked with aversion upon the temporal elevations and adoration of this monarch, whose government had "absolutely Debaucht the World," and concluded that "God and wise Nature were never Propitious to the Birth of this Monster."

Wise would be willing to trust church power to an aristocracy were he assured that the councillors "would make the Scripture, and not their private Will the Rule of their Personal and Ministerial Actions." But Wise was dubious of such trust, for even in good men there was to be discovered "much ignorance, abundance of small ends, many times cloked with a high Pretence in Religion; Pride Skulking and often breeding revenge upon a small affront; and blown up by a pretended Zeal; Yet really and truly by nothing more Divine than Interest, or ill Nature." And if a few good men were not too "frail a bottom" to carry so great a cargo as the government of the churches, there remained the difficulty of successors. But Wise, remembering Christianity by such management had been "peel'd, rob'd and spoiled already," lost patience with it and sought "a safer way home."

This safer way, there was no doubt in his mind, was democracy. Wise's preference was his own. He did not derive it from Pufendorf, whose judgment favored monarchy, perhaps because he was much in the service of rulers.[38] Pufendorf, doubtless having in mind a universal participation, did not think democracy was the right government for a large country.[39] Wise, however, conceived of democracy in the framework of a representative government.

The natural liberty and the natural equality of man were to be preserved as far as possible in the state, Wise believed, for "Government was never Established by God or Nature, to give one Man a Prerogative to insult over another." He assured his reader: "The End of all good Government is to Cultivate Humanity, and Promote the Happiness of all, and the good of every man is all his Rights, his Life, Liberty, Estate, Honor, &c. without injury or abuse done to any." And it was "as plain as daylight" to him there was "no Species of Government like a Democracy to attain this End." Because of the responsibility of its officers and ministers to the whole assembly there was the least danger in a democracy that the people would suffer "either from the fraud, or Arbitrary measures of particular Men." To look upon democracy as a kind of Brownism or anarchy was to view it falsely, for if a monarchy could have officers to execute its decrees, so could a democracy have public servants to implement the decisions voted by the assembly. Wise went so far as to say that if either monarchy or aristocracy was meant to be the accepted form of church government, the Reformation was "a meer Cheat, a Schism, and notorious Rebellion" and all its leaders must be accounted "a crew of Rebels against God and Government," for this movement and these men, generally speaking, sponsored a return to democratic procedures. If in the formation of civil government, power originated with the people, so did it in the churches, and all instruments of church government—synods, and so forth—ought, on original principle, to be operated democratically. And by a series of "Particulars," answers to "Objection," and "Consequences," Wise rounded out his argument in favor of democracy according to the light of nature and proceeded to his third demonstration.

The third demonstration—drawn from the Scriptures— Wise was willing to admit already proved in the work of many learned men; and he would present, to avoid unnecessary repetition, only a brief summary. Wise did not hesitate to state that religion not only failed to "Diminish any of Natures just Prerogatives" but rather "cultivated" and "increased" them. Man "as the Subject of Grace" seemed to Wise "not to have the least speck of Vassalage in him," but according to the Bible was lord of himself and heaven and earth. Wise pointed out the language of persuasion God used in endeavoring to turn man to His ways. God would have man seek Him through "Reason, Liberty and Nobleness of Nature" and appealed to those qualities in man.

Moreover, the churches did not have to resort to harsh measures of government as the civil state often did. Their sway was acknowledged and served by reason. Coercion in the churches would be an abuse of power. A further abuse of power, Wise thought, would be that which would restrict the formation and operation of congregational churches.

What power there was in churches resided in the single church. Wise attempted to prove this individual possession of power by a recital of certain prerogatives each church had been granted according to the Scriptures. He showed that in the election of officers, in censures and judgments, there was ample scriptural precedence for the allowance of such powers to the individual churches. And he saw it as additional evidence of the strength and dignity of the body of each church that every church epistle of Paul was directed, not to the clergy, but to the whole of the church addressed. Thus, each church maintained within itself a democratic government. Of the rights of the churches meeting in synod he saw no need to speak, since there existed an adequate statement recently published, and he referred the reader to that "Excellent Treatise" Increase Mather's *Disquisition concerning Ecclesiastical Councils*, printed in 1716.

In his fourth demonstration Wise found it easy to praise the constitution—that is, the Cambridge platform—whereby, it seemed to him, the churches of New England possessed a democratic form of government. He believed that constitution the most excellent yet provided in the Christian world and declared that no other bore so exactly the designs of the Gospel. This constitution afforded "no lurking place for *Symony*," sponsored "no buying and selling of Offices," and provided "no back Stairs for Cousins and Favourites to Climb up to high Seats without Desert." Wise rejoiced that "merit and intrinsick Worth set ... the value" and made "the strongest plea for Preferment." Nor did the constitution play any favorites in granting power to clergy and brethren. Wise saw New England church government as the best balanced in the world. Offsetting "the Venerable Major Vote" of the brethren were the universal respect paid the ministers and the extent of their commission to do the church's will.

Another means Wise used to illustrate the excellence of the constitution and defend it from "the Scandalous Title of Anarchy" was to plead its "near Affinity ... with the Civil Governments of some of the most flourishing Common-wealths in the World." He instanced three such communities, where "Liberty and Property, with the rest of the great Im-munities of Man's Nature [were] nourished, secured, and best guarded from Tyranny." These were "the *Venetian* Commonwealth," which he would not call as some an aristoc-racy but "a limited Democracy"; "the *Belgick* Provinces," where the independent states and cities went to make up "one Republick, the most considerable in the World"; and the English commonwealth, whose people were "the Subjects of the finest and most incomparable" of earthly governments. He extolled "this Original happy Form of Government" at some length. The English constitution was "Truly and properly called an English Mans Liberty." By it he received a greater inheritance than from his parents, for therein was proclaimed the privilege "to be freed in Person and Estate from Arbitrary Violence and Oppression." And this privilege was founded on two things: the legislative power of parlia-ment, wherein the Englishman through his representatives made his own laws and disposed of his own money, and the executive power of the jury, whereby each was tried and judged by his equals in rank or condition. For juries and parliaments Wise gave thanks and warned against their corruption:

These two grand Pillars of *English* Liberty, are the fundamental vital Priviledges whereby we have been, and are still preserved more free and happy, than any other People in the World; and we trust shall ever continue so. For whosoever shall design to impair, pervert, or undermine either of these, do strike at the very Constitution of our Government, and ought to be prosecuted and punished, with the utmost zeal and vigour. For to poyson all the Springs and Rivers in the Kingdom, could not be a greater mischief; for this would only affect the present Age, but the other would Ruine and Inslave our posterity.[40]

Wise concluded the demonstration by several queries, the gist of which was if Englishmen were vigilant for the preservation of their civil liberties, so should the New England churches be alert in guarding their liberties.

Wise's last demonstration was the briefest of all. He had said almost all that he wanted to say, and perhaps now he wished to be done. But he fulfilled his plan. To exemplify the dignity God had put upon the constitution of the New England churches, he drew illustrations from the present and early Christian eras—the correspondence of which he had already emphasized. Some of the distinguishing marks of God's favor in the first era were the rapid spread of the Gospel to the nations, the goodness of the early Christians, and their stanchness of spirit under suffering. Wise said as martyrs the Christians "baffled the bravery of the old *Roman* Spirit, and were quite too hard for those who had vanquished the World." He could well believe the story of the executioner tired from tormenting them. But after the first era God withdrew his favor, and as signs of diminishing grace, Wise cited the popularity of the Arian heresy,[41] especially among the clergy, and the universal apostasy that came to prevail in the next era. This was not to deny that there was a remnant of God's people faithful throughout the ages. But gradually the apostasy extended over all the Christian world and was halted only by the Reformation. The blessings of the New England churches derived from that time and from the purity of the government they had adopted; and though some of the churches had made "a Defection from the Constitution," yet they had not gone so far that they could not be brought back "to their old Basis again."

Wise thought it a fitting conclusion to his "small Treatise" to append "the Joynt Testimony" of two men who had been ministers in New England for many years. This was the exhortation to congregational orthodoxy left by John Higginson, of Salem, and William Hubbard, of Ipswich.[42] Cotton Mather had first sought it as a bulwark to his father's *Order of the Gospel*,[43] and Wise, bearing witness to the wish of his neighbor of Ipswich that "A Testimony" might live printed with a compatible companion, was "well satisfyed" that his book was the most proper traveling companion in the world. That he put "A Testimony" at the end of his book offered it no indignity, but rather accorded it an honor, for he believed it could, while he retreated in triumph from the field, hold the rear with distinction against any "forlorn party" that out of a "desperate fortune" might rally and attack.

Just before he ended his book, Wise wrote a grand hortatory subjunctive, and since *A Vindication* will be quoted from only a few more times, this quotation may be set down as a final exemplification of his concern for the churches and their platform.

Let the Holy Churches . . . flourish in their Strength, Beauty and Order, after this Triumvirate [Higginson and Hubbard's testimony and Wise's book] shall sink under the Tyranny of Moths, and Humane forgetfulness, and lye down in the House of oblivion;

where I hope the Enemies of the Constitution will be gotten down before them, and there fast Buried in their own Bones and Dust."

The publication of *A Vindication* early in 1717 did not pass without comment. Cotton Mather made vindictive note of it, questioning himself: "Should not I take into Consideration, what may be done for the Service of the Ministry and Religion and the Churches, throughout the Land, that the Poison of Wise's cursed Libel may have an Antidote?"[45] Nothing came of his question, and some regretted that Wise went unreproved. One Nathaniel Stone, minister of Harwich, complained in January, 1718, to Benjamin Colman that nothing had been written to refute Wise. Stone had just read *A Vindication* and thought it "something strange" that one of Wise's books had not been answered. Stone argued:

If he has right and truth on his side, why doe we not all lay our hands on our mouths and plead guilty? If not, why does he goe on triumphing as coming conqueror out of ye field of battle? as he himself boasts. For the ministers of ye Province, from year to year, to make no reply looks like an implicit acknowledgment yt their cause is bad, wheron they let it sink in silence; at least this is too likely to be ye general construction yt will be put on their making no Answer. I cant but think yt a reply as brief, summary and plain as might be, would be very proper.[46]

Stone seemed to think that his living in one of "ye obscure corners of ye country" excused him from the task and passed it on to one of the ministers who lived in Boston, "our metropolis," because they had "divers waies the greatest advantages therfor," a telescoped and unintelligible phrase that seemingly did not convince. Certainly no one appeared to confute Wise, and *A Vindication* was not answered until 1774.

Wise's debt to Pufendorf was great. "His author," as Wise called him, doubtless brought him into the possession of ideas that he would otherwise not have attained to. Certainly he acknowledged a debt, but he did not plainly exhibit its extensiveness. Much of what he wrote in the second demonstration was derivative, and because of carelessness about acknowledging Pufendorf's book or an unconscious saturation in his language, drew perilously close to plagiarism.

Yet Wise was far from being a one-author man. He was, of course, acquainted with the literature of ancient Greece and Rome and made references to Plato, Aristotle, and Plutarch, and quoted from the *Aeneid*. The writers of the early church he either knew firsthand or from the compilation that he admitted using. He called upon the authority of more than a dozen of them, referring six times to the writings of Cyprian[47] and five times to Eusebius's[48] history of the early church. He showed himself cognizant of the productions of the New England Puritans by seeking out the testimony of Thomas Hooker, John Cotton, Urian Oakes, and Increase Mather, and he did not leave unmentioned English writers. Indeed, he seemed to show a preference for Dr. John Owen, English Puritan divine who favored the congregational way in church government. It could be expected that he would cite the Cambridge platform a number of times and, since he was a minister, that he would mention repeatedly Biblical authority. In all, he set down about twenty-five separate textual allusions, nearly all of them references to the New Testament.

Here was a formidable array of authors. So wide and varied could have been his reading, if one is to judge from the allusions, that there may not have been one idea in Wise's book that was original with him. Almost everything that Wise thought had been thought before. Besides the similarity of Pufendorf's thought, which Wise said he knew, there was a similarity of idea and expression to other authors' works that Wise gave no hint of ever having seen. For instance, from

John Locke's *Two Treatises on Government*, published in 1690, Wise could have obtained almost the same conceptions that he got from Pufendorf. In the following quotations from Locke, a resemblance to Wise's words and ideas can easily be discovered, and yet Wise, so far as is known, never read Locke. Locke wrote:

Men living together according to reason without a common Superior on Earth, with Authority to judge between them, is properly the State of Nature.

Men being . . . by Nature, all free, equal, and independent no one can be put out of this Estate, and subjected to the Political Power of another, without his own Consent.

And hence it is that he who attempts to get another Man into his Absolute Power, does thereby put himself into a State of War with him; It being to be understood as a Declaration of a Design upon his Life.

But Government being for the Preservation of every Mans Right and Property, by preserving him from the Violence or Injury of others, is for the good presumably, of the Governed.[49]

Wise presumably did not echo Locke; if he had done so, he would probably have admitted as much, for he did not hesitate to name Pufendorf as a source. No, the ideas that were found in Pufendorf, Locke, and Wise had begun to permeate the times. Such writers, in recording them and extending their application, increased the popularity of these ideas and stimulated men's minds to further flights. In New England others did not write as Wise wrote, because there was a lag in the passage of ideas from Europe to America of sometimes nearly fifty years, a phenomenon that persisted into the nineteenth century. Wise was not subject to this lag, because he had read Pufendorf.

That Wise arrived independently at some of his ideas was probably true. Certainly on the basis of his studies he was led to express a point of view different from almost any other that was then being expressed in New England. In his unabashed recognition of man's natural rights and warm espousal of democracy he wrote for an age fifty years later. The earliness of his contributions to democratic thinking in America has not been sufficiently noted, and the influence of his writings is too little appreciated. After all, their vitality was such that they lived through the century, and two printings of five hundred copies each were called for during the fiery '70's just before the Revolution. In the following century Wise was even cited as authority in a judgment emanating from the Supreme Court of Massachusetts.[50]

Scholars were once disposed to give Wise credit for influencing the leaders of the Revolution—for example, Samuel Adams and John Hancock.[51] Now the disposition, because it cannot be proved that Adams and Hancock ever read his books and because the publication of tracts relating to church controversy was a feature of the times, is to discredit the probability that Wise influenced Revolutionary thought.[52] It is true that the names of Adams and Hancock were not on the list of subscribers that was appended to the copies from the second printing of 1772; but, as it has been pointed out,[53] a number of patriots' names were there none the less. The name of the commander of the minutemen in the battle of Concord was there, the Reverend Edward Emerson's name was there, and that of Timothy Pickering, lawyer of Salem, who was afterwards adjutant-general and quartermaster-general of the Continental Army and held several cabinet posts during the administrations of Washington and Adams. The number of military men who subscribed almost equaled the number of ministers, two colonels buying twelve copies apiece. Laymen bought almost seven times as many copies as did the clergy.[54] Of course, all these copies could have been bought because of an interest in church affairs.

Certainly Wise's books were appreciated by some because of an interest in ecclesiastical argument. Presbyterian Nathaniel Whitaker, pastor of the Third Church in Salem, assumed they were a narrow attack upon Presbyterianism and so sought to quash them as well as undermine the Cambridge platform. He succeeded in neither. He called names, blundered about, and contradicted himself. He took issue with Wise over the expense of gathering in consociations, condemning Wise for appealing to man's love of money. Then he appealed to the same interest, saying the practice would not cost much.[55] Deacon Samuel Gatchel, across the bay, in Marblehead, took a dim view of Dr. Whitaker's *Confutation*. In a little pamphlet he challenged Whitaker's declaration that Christ's church was an aristocracy, for to say so was to follow the law of Aaron that Christ had put aside. Gatchel strung out Biblical texts to prove that the government of the church was democratic.[56]

Church disputation was in the air at the time. In the lists of Isaiah Thomas a number of pamphlets on church government were set down,[57] and the Boston *News-Letter* advertised publications other than Wise's having to do with it. One such entry in the issue for March 25, 1773, advertised the printing of *A Treatise on Church-Government*. It is interesting to note, though, that a few weeks earlier, the paper advertised the reprinting of *The Revolution in New England Justified*, which, it will be remembered, defended the overthrow of the Andros party.

In the advertisements that appeared in the Boston *News-Letter* for his books, Wise was portrayed as a defender of church liberties. The assertion was made that "a new System of Church Government would have taken place, had not that reverend and bold Champion, the Author, stept forth for the

Churches Defence."[58] This edition of Wise's books may have been meant only for those interested in church affairs, but it seemed that the publisher John Boyle, in representing Wise as a brave figure, was not above enhancing the book's sale by an appeal to the public's current taste for heroes. In the advertisement put at the end of the copies made from the first printing of 1772, Boyle capitalized all the letters of "liberty" in the phrase "ecclesiastical liberty." This emphasis on a catch word—a practice followed by others than Boyle[59] —would also seem to be an appeal to the interest in liberty and human rights. The March 19 supplement of the *News-Letter* carried an enlarged version of the earlier advertisements, which embodied the same pointed capitalization of the word "liberty" and had the following heading so printed:

To all Friends to Ecclesiastical

LIBERTY.

Herein the usefulness of Wise's book was stressed, and the gentlemen who had "hitherto appear'd as Encouragers of this Work"—perhaps the subscribers—were urged to promote the second subscription in order that by a more general use of the book mankind might be universally informed "wherein their Ecclesiastical LIBERTY" lay.[60] In seeking a second printing, Boyle promised to list the names of the subscribers and capitalized this description of them: "who so nobly distinguish themselves as zealous advocates for the liberty of the churches, and whose memory posterity must respect." He could almost be charged with setting up here an approved list of church members—perhaps patriots.

As patriots, they must have found Wise speaking for the times when they read these words: "the Prince who strives to subvert the Fundamental Laws of the Society, is the Traytor and the Rebel, and not the People, who endeavour to Preserve and Defend their own."[61] Wise considered this condemnation "very applicable to particular Men in their Rebellions or Usurpations in Church or State." Wise had no need, of course, to speak for lawful rebellion in *A Vindication;* if he had so spoken, the patriots of the Revolution would have had a lively and useful primer. As it was, *A Vindication* must have been one of several timely influences in Revolutionary New England. Though the Cambridge platform was added to both printings and *A Confession of Faith* to the second, *A Vindication* did come first. The edition, too, was a large one, and the book could have had wide circulation among both church members and patriots. Moreover, one might reasonably ask why contemporaries of Wise, who wrote diffusely upon church government, were not resurrected and republished?[62] Could it be that Wise's arguments had a wider application than the purely ecclesiastical?

The role of *A Vindication* in influencing the leadership of the period could be easily overestimated. But its second demonstration was entirely in keeping with the liberty-loving sentiment of the times. The sympathetic reader would not need special instruction to apply to current events such statements as these:

It wants no farther Demonstration, for it's most apparent, that Nature is so much Mistress of her self, that man in a Natural State of Being, is under God the first Subject of all Power, and therefore can make his own Choice, and by deliberate Compacts, settles his own Conditions for the Government of himself in a Civil State of Being: And when a Government so Settled shall throw its self from its Foundations, or the Subjects of Sovereign Power shall subvert or confound the Constitution, they then degrade themselves; and so all Power returns again to the People, who are the first Owners.[63]

The harmony of Wise's work with the strains of martial liberty that were then being heard can easily be perceived.

CHAPTER XI

Liberal Notions

THE SAME YEAR that *A Vindication* was published, Wise drew up his will. But he was far from being on the verge of the grave. Affairs within and without his parish required his energies, and he was not one to shirk. The construction of a new meetinghouse in Chebacco presented its problems. Neighboring churches sought him out to settle disputes. The right way to sing psalms was becoming a subject of dissension. How should the Chebacco people sing them? Surely his views would be requested. And inoculation. In 1721 an epidemic of smallpox raged in Boston and vicinity. In the face of a fearful mortality, it was no wonder that the desperate and dreaded experiment of inoculation had been tried. Yet, though praise of the method proclaimed its successes, whispers of failure and death spread throughout the region. It was denounced as a heathen practice, and public opinion was set against it. Would Wise dare oppose the popular view? The paper money crisis was also at hand. Those who depended on paper money for payment of salaries and income found its value rapidly depreciating, and their livelihood seriously threatened. Wise received no longer a third of his salary in money and the remainder in the country's produce, but the whole amount was now paid in province currency. He would not like to receive province bills of dubious value.

He could not, of course, as one who depended on a fixed salary, miss being affected by the diminishing value of paper money. Mounting inflationary pressure upon people like him who had unfluctuating incomes had been expected. In a pamphlet of the times it was prophesied "that *Salary men, Ministers, School-Masters, Judges of the Circuit, President & Tutors at Colledge, Widows* and *Orphans, &c.*" would be "pincht and hurt more than any," and an increase in salaries was recommended.[1] Another pamphleteer commented:

there is hot talk that our Salary-Men, who (particularly the Ecclesiasticks) have hitherto had an Honourable Support and suitable to their Character, must *lower their Topsails,* and be Content to take their pay in the *produce of the Island.*[2]

Wise had doubtless experienced something of the decreased purchasing power of the province bills, for it is hardly conceivable that he had been paid wholly in coin up to this time. At any rate, he sought now to be relieved of the risk involved in taking paper money and requested his parishioners to pay him in hard coin, but they found their supply of silver so limited that they could not comply and by way of compromise, in May, 1719, voted Wise ninety pounds in bills of public credit for the seventy that was owed. This offer Wise rejected, and his salary had gone unpaid for seven months when he applied for redress to the court at Newbury, in this same year.[3]

In this petition Wise declared that his salary "in the Original Grant" was "but a poor business to maintain a Family Sick & Well" and any step "to diminish, or any ways weaken it must needs stand under the head of Oppression if not a heavier denomination." He spoke of his parishioners in a respectful and sympathetic manner; he seemed aware of the straits they were in because of the inflation and was not uncompromising in his desire for hard money. He wanted only satisfaction—which finally came in paper money at a rate higher than the ninety to seventy his parishioners had so far tendered him. The court directed Chebacco church to accord him satisfaction, and in November the church granted Wise ten more pounds in province bills in addition to the ninety already voted him. Another adjustment was sought in 1722, and a second petition was submitted.[4]

But Wise did more about the paper money situation than petition court. He wrote a long pamphlet sponsoring the further emission of bills of credit and, because of this expression of his views, was drawn into penning a number of controversial advertisements. Wise was only one of several who were writing on the currency issue. The merchants, according to the pamphlets, were generally deploring the scarcity of bills for trading purposes, notwithstanding the issue of almost four hundred thousand pounds in province bills since 1690, of which number perhaps half had been redeemed. In 1716 alone there had been issued a hundred thousand pounds in bills. Still, according to some, there was a dearth of a medium of exchange, and silver and gold had been flying out of the country at a prodigious rate. Some believed hoarding caused the scarcity of bills, and others discredited such an explanation. One offered as a remedy additional issues of paper money, but from a private land bank supervised by the colonial government. Another was convinced that the importation of luxuries was the cause of the whole trouble and warned that unless the country became frugal and worked to make its exports exceed its imports, the situation would worsen.[5]

One pamphleteer saw "the blood and vital Spirits of the Body-politick"—the medium of exchange—nearly exhausted and predicted "a Certain, & speedy dissolution" of trade, all because of "a few *wretched Misers*" who practiced usury upon "their Indigent but honest Neighbors."[6] But at the proposal to issue more paper money, some were aghast. One said of paper money, "The more 'tis *increas'd*" the less "'tis *valued.*"[7] Another thought "that if it were possible to get out *Five Hundred Thousand Pounds*, it would not fetch so much as *Two Hundred Thousand Pounds* now doth." This writer was assured that a few years would set everything to rights if "People would be content to wear their Old Clothes over again."[8]

Wise advocated more bills of credit. He apparently had no reticence about entering the controversy, although some might have felt as did a pamphleteer who wrote:

Some of our Ecclesiasticks of late, (for want of *Discretion*, without which *Learning* is *Pedantry*, and *Wit, Impertinence*,) have been guilty of *too officious* a meddling with *State Affairs*. The great substantial Duties of *Faith, Repentance*, and a *good Life*, are what they *may* and *ought* with utmost Warmth and Energy to *Inculcate*: but whatever is not compris'd in these, is *beside the Text, foreign to their Province, and another Gospel*.[9]

Wise was well known for his public spirit. His interests had never been circumscribed by the limits of Chebacco parish. Neither would he be too concerned for what people might think if he wrote on the currency question.

In *A Word of Comfort to a Melancholy Country*, published early in 1721, Wise, under the penname Amicus Patriae, urged the establishment of a sufficient medium so that the merchants and farmers, "the Grand Pillars of the Flourishing State of this Common Wealth" who joined together were the Atlas which bore up "the Great Globe of . . . Temporal Business," might stand "Strong, Steady & Firm."[10] For if they "slumped and plunged," all the country sank with them. To establish that medium Wise recommended the founding of a land bank under government or private management.

Wise recognized that trade must have its greatest fluidity in the most populous region of the colony, that is, the capital;

therefore, a medium of exchange must be plentiful to speed the flow of trade. Though he saw the colony blest by the reign of "a Protestant Prince" and the direction of an honorable governor, yet the medium of trade was "so exceeding short" that business had begun "to Clogg." As a medium Wise especially approved of paper money, if it were "upon good Security and sound at Bottom," for he saw silver and gold as too costly, too "volatile," and too corrupting a means of exchange. He attributed the progress and the successful enterprises of the last thirty years in large part to the easy medium of trade, that is, bills of public credit, or paper money. He illustrated with what distress in former years money had been expended. "Oh what Begging, and Contributing was there; even from every poor Girl and Boy, that had but a Penny to part with to a Beggar, to bring Venerable *Harvard* into its first Brick?"[11]

If bills had been of benefit in the past, Wise thought, they could continue to be. There could be no reversion to a system of barter; the country was too far advanced in civilization to submit to such a cumbersome business. The farmer, Wise believed, was especially benefited by the medium of paper money because of the ease of handling it. Then, he argued, the farmer was more likely to get a fair price if he took his pay in bills, for coin was more subject to the grasp of avarice than a paper medium. Wise urged the particular care of the farmer.

You must [he said] keep up your Farmers heart; for if he fails, you are in danger to starve all; and also he is the best Wall to his Conntry; the King and all Men must be maintained out of his field; and defended too; for from hence Muster-Rolls are filled up, and Armies are Reinforc'd with the Best Souldiers, and most Effective Men.[12]

Wise believed that bills coupled with the industry of men

could do much to settle the wilderness, increase the manu-
facture, and add to the variety of products. He was of the
further opinion that a good medium of trade, insuring as it
did a way to make a living, would encourage young people to
marry early and take up homes on unimproved lands. There
were enough "Old Batchelours, with Dames to Match them,"
Wise averred, "to settle several Towns."

People might have complaints against bills, but inasmuch
as bills were so serviceable, Wise, with an eye to the facetious,
offered the following advice. *"Gentlemen!* You must do by
your Bills, as all Wise Men do by their Wives; Make the best
of them."[13] A decrease in the purchasing power of the bills
need not be looked upon as a decrease in their value. The
scarcity of commodities themselves might have brought
about the rise in prices.

For stabilizing the value of the bills Wise believed a bank
must exist. Mere convenience in their handling and safe-
guarding would argue for its existence. Both government and
private banks under the direction of judicious and public-
spirited men could work for the good of the colony; but Wise
favored the private land bank, subject, of course, to government inspection, over the government land bank. His reason
was that the government-backed bills could be too easily
called in and the country left without an adequate medium
of exchange. A private bank, he thought, would find the
maintenance of the value of the bills always to its advantage.
Who should sponsor the private bank? The rich city merchants were the ones who had lands and estates upon which
to issue bills; Wise proposed that they set up the land bank.[14]

For writing *A Word of Comfort* Wise was to have both
detractors and admirers. Some of them, of course, appeared
in print. One of his critics inserted an advertisement in the
Boston *Gazette* in the weekly issue of February 13-20, 1721.[15]

This bit of criticism—only a paragraph—from an anonymous author who wrote at Castle William, a fort on Castle Island, in Boston harbor, impugned Wise's motives for writing *A Word of Comfort*. It represented him, not as "Amicus Patriae," but as a "Worldly Wise Man" seeking his own interest. This, perhaps the first of many puns on Wise's name— Wise himself was not above making them—indicated that he was known as the author of *A Word of Comfort* almost from the time of its publication. The advertisement—in bad taste, of course—called to public attention the business entanglements of Wise. It declared him defaulting in interest payments on private loans outstanding for twenty years and stated that, of the twelve hundred and fifty pounds Wise and two of his sons had borrowed from the government, only two hundred and fifty had ever been repaid. No wonder Wise wanted another issue of "his Miracle working Paper Money," the advertisement read. For all his "bustle of words" about enriching the country, he was only interested in another emission of bills for the purpose of easing his burden of debt.

The next week Wise answered this advertisement. His answer was announced in the Boston *Gazette* along with the publication of an anonymous pamphlet which probably addressed Wise in its title, *A Letter to an Eminent Clergy-Man in the Massachusett's Bay*.[16] Wise's answer—though not without puns on the word "wise"—was also anonymous. It enclosed a letter from "Amicus Patriae" to his son and reprinted the Castle William advertisement to make clear the references to it. The title of this short pamphlet was *A Friendly Check, from a Kind Relation, to the Chief Cannoneer, Founded on a Late Information, Dated N. E. Castle-William, 1720, 21*. The "Late Information" was, of course, the Castle William advertisement. Up to the letter of "Amicus Patriae" the content of the pamphlet was highly satiric, and the title gave the plan the satire would follow. The pamphlet portrayed the writer of the Castle William advertisement as "the Chief Cannoneer" and called the advertisement the firing of only "a few Curnels of Old-spent-Powder," the flushing of the cannon's "Touchhole with the Dust, or sweepings of the Powder-Room." He was very much of the opinion that some stronger charge was needed if "that Capital Enemy, *Amicus Patriae*," who had boldly sailed his ship into Boston harbor, was to be discouraged from his attack on "many Principal Gentlemen" who were "eminent Benefactors to the Publick" as hoarders of the province bills. Why, the "Kind Relation" declared to the "Chief Cannoneer,"

[Amicus Patriae] has Cast our Gentlemen hoarders into miserable Paroxisms in the Lower Bowels, that they are in hazard of falling into Old King *James's* Pickle; which will be a great Misfortune to their Ladies, &c. And also he has so awakened, and universally Alarmed our Country that they are fully Resolved not to be Hectored or wheedled into unsolvable Penury and Vassalage, for want of a Plentiful Medium, whence it is in their own Power to Remove those who stand in their way, and supply themselves.[17]

The cannoneer, his kinsman decided, deserved a severe punishment for his weak and cowardly advertisement and was exhorted to a braver conduct in the future.

Wise then threw off the garb of satire and excused its adoption by quoting one of the *Proverbs*: "Answer a fool according to his folly, lest he be wise in his own conceit."[18] "Amicus Patriae," Wise said, would welcome any criticism written "Solidly and not Pevishly" and would give "his Thanks to any Man" who would "fairly subvert him."

The letter that followed was doubtless autobiographical, but not completely so. There was probably no one of Wise's sons who needed to be informed of the family's financial affairs. Jeremiah, of course, had served for many years in the

somewhat distant parish of Berwick, Maine, and his father
might have had him in mind while he was writing, but the
letter was doubtless a pretext for answering the Castle
William advertisement and did not arise out of any necessity
for informing Jeremiah. In this letter there was no mention of
private loans, and the government loan Wise acknowledged
having held only three years. Moreover, it was a loan of but
one thousand pounds lent upon an estate valued at two
thousand, which Wise believed to be worth much more. As to
the amount paid back, Wise's account agreed pretty well with
the estimate of "the Pevish Gentleman" of the advertisement.
Wise divulged that these bills "furnished the business of the
Family (under your Brother's Sole management) to very
great purpose," and he admitted to an income of three hundred pounds a year. What the business of the family was or
what brother had "Sole management," it is difficult to say.
Joseph was a shopkeeper in Boston and might have watched
over his father's interest in two or three merchant vessels.[19]
After Joseph's belated attendance at Harvard, he supposedly
turned physician if he had not already practiced as a surgeon.
Henry was master of the Ipswich school at the time, and John
was the farmer of the family. Ammi Ruhamah, though he was
later a well-to-do merchant and the recipient of several hundred pounds from his father, had sometime to earn his
majority in the militia and was then probably about it. Wise's
description most closely corresponded, perhaps, to Joseph's
situation and the family's shipping interests, but could have
been written with deliberate ambiguity in order that the
writer might escape identification. Besides the estate under
mortgage, there stood free of encumbrance "Rich housen,
homestead, Remote Lands, and other Estates to the Value of
One Thousand Pounds, or not much under." Wise would not
admit to being a poverty-stricken gentleman who would

benefit by the emission of bills of public credit but insisted
that he wrote unselfishly, "purely in Love to . . . [his]
Country."[20]

*A Letter to An Eminent Clergy-Man in the Massachusett's
Bay*, written by "Yours Unknown" and published on the
same day as *A Friendly Check*, could have been addressed to
Wise. In an advertisement printed at the end of the pamphlet, "Yours Unknown" took thoroughly to task the writer
of the Castle William paragraph for attempting "to stain the
unblemish'd Reputation of a Worthy Gentleman, and a
hearty Friend to his Country." Then he had a fling at identi-
fying the Castle William author, who might belong to a Top-
ping family engaged in the odious business of usury, and offered him, for the next time he fired "a Ground-Teer from
Castle William," the following harshly-expressed caution. "If
he can Muster no stronger Arguments, than first Impudence;
secondly Nonsense; thirdly Tautology; and fourthly Fals-
hood; he is Desired to Imprison his forked Tongue within his
Teeth, and further to say nothing."[21]

Another circumstance pointing to Wise as the "Eminent
Clergy-Man" was the tenor of the argument in *A Letter*. It
echoed the cries Wise raised in *A Word of Comfort* about the
scarcity of bills of credit. In the postscript a parlous state was
described.

Through the extream Scarcity of Bills things are come to such a
pinch, that if something be not speedily done, all prudent fore-
seeing Men greatly fear the Event. The whole Province is in a
Flame at this time. Every Man's Hand is against his Brother:
Bonds and Mortgages are sued; and Men are pulling one another
by the Throat, without any Mercy.[22]

A Letter showed also an antipathy to hoarders, as did Wise
in *A Friendly Check*. "Indeed it is now confess'd by all, except a few of the most Screwing Misers who are for no Bank

at all, but the Clam bank, that something or other must speedily be done."²³ The fact that *A Letter* and Wise's answer to the Castle William author were mentioned together in a newspaper advertisement would add to the likelihood of Wise's being the minister addressed.

Whether or not he was "the Reverend Person" to whom *A Letter* had been written, that person had perused it "with great Satisfaction" and desired that it be sent to the printer. The first paragraph was one of praise for the clergyman, and, since it might have been meant for Wise, should be set down here.

That you are deservedly Esteemed a Bright Ornament, and in many respects a Father to your Countrey; a Patron of Great and Worthy Actions; and a Sincere Lover of all Good Men; a true Friend to Peace, and a Sorrowful Mourner for the Wounds and Divisions your Countrey is groaning, and Bleeding under; and bear a Tender Sympathy with the indigent and Miserable; has Emboldened me at this time to write to you, and will (I hope) Sufficiently Apologize for the same.²⁴

"Yours Unknown" went on then to describe a handful of pamphlets he had received early in February. His criticism was that they were too partisan, given over to dissension, and lacking in public spirit. The writer of *A Letter*, though he held in scorn the quarrelsome and libelous pamphleteer, was upon publication charged with such a character himself and if he could have been found would have been brought to account by the Council of the colony. The Council denounced *A Letter* for containing "many Vile, Scandalous and very Abusive Expressions which greatly Reflect[ed] on his Majesty's Government and People of this Province, and tend[ed] to disturb the Public Peace." While "Yours Unknown" could not be found, the poor bookseller was, and prosecution was directed against him by the Council. The

Council's action was voted to be printed "in the Weekly Papers."[25]

There was another anonymous *Letter* that defended Wise from the Castle William advertisement. This was *A Letter from a Gentleman in Mount Hope, to His Friend in Treamount*. It was probably published about the same time that *A Letter to an Eminent Clergy-Man* and *A Friendly Check* were published, for the date set down at the end was February 27, 1721. From the first paragraph of this pamphlet it is evident that Wise was still gratefully remembered, though some thirty years had passed, for the part he had played in the tax protestation while Andros was governor. The author remarked his indignation against the Castle William writer for daring

to Ill-Treat and Villify, whom we ever deemed a true and faithful Friend to his Conntry; and who shew'd himself to be such an One, some Years past, when many Others (considering their Stations in Government) were under stricter Obligations to appear, were afraid to be Gap-men, and protest against the Gross Injuries, Arbitrary and Illegal Actions of the then Government.[26]

Wise's injuries from the government of Andros were then recited, and his present esteem in the country and his recent pamphlet in its behalf noted. The Mount Hope gentleman, it was apparent from his *Letter*, thought of paper money as Wise did.

An answer was made to Wise's *Friendly Check*. It turned up as an advertisement in the *Gazette* the second week of March and was prepared in response to Wise's request for solid opposition.[27] The anonymous advertiser thought the best possible answer to Wise's arguments for more paper money would be to show Wise seemingly in the act of repudiating bills of public credit. Therefore, he caused to be printed in full Wise's petition to the court of Newbury for a salary adjustment. It will be remembered that less than two years before Wise had refused to accept payment in paper money and for a salary of seventy pounds would not take ninety pounds in province bills. The advertiser hoped that the reprint of this petition would "meet with a very Candid Entertainment, as well from *Amicus Patriae*, as his Imployers and Admirers," and with that hope, ceased to speak, letting the petition be his argument.

In the next number of the *Gazette* Wise "advertised."[28] He took issue with the phrase "Imployers and Admirers," and reasserted the purity of his motives for writing. He had written, not for "Bribes, Fees, Personal Influence, or anything like Espousing a Party or Faction," but averred that "the State of his Country . . . [had] lain as near to his Heart, as ever Calis [Calais] did to Queen Mary's" and that his pamphlet had not been under "the direction of any, but the Innocent Dictates of his Affections and Mind." As to admirers, Wise took the word in its narrow sense of wonder—as a way of turning off a compliment he did not want—and pointed to those gentlemen defective in understanding fundamental civil law, which, he implied, spoke for paper money, as the more proper objects for wonderment. Wise denied any inconsistency between his stand in *A Word of Comfort* and the content of the Newbury petition; instead, he argued their harmony by noting pages in his currency pamphlet, where agreement could be found. From these pages it could be demonstrated that Wise never meant to repudiate bills, but only to have salaries raised to fit the value of the paper currency. And in his petition that point of view could be discovered, he thought, for, while he rejected bills as equal to hard money, he recognized that they had a certain ratio to money (twelve shillings per pound), and he wanted only payment "in a full Equivalent." Since the petition carried his name, Wise must

have realized that his disguise had been thoroughly pene-
trated. In his answer he threw off all anonymity and showed
his willingness to be identified with "Amicus Patriae."

Another pamphlet that made "some Remarks on *Amicus
Patriae*" was *A Discours,* said to have been written by
Thomas Paine, a young man who, after graduating in Henry
Wise's Harvard class of 1717, preached for a number of years
at Weymouth. Paine agreed as to the convenience of paper
money, but joined other pamphleteers in criticizing the
people for the extravagance that had brought the country
into difficulties. His plan for saving the country was to establish a government land bank which would emit the desired
number of bills. He wanted nothing to do with a private land
bank, for he did not trust the merchants. Paine, bitter against
Wise because he had proposed a private land bank, took the
opportunity to be quarrelsome, using over again the phrases
of the Castle William advertisement. Readdly Paine took a
stand not unlike Wise's, but was too jealous and resentful to
admit to any similarity in point of view.[29] Whether or not
Wise ever saw *A Discours,* he made no answer to it, nor did
any other pamphleteer.

What was the answer to this vexing problem of paper
money? How right was Wise? For his motives in writing *A
Word of Comfort to a Melancholy Country* there need be no
doubt of their disinterested nature. His differences with his
congregation about money had been settled to his satisfaction, and in the letter of "Amicus Patriae" to his son he expressed thanks for his good fortune and was pleased to have
an income of three hundred pounds a year. Though this letter
was not entirely autobiographical, the facts about his finances
should have been accurate since they answered the slurs of
the Castle William writer. Wise wrote them, evidently, not
to help his own affairs, but those of his country, and he was

probably moved to write because of his anxiety over the straits of the farmers and the tradesmen whom he, as a country minister, knew and talked with. Despite the issue of large batches of paper money, there was still, no doubt, a scarcity of bills in many areas; and hoarding as an explanation was often enough advanced to give it some credence. But coupled with a disappearing medium went inflation. The worth of the bills was steadily sinking. They had lost the confidence of many people. Any further issue of bills, unless their value could be insured—and the government had no resources to insure them—would only contribute to greater depreciation. Wise probably did not have an accurate conception of the extent of the inflation, the limited resources of the government to curb it, and the bad reputation of bills throughout the colony. But then, how many in the country did? Its legislators seemed not to have been particularly enlightened, for the government went on trying to issue more bills. Wise, at least, believed that the bills must have security; and what better security, he thought, than the reputations and estates of substantial merchants who would set up a private land bank and find it to their interest to keep up the value of the bills? How to put the plan into operation, that was the question. But that was not Wise's province. He had set forth a plan, and it was the task of others to put it to work.

The agitation for paper money probably subsided a little after an issue of fifty thousand pounds and the decision of the government to accept produce once more as legal tender for the payment of rates.[30] But the bills of credit would occasion much debate for years to come, and the cries of "more paper money" would go up again.[31]

Another circumstance that, perhaps, took the minds of the people off the money crisis—at least occupied people in Bos-

ton and vicinity—was the smallpox epidemic in the summer
of 1721. Inoculation was one of the means proposed for
halting it, and Wise was among those who endorsed inoculation.

The evidence that Wise supported "inoculating or trans-
planting the smallpox" may be found in a pamphlet written
by Increase Mather in November, 1721. Mather wrote this
pamphlet only a week after an enemy of inoculation had
attempted to blow up his son's house. Increase probably felt
it was high time that some recommendations of the treatment
be set forth and wrote forthwith three pages full. One argument he used to gain friends for inoculation and belief in its
good works was to demonstrate the approval accorded it
by men of esteem and authority. This passage he wrote as
follows.

It cannot be denied but that some wise and judicious persons
among us, approve of inoculation, both magistrates and ministers.
My sentiments, and my son's also, about this matter are well
known. Also we hear that the reverend and learned Mr. Solomon
Stoddard of Northampton concurs with us; so doth the reverend
Mr. Wise of Ipswich, and many other younger divines, not only
in Boston, but in the country, join with their fathers.[32]

How Increase Mather learned of Wise's sentiments, he did
not divulge. Wise could have written his views, of course, in
a letter to the Doctor, but his opinion spoken in public on
such an eristic subject as inoculation would easily have
attracted notice and could have reached Boston by word of
mouth. So that the cause might have two "witnesses,"
Mather added to his own pamphlet a brief anonymous essay
written by his son Cotton.[33]

The smallpox epidemic that had called forth these pamphlets was a particularly virulent one. The first since 1702,
it had started slowly enough, the earliest cases being reported

on board a ship in Boston harbor. The town authorities were vigilant in the inspection and regulations of ships, and at one time the infection seemed to have been entirely extinguished.[34] But by midsummer the disease was spreading rapidly. The thirteenth of July was set aside as "a Day of Publick Fasting and Prayer to Almighty GOD to Avert the spreading of the Small-Pox," and on the twenty-ninth 168 persons were reported to have been stricken; eighteen of them died.[35] Some inhabitants fled Boston, but the disease extended into the outlying towns and continued to increase its toll until late fall.[36]

Early in the epidemic, Cotton Mather, concerned for the well-being of his two young children, had brought to the attention of the Boston physicians the successful use of inoculation in foreign countries. Only one of the ten or more doctors, Zabdiel Boylston, believed enough in the method to try it.[37] Though he treated successfully his small son and two Negro slaves, the people of the town were blinded to the success of the treatment by their own fears, the wild testimonies of ignorant sailors, and the active opposition of most of the other doctors. On July 15, in the Boston *Gazette*, Boylston published a report on his "Artificially giving the Small-Pocks by Inoculation" and sought to justify the method.[38] It was good that he did so, for in the following issue of the *News-Letter* his recent success was disparaged and he was slightingly referred to as "a certain *Cutter for the Stone.*" The article was signed by "W. Philanthropos," a pen name for a leading physician of the town, William Douglass.[39] In answer to this attack, the ministers of Boston, including the two Mathers, Benjamin Colman, and Thomas Prince, took up the cudgels and published a letter in Boylston's defense. They wondered why inoculation should be so scorned and feared as a terrifying and ungodly act.

For, [they asked] what hand or art of *Man* is there in this Operation more than in *bleeding, blistering* and a Score more things in *Medical use?* Which are all consistent with *a humble Trust in our Great Preserver, and a due Subjection to His All-wise Providence.*[40]

The town council was hostile to inoculation and passed an ordinance, in the face of the increasing use of the method,[41] to confine those who came to town to be inoculated to the hospital or pest house.[42] There was, at this time, in Cotton Mather's house his relative and the minister of Roxbury, Thomas Walter, who had come to town for the inoculation treatment. Mather's disregard for the law and forthright espousal of the new practice had already attracted criticism and threats,[43] and now one or more "franticks" threw a bomb into his house. Mather reported the occurrence in his *Diary* as follows.

Towards three a Clock in the Night, as it grew towards Morning of this Day, some unknown Hands, threw a fired Granado into the Chamber where my Kinsman lay, and which used to be my Lodging-Room. The Weight of the Iron Ball alone, had it fallen upon his Head, would have been enough to have done Part of the Business designed. But the *Granado* was charged, the upper part with dried Powder, the lower Part with a Mixture of Oil of Turpentine and Powder and what else I know not, in such a Manner, that upon its going off, it must have splitt, and have probably killed the Persons in the Room, and certainly fired the Chamber, and speedily laid the House in Ashes. . . . The *Granado* passing thro' the Window, had by the Iron in the Middle of the Casement, such a Turn given to it, that in falling on the Floor, the fired Wild-fire in the Fuse was violently shaken out upon the Floor, without firing the *Granado*. When the *Granado* was taken up there was found a Paper so tied with String about the Fuse, that it might out-Live the breaking of the Shell, which had these words in it; COTTON MATHER, *You Dog, Dam you: I'l inoculate you with this, with a Pox to you.*[44]

In quiet Chebacco parish, beyond the reach of the epidemic, there was, of course, no resorting to bombs; and when Wise championed inoculation, he probably met with little opposition. He merits praise for his advanced opinion, and in his own time Increase Mather's letter cited him for the courage of his convictions. But unlike Increase and Cotton Mather and Dr. Zabdiel Boylston, since he lived in an area untouched by the epidemic, probably he did not have to put his theories to the test of practice. That he would have remained resolute in his intellectual commitment, even as they, is probably not to be denied, and so posterity is not wrong in according him some praise for his belief in inoculation.

There was still another topic of the early 1720's that drew forth a public pronouncement by Wise. This was the project for singing by note. Wise wrote no pamphlet in favor of singing by note, but his words were remarked and quoted. The Reverend Thomas Symmes, of Bradford, cited Wise as an authority in the second of his discourses promoting regular singing. His first was *The Reasonableness of Regular Singing; or, Singing by Note*, published in 1720, avowedly "an Essay, to Revive the True and Ancient Mode of Singing Psalm-Tunes."[45] This practice Symmes thought "greatly decay'd in most Congregations," a regrettable situation which he tried to remedy by the publication three years later of a second work, entitled *Utile Dulci; or, A Joco-Serious Dialogue, Concerning Regular Singing*. This pamphlet purported to be a conversation between a minister who approved singing by rule and a neighbor who did not. The minister had by far the better of it, shamelessly monopolizing the conversation and crushing his poor neighbor's objections with practiced ease.

Symmes was treating a topic just then up for consideration in a good many churches. The practice of "lining"—reading the psalms line by line before each line was sung—had been growing in disfavor for some time. Frequently the deacon or elder who did the lining would also "set" the tune. Gradually the tunes got away from the notes meant for them and developed local "traditional" airs that in passing from generation to generation met with further corruption. Thus, the same psalm might be sung in as many different ways as there were churches. Some churches had already discarded the practice of lining and, importing a singing master or learning the tunes by some other means, had adopted the new way of singing. The Brattle Street Church, in Boston, was one of these.[46]

In his first book Symmes offered the following reasons for singing by note.

1. THE Total Neglect *of Singing Psalms, by many Serious Christians, for want of Skill* in *Singing Psalm Tunes.* . . .

2. THE imperfect *and* irregular manner *of Singing* Psalm Tunes *in most Places.* . . .

3. THE *Difficulties & Oppositions which some Congregations* . . . [*had*] *met withal, in their attempting & accomplishing a Reformation in their singing.* . . .

4. [The success which singing by note had met with everywhere it had supplanted singing by rote.][47]

The second reason of this group Symmes took pains to emphasize. The different "patterns" or "*Modes* of Singing" were "hurtful," he declared.

Many who have some Ability to Sing in the Usual Way, are blunder'd when they go to a Congregation they have not been us'd to Sing withal; and if they move their Habitations they have their Tunes to learn again, as much as if they knew nothing about them, or at least to learn in a different manner; whereas they who learn by Rule, let them learn where, and of whom they will, yet they Sing alike.[48]

Any omission of singing the proper tune for lack of quali-

fied singers Symmes would not allow. As an argument on this
point, in his second book he brought to mind what Wise had
written and thus reported the correspondence.

I receiv'd a Letter from the Reverend and Aged[49] Mr. *Wise* of
Ipswich, wherein he gave it, as *His Judgment,* That *when there
were a Sufficient number in a Congregation to carry away a Tune
Roundly, it was then proper to introduce that Tune*: Which Letter I read to the Church; and I never yet set any Tune Publickly,
but there were (as I said before) eno to carry the *Tune,* without
the least hazard of making a Blunder.[50]

This report of Wise's letter was fragmentary, of course. It
would be interesting to observe, had the letter come down to
this day, how completely Wise had given himself to the cause
of singing by note. Evidently it was a commitment strong
enough to allow Symmes to view him in the light of a kindred
spirit and co-worker. In Cotton Mather, also, Symmes found
a sympathetic point of view, and he quoted the close of *The
Accomplished Singer.*

Symmes felt that the prejudices against regular singing
would be quickly overcome once it was tried, for he avowed:

I've said to some of my Hearers, that if any of you A.R.S.'s[51]
would take the pains to *acquaint yourselves* with the *Rules* of
Singing, so as to be able to Sing 6 or 7 tunes tolerably by Art, *If
they did not then say as I do,* that singing by Note is Unspeak-
ably preferrible to singing the Usual way; *I'd give up the Cause as
to them.*[52]

The young people especially he urged, as did Cotton Mather,
to learn singing by note. They should be "encouraged," he
thought, "to improve the long *Winter-Evenings* in Learning to Sing." In a final recommendation, he exhorted his
"Hearers": *"Sing at your Work,* when you can do it De-
cently; and learn to Sing *as well as ever you can."*[53]

CHAPTER XII

The Lamp Burned Out

WISE'S ACTIVITY continued undiminished into the last year of his life. By this time he was venerated as "Father" Wise,[1] and his name and ideas were well known in the colony. One contemporary said of him: "He was a Great Divine, and an able Minister of the New Testament, and had a peculiar Talent for Composing Church Controversies, and Ecclesiastical Difficulties, and was happy in a constant Success in it."[2] His preaching was sought after. In 1719 Samuel Sewall reported him chosen to preach the Election Sermon for the opening of General Court, but he refused.[3]

In the glow of such esteem Wise's declining years must have been benign. The comfortable and flourishing state of his family also doubtless added to his sense of well-being. He had a son and a son-in-law settled in his chosen profession. His daughter Mary remained at home, providing him and her mother with care and companionship. John and Henry were close by. None of his children lived so far away that they could not come home often. And with the children would come his grandchildren. They were a numerous brood, and they must have delighted him. Before his death there were between fifteen and twenty.[4] It is reasonable to suppose that Wise was like other grandfathers and proud of his descendants. If descent took its normal course, the country today nourishes an abundant progeny sprung from them.

Among his old and trusted friends were many of his parishioners. He had labored long in his vineyard, and it had borne good fruit. Chebacco church, after his ministry of forty-five years, boasted ninety-one members,[5] and the congregation numbered a good many more, for membership in New England churches was not obtained by any easy course. A new meetinghouse had been built for his ministry, and a good living was provided him. He dwelt in a comfortable two-story frame house and raised crops and livestock on sixty acres of his own land. In the house was a favorite chair, which allegedly survives to this day and still keeps its place before the living-room fire.

When Wise died, he left his wife in comfortable circumstances. She was to have "an Honourable & Sufficient Maintenanc . . . out of ye Income of my Estate, as she herself, and my Executer shall Adjust ye Terms."[6] It will be remembered that the executor was his son John. Wise's wife survived him by about ten years, and his daughter Mary died the year following his wife's death.[7] It seems probable that they lived together and that Mary looked after her mother until her mother's death in 1735. All this time, no doubt, Wise's wife benefited from another stipulation of his will. Wise, like Shakespeare, left his wife some bedding. He must have had in mind her comfort, just as Shakespeare had concerned himself for the comfort of his. Wise willed to his "Beloved Wife" "that Bed, Bedstead, & Beding belonging to it, standing in my studie, wch we commonly lay on."[8]

It was only a week or so before Wise's death on April 8, 1725, that the Chebacco people convened for the purpose of procuring a substitute to preach during his illness.[9] Scarcely had their choice of substitute, the Reverend Theophilus Pickering, a resident of Salem and a Harvard graduate in 1719, arrived when Wise died. Wise had probably been ill only a short time before Pickering was called, for a church in those days would not long do without ministerial inspiration. Pickering stayed on after Wise died, and a couple of years later he assisted in the entry of a number of people into a state of grace. Joseph Felt, historian of Ipswich, Essex, and Hamilton, was convinced that the earthquake of 1727, since it was "immediately followed by a powerful reformation" calling for the minister's "abundant labors," contributed substantially to Pickering's harvest of souls.[10]

The parish paid thirty pounds toward the funeral expenses, and it was probably urged upon John White—if he did not think of publication himself—that he have the funeral sermon printed. The sermon's title, *The Gospel Treasure in Earthen Vessels*, White got from Corinthians *II*, chapter iv, verse 7: "But we have this treasure in earthen vessels, that the excellency of the power may be of God, and not of us." "The Mournful Occasion" for its delivery was taken less as an opportunity to honor Wise than as a chance to direct the minds of the hearers to the proper thoughts for salvation and grace. This was a usual practice. The concern of the ministers was for the living. White urged his listeners to seek after the Gospel, which, of course, was the greatest treasure on earth. His exhortation to the congregation to grieve for Wise's death was probably not needed, but it showed clearly his ideas of the fitting response for the bereaved and something of his admiration for his father-in-law.

LET *us be duly affected, and deeply Humbled, when these Earthen Vessels are broken to pieces; and can hold this Treasure no more. 'Tis not so much to be wondered at, as Lamented, when Earthen Vessels are Dissolved. They are Frail and Infirm, and liable to many Disasters. And the more Capacious and Serviceable any such Vessel was, the more reason we have to lay their Dissolution to heart.*[11]

The last few pages of the forty-page sermon White gave over to a eulogy of Wise, and it was thorough enough. He spoke of Wise's personal charm:

His kind, condescending, and most generous and obliging Carriage, has often brought to remembrance, what is said of *Titus Vespatianus,* the *Roman* Emperor, viz. That no man ever went out of his Presence Sorrowful. And some who had viewed him at a distance thro' a false Glass, when they have Visited him, have been Charmed, and even Ravished.[12]

He described the regard Wise had for the ministerial office and reported a last speech that attested not only to Wise's esteem but, possibly, to Wise's recognition of the separation of church and state as well.

He had a high Value and Veneration for Men of his *Character* and *Order*: And this was his Language on his Death Bed, *viz.* I would have you pay a special Veneration to your *Ministers*: They are your great Interest. *Magistrates* indeed preserve your Lives & Estates; but your Ministers Business is to Save your Souls: *Therefore esteem them highly for their Works sake;* and Cultivate this Spirit and Principle into your Children.[13]

White also reported other last words of Wise, which showed his concern for the liberties of congregational church policy and echoed the words of Paul in second Timothy.

He told me in the beginning of his Sickness, that he had been a Man of Contention, but the State of the Churches making it necessary; upon the most serious Review, he could say he had *Fought a good Fight;* and had comfort in reflecting upon the same: He was conscious to himself of his acting therein sincerely.[14]

To White's sermon was added an anonymous offering called: "A Character of the Reverend Mr. *John Wise.* By another Hand." That this was spoken at the funeral on the eleventh of April is to be doubted, but it was thought good enough for printing. It contained some sound information about Wise's life and crammed into two pages laudatory paragraphs—many of them already quoted—on all of the major undertakings of his life.

The Boston *News-Letter* made brief note of his death, saying only: "On Friday last dyed the Reverend Mr. John Wise, Pastor of a Church in Ipswich."[15] His parishioners saw him buried on the twelfth and set up a monument[16] to his memory, on which these words of praise were inscribed.

> For Talents, Piety & Learning he shone
> As a Star of the first magnitude.

Wise had worked hard at being a minister during a period when a minister's life was more than ordinarily difficult. For that time Cotton Mather has left a number of descriptions of the work of ministers. One of them goes as follows.

They must sit much in their *Libraries,* until they become themselves *walking Libraries.* Besides all this; the *Government* of their *Churches,* takes up no little share of their Time. And they must *Visit* their Flocks, to pray over the *Sick & Comfort* the *Bereaved, & Instruct* the *Ignorant, & Relieve* the *Tempted,* & give their best Advice unto the *Unadvised.* Yes, they must on frequent occasions give themselves to *Fasting & Praying* in their own Retirements, lest the *Devices of* Satan (Who *Desires* to *Sift* them) should in anything prevail against themselves, & their Flocks.[17]

Both Mather and Wise's son Jeremiah saw ministers as "the *Lamps* of the Churches," burning that others might prosper. Jeremiah said in one of his sermons:

A *Minister's* Life and Work, must, ordinarily cease together. They are *Lights* that must *waste* themselves and *burn out* in giving Light to others. Their work is a *painful Work*; and Wo unto us if we spare our Pains for fear of shortning our Days, and hastning our End. Verily the Lamp of our Life can *never* burn out better, than in lighting others to Heaven.[18]

Wise would doubtless have seconded his son's remarks and would have rejoiced that the ministerial life had been so truly described. Wise himself was content that his own life should thus burn low, flicker, and go out.

Notes

INTRODUCTION

1. Massachusetts, "Archives," Manuscript, XXXV, 138.

2. The best accounts of him are Mackaye, "The Founder of American Democracy," *The New England Magazine*, XXIX (September, 1903), 73-83; McElroy, "John Wise: the Father of American Independence," *The Essex Institute Historical Collections*, LXXXI (1945), 201-26; Rossiter, "John Wise: Colonial Democrat," *The New England Quarterly*, XXII (March, 1949), 3-32; and Story, "John Wise: Congregational Democrat," *Pacific University Bulletin*, XXXVI (1939), 1-11.

3. Representing the three fields are, in order, Parrington, *Main Currents in American Thought*, I, 118-25; Tyler, *A History of American Literature: 1607-1765*, pp. 104-15; and Walker, *The Creeds and Platforms of Congregationalism*, pp. 490-94. To these in the field of thought may be added Baldwin, *The New England Clergy and the American Revolution*, pp. 28-30, 47-53; and in the history of Congregationalism, also Walker, *A History of the Congregational Churches in the United States*, pp. 198-213, and Dexter, *The Congregationalism of the Last Three Hundred Years, As Seen in Its Literature*, pp. 488-507.

4. *Dictionary of American Biography*, XX, 427-28, and Sibley's excellent summary in *Biographical Sketches of Graduates of Harvard University*, II, 428-41.

I. ANCESTRY AND EARLY LIFE

1. Boston Record Commission, *Report of the Record Commissioners*, VI, 86.

2. Savage, *A Genealogical Dictionary of the First Settlers in New England*, IV, 614.

3. Boston Record Commission, *op. cit.*, VI, 86.

4. Morris, in *Government and Labor in Early America,* p. 390, states that the term of indenture for adult servitude designated one to seven years or more but on the average three to five; and Smith, in *Colonists in Bondage, 1607-1776,* p. 17, says "generally four."

5. *New England Historical and Genealogical Register,* II, 104.

6. Smith, *op. cit.,* pp. 16-17.

7. Morris, *op. cit.,* pp. 393 ff.

8. Roxbury, Mass., "First Church Records," Manuscript (in the possession of the First Church of Roxbury, Boston, Massachusetts); Boston Record Commission, *Report of the Record Commissioners,* VI, 76.

9. It was then often the practice to have two ministers for each church. The Cambridge platform of 1648 (Wise, *A Vindication of the Government of New England Churches,* 2d printing of 1772, p. 203) defined their duties thus: "The pastors special work is, to attend to exhortation, and therein to administer a word of wisdom: The teacher is to attend to doctrine, and therein to administer a word of knowledge. . . ." Both were to administer baptism and communion, to execute censures, and to preach. Though the division of duties was not always rigidly followed, the teacher usually occupied the position of greater authority and dispensed the Puritan theology, leaving the tasks of visitation and the like to his lesser brother called variously the pastor, preacher, etc. But most parishes found the maintenance of two ministers too heavy an economic burden, and only the larger and wealthier churches continued the practice.

10. Cotton Mather in Book III of *Magnalia Christi Americana,* 64, spoke thus of Hooker: "He was a Person who while doing his Master's Work, would put a King in his Pocket."

11. It was from this George Alcock that Bronson Alcott claimed descent, and it is reported that for many years Alcott had in his possession the Harvard diploma of Alcock's grandson George, who was a classmate of John Wise. See Cook, "John Wise, the Preacher of American Insurgency," *Proceedings of the Bostonian Society,* 1924, p. 29.

12. Smith, *op. cit.,* p. 337. Also, Pope, *The Pioneers of Massachusetts.* p. 524.

13. Savage, *op. cit.,* IV, 615.

14. Pope, *op. cit.,* p. 509. The Boston Record Commission's *Report* (VI, 45) describes this property.

15. Colonial Society of Massachusetts, *Publications,* XXXI, 5, 149.

16. Massachusetts, "Archives," Manuscript, XXXIX, 464.

17. Drake, *The Town of Roxbury.* Boston Record Commission, *Report of the Record Commissioners,* XXXIV, 48.

18. The name had a variety of spellings; see Sibley's note: *Biographical Sketches of Graduates of Harvard University,* I, 354.

19. Savage, *op. cit.,* IV, 614-15; Pope, *op. cit.,* p. 509; Hurd, *History of Essex County, Massachusetts,* II, 1163.

20. Both Benjamins died in infancy. See Roxbury, Mass., "First Church Records," Manuscript, pp. 476, 478; Boston Record Commission, *Report of the Record Commissioners,* VI, 177, 178.

21. *Ibid.,* Manuscript, pp. 468, 469, 470, 472, 473, 474, 475, 476, 477, 478, 479; VI, 116, 117, 118, 119, 121, 122, 123, 124, 125, 126.

22. Mather, *Magnalia Christi Americana,* III, 187.

23. Mather wrote, "He had once, I think, a pleasant Fear, that the Old Saints of his Acquaintance, especially those two dearest Neighbours of his, *Cotton* of *Boston,* and *Mather* of *Dorchester,* which were got safe to Heaven before him, would suspect him to be gone the wrong way, because he staid so long behind them." (Mather, *op. cit.,* III, 208).

24. Adams says, "For over forty years he [Eliot] was sole pastor," in *Dictionary of American Biography,* VI, 79. Adams is following Byington, *(The Puritan as a Colonist and a Reformer).* The facts are these: Thomas Weld was pastor 1632-1639, Samuel Danforth, 1650-1674, and Nehemiah Walter, 1688-1690. See *Report* of Boston Record Commission, VI, 170.

25. *New England Historical and Genealogical Register,* XIV, 50.

26. Eliot, "The Indian Grammar Begun," *Old South Leaflets,* III, No. 52, 15.

27. Mather, *Magnalia Christi Americana,* III, 191.

28. Massachusetts, *Laws and Liberties,* reprinted from the copy of the 1648 edition in the Henry E. Huntington Library, p. 29.

29. "Eliot's Brief Narrative," *Old South Leaflets*, I, No. 21, 1-12.

30. Byington, *op. cit.*, p. 244.

31. Adams, "John Eliot," *Dictionary of American Biography*, VI, 80. Byington has a moving account of the plight of the Christian Indians during King Philip's War (*op. cit.*, pp. 261-66). Eliot said "The English p've [prove] a very sharp rod to the praying Indians," Boston Record Commission, *Report of the Record Commissioners*, VI, 193.

32. Johnson, *Wonder-Working Providence*, edited by Jameson, p. 72.

33. Mather, *Magnalia Christi Americana*, III, 185.

34. Exodus 18: 21-23.

35. Eliot, *The Christian Commonwealth*, preface.

36. Massachusetts Historical Society. *Collections*, 1st series, VIII, 29-30; Byington, *op. cit.*, p. 217.

37. Samuel Danforth also attained some fame as an astronomer, poet, and almanac-maker, writing some of the earliest verse in America, which he printed in the almanacs Harvard College authorized him to make. See *Report* of Boston Record Commission, VI, 196.

38. Danforth, *The Cry of Sodom Enquired Into*, pp. 14-15.

39. Thwing (*History of the First Church in Roxbury, Massachusetts, 1630-1694*, p. 13) quotes the records of Roxbury Town.

40. Roxbury, Mass., "The Old School Book," Manuscript (in the possession of the Roxbury Latin School, Boston, Massachusetts), pp. 7-11. Hale, in *Tercentenary History of the Roxbury Latin School 1645-1945*, p. 2, also quotes from this record. The charter is printed in full by Greene in a pamphlet entitled *The Roxbury Latin School*. See for illustrations concerning the school an article in *The New England Magazine*, XII (June, 1895), 388-406.

41. Roxbury Latin School possesses the original agreement. Dillaway has inserted at the beginning of his *History of the Grammar School, or, "The Free School of 1645 in Roxburie"* a reproduction of it.

42. Hale (*op. cit.*, pp. 1, 45) says Wise was R.L.S. (Roxbury Latin School) 1669, and Cook (*op. cit.*, p. 30) has him the tenth

graduate of the school, being the only member of the class of 1669. Hale, however, lists at least one other graduate for that year, George Alcock; certainly Alcock was a member of Wise's college class. (See Sibley, *op. cit.*, II, 415.)

43. Mather, *Magnalia Christi Americana*, III, 187.

44. Hale, *op. cit.*, p. 17.

45. "Cotton Mather's Tribute to Ezekiel Cheever," *Old South Leaflets,* VIII, No. 177, 2-10. That Terence was then considered a proper author for schoolboys to study Samuel Sewall demonstrated by including Terence's works in an order for school books. See Sewall's "Letter Book" in *Collections* of the Massachusetts Historical Society, 6th series, I, 238.

46. Sibley, *op. cit.*, II, 144-46.

47. Ellis, *op. cit.*, p. 53. Also in Hale, *op. cit.*, pp. 39-40.

48. Hale, *op. cit.*, p. 16.

49. Roxbury, Mass., "First Church Records," Manuscript, p. 56. On March 23, 1652, Pastor Eliot wrote that "Daniel Welde [was] recommended unto us fro the church at Brantrey."

50. Roxbury, Mass., "The Old School Book," Manuscript, p. 114.

51. Johnson, *op. cit.*, pp. 71-72.

52. "Upwestward from the Towne it is something rocky whence it hath the name of Roxberry. . . ."

53. Wood, *New Englands Prospect,* edited by Boynton, pp. ii, 39.

54. Roxbury, Mass., "First Church Records," Manuscript, pp. 253, 254.

55. Drake, *The Town of Roxbury.* Boston Record Commission, *Report of the Record Commissioners,* XXXIV, 15.

56. Roxbury, Mass., "First Church Records," Manuscript, p. 255.

II. YEARS AT HARVARD

1. Increase Mather was one.

2. Wise was three years older than Samuel Angier and a year older than Edward Pelham. On the basis of information supplied by Sibley (*op. cit.*) concerning Harvard graduates entering before

John Wise, the average age of those whose age may be computed, is a little over sixteen. At least two entered at twelve and many at fourteen and fifteen; however, there was one who entered at the advanced age of twenty-seven. Samuel Eliot Morison gives corroboration to these facts in describing the median age of the seventeenth-century Harvard freshman (*Harvard in the Seventeenth Century*, I, 75n).

3. Hale (*op. cit.*, p. 47) suggests that Wise was helped to a college education by a scholarship and the generosity of the Alcock family, but gives no evidence. John Wise's oldest son, Jeremiah, enjoyed the emoluments of a Harvard scholar, but in John's class it was George Alcock who held a scholarship. See *Publications* of the Colonial Society of Massachusetts, XV, 212.

4. Of the 196 Harvard graduates before Wise, sixty per cent became ministers. The other forty per cent—83 in number—became physicians, school teachers, holders of public office, gentlemen who lived off their estates, or died before their careers could be determined. These figures are based on information that Sibley gives. See also Morison, *Harvard in the Seventeenth Century*, II, pp. 557-58, or *Three Centuries of Harvard*, pp. 23-24.

5. *A Platform of Church Discipline*, 1649 edition (photostatic copy), p. 8.

6. *New Englands First Fruits*, p. 23.

7. White, *The Gospel Treasure in Earthen Vessels*, pp. 24-25, 29.

8. Wise, *Prayer for a Succession and Full Supply of Gospel Ministers*, pp. 17-18.

9. Morison, *Harvard in the Seventeenth Century*, I, 75.

10. *Ibid.*, I, 81.

11. Colonial Society of Massachusetts, *Publications*, XXXI, 329. Mr. Walter Muir Whitehill, editor, has kindly permitted me to quote from *Publications* of the Colonial Society of Massachusetts.

12. *Ibid.*, XXXI, 331.

13. Morison says (*Harvard in the Seventeenth Century*, I, 85): "Latin was the language of textbooks, recitations, lectures, and disputations; everyone who graduated from Harvard must have been able to talk Latin of a sort; but that students used it in

familiar discourse, or even that tutors spoke it outside the class-room, is highly improbable."

14. Miller and Johnson, *The Puritans*, p. 408, excerpts from "The Journal of Jasper Danckaerts."

15. Evidence that Wise smoked is found in his *Narrative* of the expedition of Sir William Phips (Waters, *Ipswich in the Massachusetts Bay Colony, I*, 534): "Yet before I lay downe in my Straw I sat smoaking of a Pipe & discoursing with some of the Officers of the Army."

16. Colonial Society of Massachusetts, *Publications*, XXXI, 331-32.

17. Professor Morison (*Harvard in the Seventeenth Century*, I, 92), waxes enthusiastic over beer for breakfast.

18. Drawings of its probable dimensions are opposite pages 271 and 276 in Morison's *Founding of Harvard College;* see also pages 274-75.

19. See the frontispiece and the illustration opposite page 42 in Morison, *Harvard in the Seventeenth Century*, Vol. I.

20. Page 24.

21. Colonial Society of Massachusetts, *Publications*, XXXI, 342: "Whereas it is observed yt there is great discouragement put upon parents, by reason of several abuses yt are put upon their children at their first entrance, by ye senior students sending them upon their private errands & . . . for ye future due care to be taken to prevent ye same, & yt all abuses in yt kind bee severely punished, by imposeing a penalty on such person or psons as shall presume soe to doe, or by corporall punishment as to ye corporation shall seeme meet." (Adopted December 5, 1667).

22. Morison in *Three Centuries of Harvard*, pages 26-28, gives a summing up of the freshman's day.

23. Such provisions were paid to the steward and, it is hoped, went to feed the students. See "Chesholme's Steward's Book," *Publications* of the Colonial Society of Massachusetts, XXXI.

24. Morison, *Harvard in the Seventeenth Century*, I, 103.

25. "Chesholme's Steward's Book" comes down only to 1660.

26. *New Englands First Fruits*, pp. 28-30. Morison, on the basis of the information given in *New Englands First Fruits*, has drawn up a schedule of this curriculum on page 141 of *Harvard in the*

Seventeenth Century, Vol. I.

27. Colonial Society of Massachusetts, *Publications,* XXXI, 333.

28. The classes of 1670, 1671, and 1673 had a total of 19 graduates, no one being graduated in 1672, and there must have been some in these classes who did not graduate, bringing the total of undergraduates close to thirty. Sibley, *op. cit.,* II, 315, 334, 412, 414.

29. Colonial Society of Massachusetts, *Publications,* XV, 156-68.

30. Morison, *Three Centuries of Harvard,* pp. 31-32.

31. That there was extracurricular reading of the light and amorous sort, Morison gives ample evidence in *Harvard in the Seventeenth Century,* I, 124-32.

32. Morison, *Three Centuries of Harvard,* pp. 37, 39; *Harvard in the Seventeenth Century,* I, 320-39.

33. Colonial Society of Massachusetts, *Publications,* XV, 217, 219.

34. Sibley, *op. cit.,* I, 480-84; II, 148-49.

35. Morison, *Harvard in the Seventeenth Century,* I, 170.

36. Noble, "Frequenting the College: A Trial in 1685," Colonial Society of Massachusetts, *Publications,* III, 448-70.

37. *Ibid.,* XXXI, 338.

38. Noble gives a full account of this incident in *Publications* of the Colonial Society of Massachusetts, III, 452-54. The court records are also reproduced in Paige, *History of Cambridge, Massachusetts, 1630-1877,* footnote, pp. 225-26. "Middlesex County Court Records," Manuscript, p. 41, gives the sentence passed on Gibson (Clerk of Court's Office, Middlesex County Courthouse, Cambridge, Massachusetts).

39. Colonial Society of Massachusetts, *Publications,* XXXI, 335-39.

40. Jonathan Russell became the minister of the church at Barnstable; and Pelham lived off the estate inherited from his father, marrying twice, his wives being women of strange and wonderful names: Freelove and Godsgift. Sibley, *op. cit.,* II, 419, 455.

41. Morison, *Harvard in the Seventeenth Century,* I, 106.

42. Morison (*loc. cit.*, I, 110) shows that unauthorized vacations were nevertheless common.

43. Colonial Society of Massachusetts, *Publications*, XXXI, 334.

44. Mather, *Magnalia Christi Americana*, IV, 128.

45. Morison in *Three Centuries of Harvard*, pages 32-35, has an entertaining account of a seventeenth-century commencement and the events leading up to it.

III. UNSETTLED YEARS

1. Branford, Conn., "Town Records," Typescript copy in the James Blackstone Library, Branford, Connecticut, Vol. I, Part I. Hereafter referred to as "Branford TS." Up to 1689 the town and church records are one. See also Simonds, *A History of the First Church and Society of Branford, Connecticut, 1644-1919*, p. 37.

2. Trumbull, ed., *The Public Records of the Colony of Connecticut*, III, 216. Cited hereafter as "Connecticut Colonial Records."

3. "Branford TS," Typescript, Vol. I, Part I, 292, 309.

4. Branford, Conn., "Town Records," Manuscript, I, (1645-1678), 153, 163. Hereafter referred to as "Branford Records." Also in "Branford TS," Typescript, Vol. I, Part I, 152, 154.

5. "Branford Records," Manuscript, I, 31; "Branford TS," Typescript, Vol. I, Part I, 22-23.

6. *Connecticut Colonial Records*, II, 76.

7. Dexter, "The History of Connecticut, As Illustrated by the Names of Her Towns," *Proceedings of the American Antiquarian Society*, new series, III, 426-27.

8. Simonds, *op. cit.*, p. 1.

9. *Ibid.*, p. 14.

10. "Branford TS," Typescript, Vol. I, Part I, 312.

11. Simonds, *op. cit.*, pp. 13-14.

12. *Ibid.*, pp. 31-32.

13. Sibley, *op. cit.*, II, 253.

14. "Branford TS," Typescript, Vol. I, Part I, 296-97.

15. *Ibid.*, p. 303.

16. *Connecticut Colonial Records*, II, 399.

17. Morris and Ellis, *King Philip's War*, pp. 145-46; Wirner, *Events in Indian History*, p. 47.

18. *Connecticut Colonial Records*, II, 399, 402.

19. Morris and Ellis, *op. cit.*, p. 162.

20. *Ibid.*, pp. 162-63.

21. *Connecticut Colonial Records*, II, 405.

22. "Branford Records," Manuscript, I, 36; "Branford TS," Typescript, Vol. I, Part I, pp. 27, 368.

23. *Connecticut Colonial Records*, II, 408.

24. Massachusetts Historical Society, *Proceedings*, 2d series, XV, 286.

25. Increase Mather, *A Brief History of the War with Indians in New England*, p. 23.

26. Sibley, *op. cit.*, II, 415.

27. "Branford Records," Manuscript, I, 153; "Branford TS," Typescript, Vol. I, Part I, 152.

28. Massachusetts Historical Society, *Collections*, 1st series, XXXVIII, 581.

29. Sibley, *op. cit.*, II, 194.

30. Temple, *History of the Town of Whately, Mass.*, pp. 27-33; *Papers Concerning the Attack on Hatfield and Deerfield*, p. 53.

31. Wells and Wells, *A History of Hatfield, Massachusetts*, p. 106.

32. Temple, *op. cit.*, p. 32; Wells and Wells, *op. cit.*, p. 92.

33. Wells and Wells, *op. cit.*, p. 61.

34. Judd, *History of Hadley, Including the Early History of Hatfield, South Hadley, Amherst and Granby, Massachusetts*, p. 40.

35. Sibley, *op. cit.*, II, 194.

36. Temple, *op. cit.*, p. 19.

37. Judd, *op. cit.*, p. 86.

38. *Ibid.*, pp. 87, 92; Wells and Wells, *op. cit.*, p. 106.

39. *Ibid.*, p. 47.

40. The documents relative to the controversy between the East and West (Hatfield) Hadley groups are in the Massachusetts "Archives," Manuscript, X, 160-82.

41. Temple, *op. cit.*, p. 18; Judd, *op. cit.*, p. 92; Wells and Wells, *op. cit.*, p. 60.

42. Which one is not known, according to Judd, *op. cit.*, p. 91.

43. The formal gathering of the church and the ordination of Atherton, however, did not take place until after March, 1671.

44. *Papers Concerning the Attack on Hatfield and Deerfield*, pp. 46-47.

45. Wells and Wells, *op. cit.*, p. 107; Hurd, *History of Essex County, Massachusetts, with Biographical Sketches of Many of Its Pioneers and Prominent Men*, II, 1163.

46. Savage, *op. cit.*, IV, 614.

47. *Ibid.*

48. She was the second Abigail in the family; the first died "of a cough & pox" in 1649. See "Roxbury First Church Records," Manuscript, p. 470, and Savage, *op. cit.*, II, 231.

49. Thwing, *History of the First Church in Roxbury, Massachusetts, 1630-1904*, p. vi.

50. He may have fallen upon evil days in his old age though, for there is a respectful but firm dun among the letters of Samuel Sewall, Massachusetts Historical Society, *Collections*, 6th series, I, 62-63.

51. Ellis, *The History of Roxbury Town*, p. 25.

52. Roxbury, Mass., "First Church Records," Manuscript, p. 472.

53. Essex, Mass., "Records of the First Parish, 1676-1726," Manuscript copy, p. 39.

54. Massachusetts, "Archives," Manuscript, X, 132.

55. Massachusetts, "Archives," Manuscript, X, 132.

56. *Ibid.*, X, 131c.

57. Essex, Mass., "Records of the First Parish, 1676-1726," Manuscript copy, pp. 1-6.

58. *Ibid.*, p. 8.

59. Massachusetts, "Archives," Manuscript, X, 118.

60. *Ibid.*, X, 119, 120.

61. Essex, Mass., "Records of the First Parish, 1676-1726," Manuscript copy, p. 10.

62. Ipswich, Mass., "Town Records," Manuscript copy, II (1674-96), 47, 50-51; Massachusetts, "Archives," Manuscript, X, 122.

63. Massachusetts, "Archives," Manuscript, X, 121.

64. Essex, Mass., "Records of the First Parish, 1676-1726," Manuscript copy, p. 11.

65. Massachusetts, "Archives," Manuscript, X, 123-24.

66. Essex, Mass., "Records of the First Parish, 1676-1726," Manuscript copy, p. 12.

67. Ipswich, Mass., "Town Records," Manuscript copy, II, (1674-1696), 74.

68. Massachusetts, "Archives," X, 126-29.

69. Essex, Mass., "Records of the First Parish, 1676-1726," Manuscript copy, pp. 13-14, 21-23.

70. *A Platform of Church Discipline,* 1649 edition (photostatic copy), pp. 25-26.

71. Palfrey, *History of New England,* III, 525.

72. Essex, Mass., "Records of the First Parish, 1676-1726," Manuscript copy, pp. 23-24. To honor the part the women played in founding the Essex Congregational Church, its present women's society goes by the name of the Madame Varney Guild.

73. Essex, Mass., "Records of the First Parish, 1676-1726," Manuscript copy, pp. 24-27; Massachusetts, "Archives," Manuscript, X, 120b, 129a.

74. *Ibid.,* p. 35; Essex County, Mass., *Records and Files of the Quarterly Courts,* VII (1678-1680), 245.

75. Massachusetts, "Archives," Manuscript, X, 132-34.

76. *Ibid.,* X, 136-38a.

77. *Ibid.,* X, 135.

78. Essex, Mass., "Records of the First Parish, 1676-1726," Manuscript copy, pp. 35-38.

79. *Ibid.,* p. 39.

80. *Ibid.,* p. 61.

81. *Ibid.,* pp. 40-41.

82. Ipswich, Mass., "Town Records," Manuscript copy, II (1674-1696), 90-91.

83. Essex, Mass., "Records of the First Parish, 1676-1726," Manuscript copy, pp. 58-60.

84. *A Platform of Church Discipline,* 1649 edition (photostatic copy), 10.

85. Essex, Mass., "Records of the First Parish, 1676-1726," Manuscript copy, pp. 42, 63, 65, 66; Ipswich, Mass., "Town

Records," Manuscript copy, II (1674-96), 204-5.

86. The laborer in the year 1680 was paid 2s to 2s6 a day (Massachusetts Historical Society, *Collections,* 1st series, IV, 222) and in this year (1952) the unskilled worker is paid five or six dollars a day. The wage scale today compared to the 1680 rate is in a ratio of about ten or twelve to one. Wise's salary then, by this ratio, would be worth today, exclusive of his loads of cordwood and salt marsh hay and the house and land provided him, about $3600. See Wright, *Literary Culture in Early New England, 1620-1730,* p. 78, footnote 15.

87. See note 85.

88. Roxbury, Mass., "First Church Records," Manuscript; Boston Record Commission, *Report of the Record Commissioners,* VI, 135.

89. This name Wise may have learned while he was in college, for at that time Ammi Ruhamah Corlet was one of the College Corporation (Colonial Society of Massachusetts, *Publications,* XV, 235). Wise quoted *Hosea,* ii, 1, the verse that is the Biblical source for the name, on the title page of his *Vindication.*

IV. FOR A GOOD GOD AND A GOOD KING

1. Palfrey, *History of New England,* III, 285.

2. *Ibid.,* 296-305.

3. Andrews, *The Fathers of New England,* p. 167.

4. Palfrey, *op. cit.,* III, 521-22.

5. *Ibid.,* III, 277, 518.

6. *Connecticut Colonial Records,* III, 405-06.

7. Dexter, "Address on Reverend John Wise," *Essex Bicentennial Celebration,* p. 125.

8. Andrews, ed., *Narratives of the Insurrection, 1675-1690,* pp. 242-43. During the Andros administration, the Council vote was frequently disregarded, constantly so after the first six months (Channing, *A History of the United States,* II, 179) Andrews (*op cit.,* p. 226) has summarized the complaints of Council members against the arbitrariness of Andros. The complaints themselves are on pages 239 to 249.

9. *Connecticut Colonial Records,* III, 406-07. Palfrey summarized this measure in his *History of New England,* III, 520.

10. Salem, Newbury and Marblehead—Palfrey, *op. cit.,* III, 524n.

11. Adams, "John Wise," *Dictionary of American Biography,* XX, 427.

12. John White, *The Gospel Treasure in Earthen Vessels,* p. 38.

13. Massachusetts, "Archives," Manuscript, XXXV, 138.

14. Toppan, ed., *Edward Randolph; Publications of the Prince Society,* XXVII (1899), 172; Sibley, *op. cit.,* II, 429.

15. Massachusetts, "Archives," Manuscript, CXXVII, 101.

16. *Ibid.,* XXXV, 138.

17. *Ibid.,* CXXVII, 102.

18. *Ibid.,* CXXVII, 104.

19. *Ibid.,* CXXVII, 105a.

20. *Ibid.,* XXXV, 139.

21. Ipswich, Mass., "Town Records," Manuscript copy, II (1678-1696), 238.

22. Massachusetts, "Archives," Manuscript, CXXVII, 101-02.

23. *Ibid.,* XXXV, 138; CXXVII, 105, 105a.

24. *Ibid.,* XXXV, 148a; CXXVII, 158, 165, 166, 181.

25. *Ibid.,* XXXV, 119, 122a; Waters, "Two Ipswich Patriots," *Publications of the Ipswich Historical Society,* XXVI (1927), 13-14.

26. *Ibid.,* CXXVII, 92.

27. *Ibid.,* CXXVII, 96, 97, 98; Waters, *Ipswich in the Massachusetts Bay Colony,* I, 240.

28. *Ibid.,* CXXVII, 93, 103-4.

29. *Ibid.,* CXXVII, 101-2.

30. Channing, *A History of the United States,* II, 179.

31. Toppan, *op. cit.,* XXV, 40.

32. Palfrey, *op. cit.,* III, 523n.

33. Massachusetts, "Archives," Manuscript CXXVII, 156a; XXXV, 138.

34. *Ibid.,* CXXVII, 162.

35. *Ibid.,* XXXV, 139.

36. Massachusetts Historical Society, *Collections,* 5th series, VI, 36*. This is Volume II of Sewall's *Diary.*

37. Massachusetts, "Archives," Manuscript, CXXVII, 206.

38. Andrews (*The Fathers of New England,* p. 186), Palfrey (*op. cit.,* p. 526*n*), Sibley (*op. cit.,* II, 169), and other historians cite Dudley as speaking thus. See "A Memorial of the Present Deplorable State of New England" in *Collections* of the Massachusetts Historical Society, 5th series, VI, 36*. This piece, directed with venom against Dudley, has been assigned to both Cotton Mather and Sir Henry Ashurst (Palfrey, *op. cit.,* III, 492, footnote, second column). In the sentence from the pamphlet, "they saw themselves . . . turned out of the public ministry," it would seem Wise was referred to.

39. Massachusetts, "Archives," Manuscript, XXXV, 168; CCXLII, 371. There are two copies of this material; the latter reference is to the more illegible one, but it is the only one of the two that has the date inscribed.

40. *Ibid.,* XXXV, 267: "The Revd. John Wise & 5 more; affirm that sd West told Some of them that they had no priviledge left them." Page 257: "The Revd. John Wise & 5 more of Ipswich their complaint of being damnified f1000: most wickedly and without & contrary to all Law Reason & Equity and that Sr Edmund called the people of the Countrey Jacks & Toms, speaking yt he & his Crew had the Immediate dispose of our fortuns." This presentation of the statements made at the arraignment on September 21 agrees with Waters, *Ipswich in the Massachusetts Bay Colony,* I, 246, 259-64.

41. *Ibid.,* XXXV, 139.

42. Wise did not list all the judges for the trial. After naming Dudley, Stoughton, Usher, and Randolph, he put "etc." Toppan (*op. cit.,* XXV, 43) listed the judges as do the Massachusetts "Archives," Manuscript, CXXVII, 167, 168, and 169.

43. Massachusetts, "Archives," Manuscript, XXXV, 139.

44. *Ibid.,* CXXVII, 147. Waters (*Ipswich in the Massachusetts Bay Colony,* I, 249) placed this letter last among the three that were submitted by Wise and friends and dated it September 28. While there might be some doubt about the "1" in "21th Septr. 1687" on the front of the page (it looks like a "7"), there is no doubt about it on the back of the page where the date is repeated. The "th" following the date was a standard ending.

Nicety in the use of "st" and "rd" following "1" and "3" was then little regarded.

45. *Ibid.*, CXXVII, 156a.

46. *Ibid.*, CXXVII, 158a. Waters (*Ipswich in the Massachusetts Bay Colony*, I, 247) called this letter "a humorous but not wholly intelligible plea." Waters, in his quotation of the letter, left out the clause, "that I may Bedd wt my Relations at Roxburie," hence the label "unintelligible." The letter is hardly humorous.

47. Wise's father died in 1684, but his mother lived on until 1693; there were also the families of brothers and sisters who dwelt there. Savage, *op. cit.*, IV, 615.

48. Massachusetts, "Archives," Manuscript, CXXVII, 164.

49. *Ibid.*, CXXVII, 109.

50. *Ibid.*, CXXVII, 184.

51. *Ibid.*, CXXVII, 167, 168, 169; Toppan, *op. cit.*, XXV, 43.

52. *Ibid.*, XXXV, 138-39.

53. They were Boston merchants according to Toppan, *op. cit.*, XXVII, 178.

54. Massachusetts, "Archives," Manuscript, XXXV, 139.

55. Prince Society, *Publications*, XXX (1909), 307.

56. Massachusetts, "Archives," Manuscript, XXXV, 139-40.

57. Ipswich, Mass., "Town Records," Manuscript copy, II (1674-96), 299, 284, 303, 309-10.

58. *Ibid.*, II, 361-62, 366.

59. Massachusetts, "Archives," Manuscript, CCXLII, 341; also in Massachusetts Historical Society, *Proceedings*, XII, 109.

60. Waters, *Ipswich in the Massachusetts Bay Colony*, I, 255.

61. Thomas French in his charge against Andros mentioned "twenty weckes imprisonment." Doubtless he stayed in jail until his fines and court charges, amounting to over forty pounds, were paid. Massachusetts, "Archives," Manuscript, CVII, 60.

62. *Ibid.*, XXXV, 148.

63. Andrews, *Narratives of the Insurrections, 1675-1690*, pp. 167-68.

64. Palfrey, *op. cit.*, III, 579n.

65. Andrews, "Byfield's Account of the Late Revolution," *Narratives of the Insurrections, 1675-1690*, pp. 170-82. See also

Waters, *Ipswich in the Massachusetts Bay Colony*, I, 256-57; Palfrey, *op. cit.*, III, 577-79.

66. Sibley, *op. cit.*, II, 273.

67. Andrews, *loc. cit.*, XVI, 174.

68. Massachusetts Historical Society, *Collections*, 3d series, IV, 291.

69. Massachusetts, "Archives," Manuscript, CVII, 60; XXXV, 168.

70. It is this latter account that has been much referred to for information about the action that involved Wise. It is copied in full from the Massachusetts "Archives," Manuscript, XXXV, 138-40.

Complaints of Great wrongs done undr; ye Ill Governmt; of Sr, Edmond Androsse Governr; in N=England in ye year, 1687. We John Wise, John Andrews Senr, Robt Kinsman, William Goodhew Junr; all of Ipswich in N=England in ye Countie of Essex about the 22d day of Augst; in ye year above Named, were, wt Several principall Inhabitants of the towne of Ipswich, Mett, at Mr. John Appletons & ther did Discourse, & Conclude yt it was not ye townes Dutie any wayes to Assist yt ill Methode of Raising mony wtout a Generall Assembiy, wch was apparently intended by abovesaid Sr Edmond, & his Councill, as wittnesse A Late Act Issued out by them for Such a purpose.

The next day in a Genll. towne meetting of ye Inhabitants of Ipswich wee ye above named John Wise, Jno Andrews, Robt, Kinsman, William Goodhew, wt ye rest of ye Towne yn (none Contradicting) Gave Or assent to ye vote yn made.

ye Ground of Or Trouble, Or Crime, was ye Coppie transmitted to ye Councill viz At a Legall Towne meeting Augst, 23 assembled by Vertue of an order from Jno Usher Esqr Treasurr; for choosing a Comissionr, to Joyne wt ye Selectmen to Assesse ye Inhabitants, according to an act of His Excellie; ye Govrnr; & Councill fr, Laying of Rates; ye Towne yn Considring yt ye Sd act doth Infringe yir Libertie as free=borne English Subjects of his Majestie by Interfeiring wt ye Statute Lawes of ye Land, by wch it was Enacted yt no taxes Should be Levyed on ye Subjects wtout Consent of an Assembly Choasen by ye free=holders, for Assessing of ye Same, they Do therfore Vote yt they are not willing to

Choose a Comissionr for Such an End wtout Sd Previledge; &
more over Consent not yt ye Selectmen do proceed to Lay any
Such Rate untill it be appointed by a Genll; Assembly Concurring wt ye Govrnr & Councill.

We ye Complainants wt Mr Jno Appleton, & Thos French, all
of Ipswich were brought to Answer for sd vote, out of Or Owne
cowntie 30ie or 40ie miles into Suffolk, & in Boston kept in Goale
only for Contempt, & high misdemeanr, as Or mittimus Specefies,
and upon Demand denyed ye previledge of an habeas Corpus;
and from prison over=Ruled to Answer at a Court of oyer &
Terminr in Boston aforesaid.

Our Judges were Mr Joseph Dudly of Roxbury in Suffolk, in
N=England, Mr Stoughton of Dorchester, John Usher of Boston
Treasur; & Edward Randolfe &ca

He yt officiates as Clerke & Attorny in ye Case is Georg; Farewell. The Jurors only 12ve; men, and most of them as is said non=
freeholders of any Land in ye Colony, Some of ym Strangers, &
Foreigners (as we Suppose) geathered up to Serve ye present
turne.

In Or, Defenc was pleaded ye Repeal of ye Law of Assesmts;
upon ye place. also ye maga; Charta of England, & ye Statute
Lawes yt Secure ye Subjects proprties, & Estate &ca to which was
Replyed by one of ye Judges ye Rest by Silenc assenting; yt we
must not think ye Lawes of England follow us to ye Ends of ye
Earth, or whether we went. and ye Same Prson (Jno Wise above-
said testifies) Declared in open Councill upon Examination of
Said Wise, Mr. Wise you have no more previledges Left you yn
not to be Sould for Slaves. & no man in Councill Contradicted.----
By Such Lawes Or Tryall & troubles began, & Ended.

Mr. Dudly aforesd; cheif Judge, to Close up ye Debate, &
Tryall trimed up a Speech yt pleased himself (we suppose) more
yn ye people: amongst many other Remarkable Passages to this
purpose he bespeakes ye Juryes Obedienc, who (we suppose)
were very well preinclined. Viz I am glad (Sayes he) ther be so
many worthie Gentlemen of ye Jury so Capable to do ye King
Service, and we Expect a good verdict from you Seeing ye matter
hath been so sufficiently proved against ye Criminalls.------Note
The Evidenc in ye Case as to ye Substanc of it was yt we too

bouldly Endaivred to perswade Orselves we were English men, &
undr previledges; and yt we were all Six of us aforesd; at ye towne
meetting of Ipswich aforesd; and as ye wittnesse Supposed we
assented to the foresd vote: and also yt Jno Wise made a speech
at ye Same time & said we had a good God, & a good King, and
Should Do well to Stand for Or Previledges.------Jury Returnes
us all Six guiltie, being all involved in the Same Information.----

We were Remanded from Verdict to prison, and ther kept one
& Twentie Dayes for Judgt; yn wt Mr Dudlyes approbation as
Judge Stoughton sd this Sentence was passed. Viz-----

Jno Wise suspended from ye ministerial function: fine 50£
mony, & pay Cost; 1000£ bond for ye good behavr one year.

Jno Appleton: not to bear office; fine: 50£ mony: pay ye Cost:
1000£ bond for ye good behavr one year.

Jno Andrews: not to bear office: fine: 30£ mony: pay ye Cost:
500£ Bond for ye Good Behavr one year.

Robt Kinsman: not to bear office: fine 20£: mony: pay Cost:
500£ Bond for ye Good behavior one year.

William Goodhew: not to bear office: fine 20£: mony: pay
Cost: 500£ Bond for good behavior one year.

Thos French: not to bear office: fine: 15£ money: pay Cost:
500£ Bond for good behavior one year.------

The total fees of this case, upon one Single Information De-
maned by Farewell abovesd amounts to about 101£--17s--0. who
Demanded of us Singly about 16£--19s--6d: ye Cost of prosecution. The fines Added make up this two hundred eightie & six
pounds; seventeen shillings. Suma totalis: 286£--17s--0d

To all wch we may add a Large acct; of other fees, of Messengers prison Charges, & mony for Bonds, and transcripts of Records
Exhausted by those Ill=men one way, and another to ye vallue of
three= or foure Schoar pounds, besides our Expenc of time & Imprisonment.----

We Judge the Totall Charge for one Case, & Tryall undr one
Single Information Involving us Six men abovesd; in Expenc of
time, & monyes, of us and or Relations, for our necessary Succour,
& Support to Amount to more; Bute no Lesse then four hundred
pounds Mony.

------400£—00s—00d Mony.——

Too Tedious to Illustrate more amply at this time, & so we Conclude.---

John Wise: John Andrews Senr: William Goodhew Jur: Thos French, and Robert Kinsman

Those fower persons first named apeared ye twentieth of December and Robert Kinsman appeared ye one & twenty of December one thousand six hundred eighty nine and gave in their testimonies upon oath unto me Samel Appleton Assist for ye Colony of ye Massachusetts in New England.

71. Andrews, *Narratives of the Insurrections, 1675-1690,* pp. 165-269.

72. Massachusetts Historical Society, *Collections,* 4th series, VIII, 699-700.

73. Prince Society, *Publications,* XXX (1909), 307.

74. Massachusetts, "Archives," Manuscript, XI, 56a.

75. "The Narrative of Mr John Wise, Minister of Gods Word at Chebacco," Massachusetts Historical Society, *Proceedings,* 2d series, XV (1902), 283.

V. CHAPLAIN AGAINST QUEBEC

1. A small number of men from Winthrop's force would not give over fighting and moved into Canada where they had a little success (Massachusetts Historical Society, *Proceedings,* 2d series, XV, 305).

2. Massachusetts Historical Society, *Proceedings,* 2d series, XV, 283, 306.

3. *Ibid.,* XV, 309.

4. *Ibid.,* XV, 313.

5. Walley himself wrote between "12 and 1300 men"; see Hutchinson, *The History of the Colony and Province of Massachusetts Bay,* edited by Mayo, I, 460.

6. "The Narrative of Mr. John Wise," Massachusetts Historical Society, *Proceedings,* 2d series, XV, 289. Walley said the field pieces were landed "contrary to order and without my knowledge" and "greatly clogg'd us" (Hutchinson, *op. cit.,* I, 462).

7. So counted by Wise; he must have started counting with the day of landing.

8. Walley reported that in this action "through hast in the retreat, a small drummer left his drum behind him." (Hutchinson, *op. cit.*, I, 464).

9. Massachusetts Historical Society, *Proceedings,* 2d series, XV, 316.

10. Hutchinson, *op. cit.*, I, 339-40.

11. Massachusetts Historical Society, *Proceedings,* 2d series, XV, 298-99.

12. *Ibid.*, XV, 299-300, 312.

13. Hutchinson, *op. cit.*, I, 460.

14. White, *The Gospel Treasure in Earthen Vessels,* p. 42.

15. Massachusetts Historical Society, *Proceedings,* 2d series, XV, 315.

16. "The Narrative of Mr John Wise," Massachusetts Historical Society, *Proceedings,* 2d series, XV, 291.

17. *Ibid.*, XV, 282.

18. Walley contemplated another landing place upon an intelligence afforded by some French prisoners, but the necessity for changing an already announced decision and the shortness of time discouraged him from any alteration of plan (Hutchinson, *op. cit.*, I, 460).

19. "The Narrative of Mr John Wise," Massachusetts Historical Society, *Proceedings,* 2d series, XV, 284.

20. Massachusetts Historical Society, *Proceedings,* 2d series, XV, 315.

21. Hutchinson, *op. cit.*, I, 467. Walley nowhere mentioned Wise or the actions of a clergyman—a strange omission if Wise's activities were as numerous as he said they were.

22. Massachusetts Historical Society, *Proceedings,* 2d series, XV, 301-3.

23. Walley had quite a different explanation about the loss of the guns (Hutchinson, *op. cit.*, I, 465-66).

24. "The Narrative of Mr. John Wise," Massachusetts Historical Society, *Proceedings,* 2d series, XV, 295.

25. *Ibid.*, XV, 289.

26. *Ibid,* XV, 290.

27. Walley gave a different account of this night (Hutchinson, *op. cit.*, I, 464).

28. Massachusetts Historical Society, *Proceedings*, 2d series, XV, 294, 301-3.

29. Hutchinson, *op. cit.*, I, 463.

30. Massachusetts, "Archives," Manuscript, XXXVI, 227.

31. "The Narrative of Mr. John Wise," Massachusetts Historical Society, *Proceedings*, 2d series, XV, 296.

32. Massachusetts, *Journal of the Honourable House of Representatives of His Majesty's Province of the Massachusetts Bay in New England*, January 8, 1736-37, p. 97.

VI. "STORMS OF WITCHCRAFTS"

1. Present-day descendants now spell their name Proctor.

2. Salem, Mass., "Witchcraft, 1692," Manuscript copy of the Essex County Court Records (Clerk of Court's Office, Essex County Superior Court House, Salem, Massachusetts), I, 75; Hurd, *op. cit.*, II, 995; Upham, *House of John Procter*, p. 10.

3. *Ibid.*, I, 74-76.

4. Massachusetts Historical Society, *Collections*, 1st series, V, 72-73.

5. Hutchinson, *op. cit.*, II, 38-39.

6. Cotton Mather, *The Wonders of the Invisible World*, p. 223.

7. Sibley, *op. cit.*, II, 433.

8. Salem, Mass., "Witchcraft, 1692," Manuscript copy, I, 74.

9. *Ibid.*, I, 74-76.

10. *Ibid.*, I, 124-25.

11. Robert Calef, [*More*] *Wonders of the Invisible World or Salem Witchcraft*, pp. 224-26.

12. *Ibid.*, p. 222.

13. Upham, *History of the Salem Witchcraft*, II, 304-5. Brattle in his letter (Massachusetts Historical Society, *Collections*, 1st series, V, 75) avowed that "excepting Mr. Hale, Mr. Noyes, and Mr. Parris, the Rev. Elders, almost throughout the whole country, are very much dissatisfied."

14. Salem, Mass., "Witchcraft, 1692," Manuscript copy, II, 37.

15. Benjamin was the only surviving child of John Procter's first marriage. See Waters, *Notes on the Manning Family*, 23-24. Procter had five other children by his second wife, the youngest of which was twenty, and four or five by his third wife. William and Sarah were children by his third wife.

16. Calef, *op. cit.*, p. 225.

17. Upham, *op. cit.*, II, 312.

18. Calef, *op. cit.*, p. 224.

19. Massachusetts Historical Society, *Collections*, 5th series, V, 363.

20. Calef, *op. cit.*, p. 236.

21. Cotton Mather, *The Wonders of the Invisible World*, p. 17.

22. John Procter's will and estate papers are on file in the Probate Office of the County Court, Salem, Massachusetts.

23. Salem, Mass., "Witchcraft, 1692," Manuscript copy, II, 132-33.

24. Abraham Hammatt, *Early Inhabitants of Ipswich, Mass.*, p. 272.

25. Salem, Mass., "Witchcraft, 1692," Manuscript copy, II, 147.

26. *Ibid., II*, 137-43.

27. *Ibid.*, 143-44.

28. *Ibid.*, 146-47.

29. *Ibid.*, 145.

30. *Ibid.*, 148-51, 186-87.

VII. LIFE AT CHEBACCO

1. Wise, "Instructions for Emigrants from Essex County, Mass. to South Carolina, 1697," *New England Historical and Genealogical Register*, XXX, 66.

2. Ipswich, Mass., "Town Records," Manuscript copy, II 1674-96), 91.

3. "Ipswich Manuscripts, 1633-1684," from the Winthrop Papers, p. 1. These manuscripts are in the Essex Institute, Salem, Massachusetts.

4. Ipswich, Mass., "Town Records, 1634-1657," Manuscript copy, Folios 7 and 8, in the Essex Institute, Salem, Massachusetts.

5. *Ibid.*, Folios 11, 13, 21.

6. Ipswich, Mass., "Town Records, 1634-1657," Manuscript copy, Folio 9.

7. White, *The Gospel Treasure in Earthen Vessels,* pp. 37-38, 41-42.

8. Essex, Mass., "Records of the First Parish, 1676-1726," Manuscript copy, pp. 96-97.

9. Crowell, *A Sketch of the History of the Second Parish in Ipswich,* p. 17.

10. There are variations of this legend. Tradition has prescribed no set form, and scholars have written their own versions of it. Its retelling here is based on the earlier accounts. See Felt, *History of Ipswich, Essex, and Hamilton,* pp. 259-60; and Mackaye, "The Founder of American Democracy," *The New England Magazine,* XXIX (September, 1903), 78.

11. Crowell, *A Sketch of the History of the Second Parish in Ipswich,* p. 17.

12. Felt, *op. cit.,* p. 259; Crowell, see above.

13. A phrase from Wise's will is echoed here. Wise's will is on file in the Probate Court of Essex County, Salem, Massachusetts.

14. Shipton, *Sibley's Harvard Graduates,* IV, 550-53; Colonial Society of Massachusetts, *Publications,* XV, 361, 363.

15. Wise's will.

16. The Boston *News-Letter,* Number 459, January 26 to February 2, 1712; Waters, *Ipswich in the Massachusetts Bay Colony,* II, 228.

17. Massachusetts, "Archives," Manuscript, VII, 486, 489 .

18. Ipswich, Mass., *Vital Records to 1850,* II, 714.

19. Waters, *An Historical Address Delivered on the 140th Anniversary of the Organization of the South Church, Ipswich,* p. 19.

20. Ipswich, Mass., *Vital Records to 1850,* II, 714.

21. *Ipswich Antiquarian Papers,* I, No. X (July, 1880).

22. Shipton, *Sibley's Harvard Graduates,* VI, 219-20.

23. These three volumes were doubtless William Gurnall's *The Christian Compleat Armour* (Wise wrote in his will "Gurnils Armour of Light"), Michael Dalton's *The Countrey Justice,* and John Speed's *The History of Great Britaine under the Conquests of ye Romans, Saxons, Danes, and Normans. . . from Julius Caesar*

to our most gracious soveraigne King James (Wise wrote "Speeds Chronicles of England"), all three volumes popular works of the 17th century.

24. Ipswich, Mass., "Town Records," Manuscript copy, II (1674-96), 394-96, III, 97; Essex, Mass., "Records of the First Parish, 1676-1726," Manuscript copy, p. 98.

25. The location of this region is unknown, but the instructions of Wise linked it with "Places near the Sea." Another group of New Englanders settled the town of Dorchester in Dorchester County.

26. Wise, "Instructions for Emigrants from Essex County, Mass. to South Carolina, 1697," *New England Historical and Genealogical Register*, XXX, 64-67; Sibley, *op. cit.*, II, 434.

27. "Letter-Book of Samuel Sewall," Massachusetts Historical Society, *Collections*, 6th series, I, 196-99. Sewall's meaning is not always clear. He said: "As for South Carolina. It pleaseth me that Christ is carrying his trenches so near Idumea." Idumea was a part of Palestine and, speaking loosely, could be identified as all Palestine, the home of orthodox Jews who rejected Christ. This would seem to be the meaning Sewall put upon it, and South Carolina was closer, at least spiritually, to the seat of sinful unbelief than New England.

VIII. THE "POPISH PLOT" IN NEW ENGLAND

1. *A Platform of Church Discipline*, 1649 edition (photostatic copy), p. 3.

2. The Saybrook (Conn.) Platform, *A Confession of Faith*, p. 1.

3. *A Platform of Church Discipline*, 1649 edition (photostatic copy), preface, p. 1.

4. *Ibid.*, p. 4.

5. Hubbard, *A General History of New England*, p. 589.

6. Besides the Cambridge association, there was one each in Essex and Bristol Counties and in the Weymouth and Sherborn neighborhoods.

7. Wise, *The Churches Quarrel Espoused*, 1713 edition, p. 102.

8. Walker, *A History of the Congregational Churches in the United States,* pp. 198-99.

9. Mather, *Magnalia Christi Americana,* V, 58-59.

10. *Ibid.,* V, 45, 52.

11. Increase Mather, *The Order of the Gospel,* p. iv.

12. Quincy, *The History of Harvard University,* I, 88-89.

13. *The Order of the Gospel,* p. vi.

14. "The Colman Papers," Manuscript, in the Massachusetts Historical Society Library, I (1697-1734), 6. Lothrop printed much material from this source in his *History of the Church in Brattle Street.*

15. *Ibid.*

16. Jenks et al., eds., *Record of the Church in Brattle Square, Boston, 1699-1872,* p. 4; also in Turell, *The Life and Character of the Reverend Benjamin Colman, D.D.*

17. *The Order of the Gospel,* p. 23.

18. Lothrop, *A History of the Church in Brattle Street,* p. 25. The Manifesto of the Brattle Street Church is printed on pp. 20-26.

19. "The Colman Papers," Manuscript I, (1697-1734), 6.

20. *Ibid.*

21. *Ibid.*

22. "Diary of Samuel Sewall," Massachusetts Historical Society, *Collections,* 5th series, VI, 291. Entry for November 28, 1710: "Mr. Pemberton quickly begun to say, What have you been holding a Court to day! Had it over again; I was a little amus'd at the word Court; however, I began to relate what had been done. Mr. Pemberton with extraordinary Vehemency said, (capering with his feet) If the Mathers order'd it, I would shoot him thorow. I told him he was in a passion. He said he was not in a Passion. I said, it was so much the worse. He said the Fire from the Altar was equal impartial, Upbraiding me, very plainly, as I understood it, with Partiality."

23. "The Colman Papers," Manuscript, I (1697-1734), 6.

24. Turell, *op. cit.,* p. 43.

25. Jenks, *op cit.,* p. 4.

26. Turell, *op. cit.,* p. 6.

27. *Ibid.,* pp. 25-26.

28. Jenks, *op. cit.*, p. 4.

29. Lothrop, *op. cit.*, p. 20.

30. "The Colman Papers," Manuscript, I (1697-1734), 11.

31. "The Diary of Samuel Sewall," *op. cit.*, 5th series, V, 509.

32. *Ibid.*, 5th series, V, 506.

33. "Diary of Cotton Mather," Massachusetts Historical Society, *Collections*, 7th series, VII, 326.

34. *Ibid.*, 7th series, VII, 332-33.

35. Jenks, *op. cit.*, p. 5.

36. "The Colman Papers," Manuscript, I (1697-1734), 11.

37. Turell, *op. cit.*, p. 47.

38. "Diary of Cotton Mather," op. cit., 7th series, VII, 333.

39. "The Diary of Samuel Sewall," *op. cit.*, 5th series, VI, 3.

40. Jenks, *op. cit.*, pp. 8-9, 95, 125.

41. "Diary of Cotton Mather," *op. cit.*, 7th series, VII, 338, 348-49.

42. *The Order of the Gospel,* p. iv.

43. [Woodbridge, Colman, and others] *The Gospel Order Revived,* viii, 36, v-vi.

44. Mather, *The Order of the Gospel,* p. 22.

45. Woodbridge, *op. cit.*, p. 20.

46. *Ibid.*, postscript and following pages.

47. Colman was probably a co-author of *The Gospel Order Revived.*

48. "Diary of Cotton Mather," *op. cit.*, 7th series, VII, 376, 377, 378.

49. *A Collection of Some of the Many Offensive Matters,* p. 9.

50. *Ibid.*, pp. 2, 4, 3.

51. Colman is meant.

52. Simon Bradstreet, thought to have been an author.

53. Woodbridge.

54. "Letter Book of Samuel Sewall," Massachusetts Historical Society, *Collections,* 6th series, I, 255.

55. Mather, *A Disquisition Concerning Ecclesiastical Councils,* pp. 37-38.

56. This church, too, had bonds of strictness that seem strange today. It could not accept the organ Thomas Brattle left in 1713. His request, "within a year after my decease procure a

Sober person that can play skilfuly thereon with a loud noise," the church would not comply with, and the organ went to King's Chapel. See Sibley, *op. cit.*, II, 496.

57. This was in 1702, according to Mather's "Diary" (*op. cit.*, 7th series, VII, 434).

58. "Diary of Cotton Mather," *op. cit.*, 7th series, VII, 522.

59. *Ibid.*, 7th series, VII, 546-49.

60. Dr. Clifford Shipton ("The New England Clergy of the 'Glacial Age,'" Colonial Society of Massachusetts, *Publications*, XXXII [1933-1937], 24-54) has interpreted the proposals as a struggle of the younger clergymen "to bring their churches to a gentler and more liberal Calvanism." From Wise's support of the office of ruling elder he has read into the proposals a major attack upon this office. Such an interpretation is a misreading. The office of ruling elder is nowhere mentioned in the proposals. Cotton Mather as well as Wise defended the office and gave arguments for its continuance (*Magnalia Christi Americana*, V [Part II], 40-41).

61. Dexter, *The Congregationalism of the Last Three Hundred Years, As Seen in Its Literature*, p. 506.

62. Page 184.

63. Allibone, *A Critical Dictionary of English Literature and British and American Authors Living and Deceased from the Earliest to the Latter Half of the Nineteenth Century*, III, 2801.

64. Evans, *American Bibliography*, I, 230. The only extant copy of this edition is in the library of the Pennsylvania Historical Society.

65. Whitaker, *A Confutation of Two Tracts, Entitled, A Vindication of the New England Churches; and The Churches Quarrel Espoused, Written by the Reverend John Wise.*

IX. THE CHURCHES QUARREL ESPOUSED

1. Dexter, *op. cit.*, pp. 495-96.
2. Wise, *The Churches Quarrel Espoused*, 1713 edition, p. 50.
3. "Diary of Cotton Mather," *op. cit.*, 7th series, VIII, 74.
4. Wise, *op. cit.*, 1713 edition, p. 11.
5. Given in Chapter VIII, p. 101.

6. Wise, *op. cit.*, 1713 edition, p. 36.

7. *Ibid.*, 13-14.

8. *Ibid.*, p. 30.

9. *Ibid.*, pp. 10-34.

10. *Ibid.*, p. 41.

11. *Ibid*, pp. 44-49.

12. Known in Roman Law as *The Digest*, "A compilation of excerpts from the writings of Roman jurists, made by direction of the emperor Justinian and published A.D. 533."—*Funk and Wagnall's Dictionary*.

13. Wise, *op. cit.*, 1713 edition, p. 49.

14. *Ibid.*, pp. 51-63.

15. *Ibid.*, pp. 55-56.

16. *Ibid.*, pp. 51-52.

17. *Ibid*, p. 69.

18. *Ibid.*, pp. 63-107.

19. *Ibid.*, p. 110.

20. *Ibid.*, pp. 119-20.

21. *Ibid.*, p. 121.

22. *Ibid.*, p. 125.

23. *Ibid.*, p. 141.

24. *Ibid.*, p. 152.

25. "The Diary of Samuel Sewall," *op. cit.*, 5th series, VII, 23.

26. Wise, *op. cit.*, 1715 edition, opposite the title page.

27. *The Essex Institute Historical Collections*, XXXVI, 326.

28. "The Diary of Samuel Sewall," *op. cit.*, 5th series, VII, 51.

29. "Diary of Cotton Mather," *op. cit.*, 7th series, VIII, 327.

30. Mather, *Ratio Disciplinae Fratrum Nov-Anglorum*, pp. 184-85.

31. Dexter, *op. cit.*, pp. 500-501.

X. WISE'S "SMALL TREATISE"

1. From the title page of the first edition.

2. Whitaker, *A Confutation of Two Tracts*, p. iii.

3. This term Wise was probably led to employ because of Pufendorf's use of it in *De jure naturae et gentium*.

4. Wise, *A Vindication of the Government of New-England Churches*, 1717 edition, pp. 4-5.

5. *Ibid.*, p. 8.

6. This military expression has today the same meaning as it had over two centuries ago when Wise used it.

7. Wise, *op. cit.*, 1717 edition, pp. 9-10.

8. This was Lord Peter King, nephew of Locke and lord chief justice under George I, who published this book in 1691. There were other editions; one Wise might have used was that of 1712.

9. Increase and Cotton Mather cited as authority many of the writers Wise referred to; so there may have been some circulation of the ante-nicene fathers. However, the Mathers could have gotten—and probably did get—many such references from secondary sources. See the appendix in Wright, *Literary Culture in New England, 1620-1730*.

10. Colonial Society of Massachusetts, *Publications*, XV, 167.

11. Compare Wise's definition of church and parish (1717 edition, pp. 11-12, 15) with King's definitions (1691 edition, pp. 7-8, 16).

12. Tertullian, born in the middle of the second century the son of a Roman centurion, was the first great Carthaginian presbyter and one of the greatest of the writers of the early church.

13. Irenaeus, bishop of Lyons at the end of the second century, was famous as a peacemaker, helping to settle the controversy over the date of Easter. His chief writing was directed against the many heresies that were springing up in his time and is commonly known as *Against Heresies*.

14. Wise, *op. cit.*, 1717 edition, p. 25.

15. *Ibid.*, p. 26.

16. *Ibid.*, p. 30.

17. In all there were four references to Pufendorf.

18. A list of books in Harvard library, compiled in 1723, included *De jure naturae et gentium*. See Wright, *Literary Culture in Early New England, 1620-1730*, p. 282.

19. For *scilicet*. Compare *A Vindication* (1717 edition, p. 35) with *Of the Law of Nature and Nations* (1710 edition, Book II, Chapter III, paragraph XV, 111).

20. Compare *A Vindication* (1717 edition, p. 43) with *Of the Law of Nature and Nations* (1710 edition, Book VII, Chapter I, paragraph IV, 499-500).

21. Compare *A Vindication* (1717 edition, pp. 40, 41) with *Of the Law of Nature and Nations* (1710 edition, Book II, Chapter III, paragraph III, 180).

22. Wise, *op. cit.*, 1717 edition, p. 40.

23. Here is the passage as it appears in *Of the Law of Nature and Nations* (1710 edition, Book III, Chapter II, paragraph I, 178):

"The word MAN is thought to carry somewhat of *Dignity* in its sound; and we commonly make use of this, as the last and the most prevailing Argument against a rude Insulter, *I am not a Beast, a Dog, but I am a Man as well as your self*. Since then Human Nature agrees equally to all Persons, and since no one can live a sociable Life with another, who does not own and respect him as a *Man;* it follows as a Command of the Law of Nature, *that every Man esteem and treat another as one who is Naturally his Equal, or who is a Man as well as he."*

24. Compare *A Vindication* (1717 edition, pp. 40-42) with *Of the Law of Nature and Nations* (1710 edition, Book III, Chapter II, paragraphs IV and VIII, 181, 184-85).

25. Compare *A Vindication* (1717 edition, p. 53) with *Of the Law of Nature and Nations* (1710 edition, Book VII, Chapter VIII, paragraph IV, 586-87, and paragraph VI, 589).

26. Pufendorf treated the qualities of self-preservation and sociability from the same point of view as Wise did. See the edition of 1710, Book II, Chapter III, paragraphs XIV and XV, 109-11.

27. Wise, *op. cit.*, 1717 edition, p. 38.

28. Pufendorf held a similar view of man, but it was not nearly so exalted as Wise's, and he seemed to be more concerned with man's natural depravity than Wise did. See *Of the Law of Nature and Nations,* 1710 edition, Book I, Chapter III, paragraph I, 19; Book II, Chapter III, paragraph XIII, 107.

29. Wise, *op. cit.*, 1717 edition, p. 41; *Of the Law of Nature and Nations,* 1710 edition, Book III, Chapter II, paragraph III, 180.

30. *Of the Law of Nature and Nations,* 1710 edition, Book III,

Chapter IV, paragraph IV, 207; Book VII, Chapter III, paragraph IX, 531.

31. This idea was in Pufendorf. See the 1710 edition (Book VII, Chapter I, paragraph VII, 502): "Therefore the true and leading Cause, why the Fathers of Families would consent to resign up their Natural Liberty, and to form a Commonwealth, was thereby to guard themselves against those Injuries, which one Man was in Danger of sustaining from another. For, as nothing, next to Almighty GOD, can be more beneficial to Man than Man himself: so nothing is able to work him greater Mischief."

32. Wise, *op. cit.*, 1717 edition, p. 46. These ideas were all taken from *Of the Law of Nature and Nations* (1710 edition, Book VII, Chapter II, paragraph XIII, 517-18), and Pufendorf quoted Hobbes.

33. Wise followed the authority of Pufendorf here: 1710 edition, Book VII, Chapter V, paragraph IV, 541.

34. *Of the Law of Nature and Nations,* 1710 edition, Book VII, Chapter V, paragraph III, 540.

35. Wise sang the praises of the government of England independent of Pufendorf.

36. Wise, *op. cit.,* 1717 edition, pp. 52-53.

37. Massachusetts, "Archives," Manuscript, XXXV, 139.

38. *Of the Law of Nature and Nations,* 1710 edition, Book VII, Chapter V, paragraph IV, 541; paragraph XXII, 557-558; Chapter VI, paragraph VI, 561.

39. *Ibid.,* Chapter V, paragraph XXII, 558.

40. Wise, *op. cit.,* 1717 edition, pp. 95-96.

41. A doctrine which stated that Christ was neither consociate with God nor eternal, but merely a divine instrument that assumed the body, not the soul of man.

42. Hubbard died in 1704 at the age of 83 after serving the Ipswich church 48 years, and Higginson in 1708 at the age of 92 after ministering to the Salem church for 49 years.

43. "Diary of Cotton Mather," Massachusetts Historical Society, *Collections,* 7th series, VII, 393-95. *A Testimony to the Order of the Gospel* was not printed until 1701 after the publication of Mather's *A Collection of Some Offensive Matters,* supposedly the closing paper in the Brattle Street Church contro-

versy, but its title was assuredly not by accident. Indeed, *A Testimony* expressly commended *The Order of the Gospel* and annexed three pages from Cotton Mather's life of his grandfather John Cotton. Were Mather disposed to answer *A Vindication,* the appendix of *A Testimony,* which included his own words, might present an embarrassing difficulty, that of seeming to contradict himself. Wise was likely aware of this difficulty.

44. Wise, *op. cit.,* 1717 edition, p. 105.

45. "Diary of Cotton Mather," *op. cit.,* 7th series, VIII, 450.

46. Manuscript letter in "The Colman Papers," Vol. I (1697-1734), dated January 29, 1717-18.

47. Cyprian, admirer of Tertullian and famous Carthaginian bishop of the third century, was the first African ecclesiastic to undergo martyrdom.

48. Eusebius, bishop of Caeserea in the first half of the fourth century and church historian, was at the time of the adoption of the Nicene creed probably the most learned man in the civilized world.

49. John Locke, *Two Treatises of Government,* pp. 179, 238, 177, 92.

50. Tyng, ed., *Reports of Cases Argued and Determined in the Supreme Judicial Court of the Commonwealth of Massachusetts,* XVI (1836), 498-99.

51. Tyler, *op. cit.,* p. 116.

52. Rossiter, *op. cit.,* pp. 30-31.

53. Mackaye, *op. cit.,* p. 82.

54. Dexter, *op. cit.,* p. 502n.

55. *A Confutation of Two Tracts,* p. 98.

56. *A Contrast to the Reverend Nathaniel Whitaker, D.D.,* pp. 10, 12.

57. *History of Printing in America* in *Transactions of the American Antiquarian Society,* VI, 599-639.

58. December 12 and 26, 1771, and January 9, 1772. The Essex *Gazette,* published at Salem, in its issue of January 7-14, 1772, also printed the advertisement.

59. In the *News-Letter* of February 11, 1773, notwithstanding the paper's being the official organ of the royal governor, a work was proposed for printing under the following head:

"To all Protestants, of every Denomination,
throughout America, and all other Friends
to religious and civil LIBERTY."

60. Boston *News-Letter,* February 27, March 19, 1772.

61. Wise, *op. cit.,* 1717 edition, p. 53.

62. Of course, there was much being written on church government at the time, and perhaps there was no need for any but the most outstanding commentary from the past. According to Thomas's lists (*Trans. of American Antiquarian Society,* VI, 638, 614, 647), *New England's Lamentations* by White, Wise's son-in-law, saw publication in 1773, Wigglesworth's *Meat out of the Eater* in 1770, Cotton Mather's *Corderius Americanus* and his father's *Elijah's Mantle* in 1774, and Cheever's Latin grammars over a number of years.

63. Wise, *op. cit.,* 1717 edition, pp. 65-66.

XI. LIBERAL NOTIONS

1. "The Present Melancholy Circumstances of the Province Considered," *Colonial Currency Reprints,* I, edited by Davis, *Prince Society Publications,* XXXII, 360.

2. "New News from Robinson Cruso's Island," *Colonial Currency Reprints,* II, edited by Davis, *Prince Society Publications,* XXXIII, 128.

3. The Boston *Gazette,* photostatic copy, No. 65, March 6-13, 1721.

4. Essex, Mass., "Records of the First Parish, 1676-1726," Manuscript copy, pp. 152, 154, 168-75.

5. *Colonial Currency Reprints,* I, II, edited by Davis, *Prince Society Publications,* XXXII, XXXIII.

6. "New News from Robinson Cruso's Island," *op. cit.,* XXXIII, 128.

7. "The Present Melancholy Circumstances of the Province Considered," *op. cit.,* XXXII, 361.

8. "The Second Part of South-Sea Stock," *Colonial Currency Reprints,* II, edited by Davis, *Prince Society Publications,* XXXIII, 331.

9. "New News from Robinson Cruso's Island," *op. cit.,* XXXIII, 134.

10. Dedication of the pamphlet. This pamphlet may be found in *Colonial Currency Reprints,* II, edited by Davis, *Prince Society Publications,* XXXIII, 159-223.

11. *A Word of Comfort to a Melancholy Country,* p. 10.

12. *Ibid.,* pp. 23-24.

13. *Ibid.,* p. 29.

14. See Dorfman's discussion of Wise's pamphlet in *The Economic Mind in American Civilization 1606-1865,* I, 147-48.

15. No. 62, photostatic copy.

16. No. 63, photostatic copy, February 20-27.

17. *A Friendly Check, from a Kind Relation, to the Chief Cannoneer,* p. 3. This pamphlet is also in *Colonial Currency Reprints,* II, edited by Davis, *Prince Society Publications,* XXXIII, 245-50.

18. *Proverbs* xxvi: 5.

19. According to public notices of November, 1713, Wise was acknowledged, along with a William Clark of Boston, as owner of the sloop *Dolphin* and the bark *Good Intent.* Massachusetts, "Archives," Manuscript, VII, 486, 489.

20. *A Friendly Check, from a Kind Relation, to the Chief Cannoneer,* pp. 5-6. Further evidence of Wise's prosperity is the advertisement in the Boston *News-Letter* during January, 1712, for a runaway servant. This advertisement also establishes Wise's son Joseph as a "Shopkeeper in Anne Street."

21. *A Letter to an Eminent Clergy-Man in the Massachusett's Bay,* p. 12. In *Colonial Currency Reprints,* II, edited by Davis, *Prince Society Publications,* XXXIII, 227-42.

22. *Ibid.,* p. 11.

23. *Ibid.,* p. 7.

24. *Ibid.,* p. 1.

25. See the Boston *Gazette,* photostatic copy, No. 64, February 27-March 6, 1721.

26. *Colonial Currency Reprints,* II, edited by Davis, *Prince Society Publications,* XXXIII, 257-58.

27. No. 65, photostatic copy, March 6-13, 1721.

28. No. 66, photostatic copy, March 13-20, 1721.

29. *Colonial Currency Reprints,* II, edited by Davis, *Prince Society Publications,* XXXIII, 279-300.

30. Weeden, *Economic and Social History of New England 1620-1789,* II, 479-80.

31. Dorfman, *op. cit.,* I, 148-65.

32. Massachusetts Historical Society, *Collections,* 1st series, IX, 276.

33. "Diary of Cotton Mather," Massachusetts Historical Society, *Collections,* 7th series, VIII, 660.

34. Boston Record Commission, *Report of the Record Commissioners,* VIII, 154, 155, 157; Boston *News-Letter,* No. 906, June 22-26, 1721.

35. Boston *News-Letter,* Nos. 911 and 913, July 10-17 and July 24-31, 1721.

36. Cotton Mather announces from time to time the number prayed for who were sick with smallpox. See his "Diary," *op. cit.,* 7th series, VIII, 652, 653, 683.

37. Fitz, "Zabdiel Boylston, Inoculator, and the Epidemic of Smallpox in Boston in 1721," *The Johns Hopkins Hospital Bulletin,* XXII (September, 1911), 314-27.

38. No. 911, July 10-17 issue.

39. No. 912, July 17-24 issue; Fitz, *op. cit., The Johns Hopkins Bulletin,* XXII (September, 1911), 316; Struik, *Science in the Making,* pp. 32-35.

40. Boston *Gazette,* No. 88, July 27-31, 1721.

41. By this time Cotton Mather's son Samuel had been inoculated and had recovered.

42. Boston Record Commission, *Report of the Record Commissioners,* VIII, 159.

43. "Diary of Cotton Mather," *op. cit.,* 7th series, VIII, 632, 634, 655.

44. *Ibid.,* VIII, 657-58.

45. From the title page.

46. Jenks, *op. cit.,* p. 5.

47. *The Reasonableness of Regular Singing; or, Singing by Note,* pp. 3-4.

48. *The Reasonableness of Regular Singing; or, Singing by Note,* p. 15.

49. He was over seventy. Symmes was forty-five, but he outlived Wise only a few months.

50. *Utile Dulci,* p. 55.

51. "Anti-Regular Singers"; the connotation was intended, of course.

52. *Utile Dulci,* p. 18.

53. *Ibid.,* p. 58.

XII. THE LAMP BURNED OUT

1. Massachusetts Historical Society, *Collections,* 6th series, IV, 5.

2. "A Character of the Reverend Mr. *John Wise.* By another Hand." In White, *The Gospel Treasure in Earthen Vessels,* p. 42.

3. "Diary of Samuel Sewall," *op. cit.,* 6th series, VII, 214.

4. Ipswich, Mass., *Vital Records to 1850,* I, 398-99.

5. Crowell, *A Sketch of the History of the Second Parish in Ipswich,* p. 17.

6. Wise's will.

7. Ipswich, Mass., *Vital Records to 1850,* II, 714; Ipswich, Mass., "Births, Marriages, Deaths, Intentions, Strays 1734-1783," Manuscript copy, p. 208.

8. Wise's will.

9. Essex, Mass., "Records of the first Parish, 1676-1726," Manuscript copy, p. 181.

10. Felt, *A History of Ipswich, Essex, and Hamilton,* p. 260.

11. Page 36.

12. Page 37.

13. Pages 37-38.

14. Page 38.

15. No. 1107, April 8-15, 1725.

16. This monument now has the form of a stone table, being a slab of rock the length of the grave and elevated on four pedestals. It has served at one time and another as a playhouse for Essex children.

17. *A Monitory Letter about the Maintenance of an Able and Faithful Ministry*, pp. 9-10.

18. *Prayer for a Succession and Full Supply of Gospel Ministers*, p. 18.

Bibliography

WORKS OF JOHN WISE

Churches Quarrel Espoused, The. New York, William Bradford, 1713.

Churches Quarrel Espoused, The. Boston, Nicholas Boone, 1715.

Friendly Check, from a Kind Relation, A. Boston, J. Franklin, 1721. Also in Colonial Currency Reprints, II, ed. by A. M. Davis, Prince Society Publications, XXXIII, 245-50.

"Instructions for the Emigrants from Essex County, Mass. to South Carolina, 1697," *New England Historical and Genealogical Register*, XXX, 64-67.

"Narrative of Mr John Wise, Minister of Gods Word at Chebacco, The." Manuscript, New York Public Library.

"Narrative of Mr John Wise, Minister of Gods Word at Chebacco, The," Massachusetts Historical Society, *Proceedings*, 2d series, XV, 281-96.

Vindication of the Government of New-England Churches, A. Boston, N. Boone, 1717.

Vindication of the Government of New-England Churches, A. Boston, John Boyles, 1772.

Vindication of the Government of New-England Churches, A. Boston, John Boyles, 1772.

Vindication of the Government of New-England Churches, A. and the Churches' Quarrel Espoused; or, A Reply to Certain Proposals. Boston, Congregational Board of Publication, 1860.

Word of Comfort to a Melancholy Country, A. Boston, 1721. Also in Colonial Currency Reprints, Vol. II, ed. by A. M. Davis, Prince Society Publications, XXXIII, 159-226.

PRIMARY SOURCES

Manuscripts

Branford, Conn., "Town Records." Manuscript, I, (1645-78), 31, 36, 153, 163, Clerk of Court's office, Branford, Connecticut.

Typescript copy in James Blackstone Library, Branford, Connecticut, Vol. I, Part I, pp. 22-23, 27, 128, 134, 152, 154, 292, 296-97, 303, 312.

Choate, Parker C., ed., "Papers in Burnham Public Library." Typescript, Essex, Massachusetts.

"Colman Papers." Manuscript, Vol. I, (1697-1734), Massachusetts Historical Society Library.

Essex, Mass., "Records of First Parish, 1676-1726." Manuscript, copied by Rufus Choate, 1902. The First Congregational Church of Essex.

Essex County, Mass., "Extracts from Records of Superior Court of Judicature," January and May Sittings, 1693. Manuscript, The Essex Institute, Salem.

——"Salem Witchcraft." Salem, Verbatim transcriptions (typescript) of Salem Witchcraft Papers, 1938, Vol. III.

Ipswich, Mass., "Town Records, 1634-1657." Manuscript, The Essex Institute, Salem, 34 folios.

——"Town Records." Manuscript, I (1664-1734, "Births, Marriages, Deaths, etc."), 238, Town Clerk's Office, Ipswich.

——"Town Records." Manuscript, II (1674-96), 44, 47, 50-51, 70, 74, 80, 83, 90-91, 170, 204-5, 238, 284, 299, 303, 309, 310, 361-62, 366, 394-96; III, 97; Town Clerk's Office, Ipswich.

——"Town Records: Births, Marriages, Deaths, Intentions, Strays, 1734-1783." Manuscript, p. 208; Town Clerk's Office, Ipswich.

——Records, First Church, 1739-1805. Manuscript, pp. 67-68.

"Ipswich Manuscripts, 1633-1684," The Winthrop Papers, Vol. I. Manuscript, The Essex Institute, Salem, Mass.

Massachusetts, "Archives." Manuscript, VII, 486, 489; X, 118-138a, 160-82; XI, 56a, XVI, 531; XXXV, 127, 138, 139, 140, 168, 255, 257, 261, 265, 267, 272; CVII, 60; CXXVII, 92, 93, 96, 97, 98, 101, 102, 103, 104, 105, 105a, 109, 109a, 147, 148, 156a, 158a, 162, 164, 165, 166, 167, 168a, 169, 170, 180, 181, 184, 187, 206, 208; CCXLII, 341, 371.

Roxbury, Mass., "First Church Records." Manuscript, The First Church of Roxbury, Boston.

Salem, Mass., "Witchcraft, 1692." Manuscript, Vols. I, II; Clerk of Court's Office, Salem, Massachusetts.

Printed Material

Andrews, Charles M., ed., Narratives of the Insurrections, 1675-
1690; Original Narratives of Early American History. New
York, Charles Scribner's Sons, 1915, pp. 165-297.

Boston *Gazette*, Nos. 62, 63, 64, 65, 66, and 88.

Boston *News-Letter*, Nos. 906, 911, 913, 1107, and the numbers
from December, 1771, through March, 1772.

Boston Record Commission, A Report of the Record Commissioners Containing the Roxbury Land and Church Records.
Boston, Rockwell and Churchill, 2d ed., 1884, VI, 45, 90, 91, 97,
116, 117, 118, 119, 121, 122, 123, 124, 125, 126, 135, 170, 177,
178, 182, 185, 193, 196; VIII, 153-60; XXXIV, 15, 45, 48.

Burr, George L., ed., Narratives of the Witchcraft Cases, 1648-
1706; Original Narratives of Early American History. New
York, Charles Scribner's Sons, 1914, pp. 1-38, 89-164, 203-87.

Calef, Robert, [More] Wonders of the Invisible World; or, Salem
Witchcraft. Boston, Timothy Bedlington, 1828.

Church, Benjamin, The History of King Philip's War, ed. by
Henry M. Dexter. Boston, J. K. Wiggin, 1865.

Colonial Society of Massachusetts, Publications, XV, 58, 156-68,
210, 217, 219, 221, 235, 361, 363; XXIX, 11; XXX, 898, 969;
XXXI, 58, 87, 128, 149, 188, 452, 329-42.

Danforth, Samuel, The Cry of Sodom Enquired Into. Cambridge,
Marmaduke Johnson, 1674.

Drake, Samuel G., ed., Tragedies of the Wilderness. Boston,
Antiquarian Bookstore and Institute, 1842, pp. 20-60.

Eliot, John, "Brief Narrative," Old South Leaflets. Boston, Directors of the Old South Work, Old South Meeting House, 1896,
Vol. I, No. 21.

——The Christian Commonwealth. London, Livewell Chapman,
1659.

——The Communion of Churches. Cambridge, Marmaduke,
Johnson, 1665, p. 17.

——"The Indian Grammar Begun," Old South Leaflets. Boston,
Directors of the Old South Work, Old South Meeting House,
1896, Vol. III, No. 52.

Essex County, Mass., Records and Files of the Quarterly Courts.

Salem, The Essex Institute, 1919, VII (1678-1680), 183, 187, 245.

Essex Gazette, The, Salem, Samuel & Ebenezer Hall, IV (No. 181, Jan. 7-14, 1772), 99.

Gatchel, Samuel, A Contrast to the Reverend Nathaniel Whitaker, D.D.; His Confutation of the Reverend John Wise, A.M.; Vindication of the New-England Churches; and the Churches Quarrel Espoused. Danvers, Mass., E. Russel, 1778.

Green, Samuel A., ed., Two Narratives of the Expedition against Quebec, A.D. 1690 under Sir William Phips. Cambridge, John Wilson and Son, University Press, 1902.

Hall, Howard J., ed., Benjamin Tompson, 1642-1714, First Native-Born Poet of America. Cambridge, The Riverside Press, Houghton Mifflin Company, 1924, pp. 1-35.

Higginson, John, and William Hubbard, A Testimony to the Order of the Gospel in the Churches of New-England. Boston, Timothy Green, 1701.

Ipswich, Mass., Vital Records to 1850. Published by the town. I, 398-99; II, 714.

Johnson, Edward, "Wonder-Working Providence," ed. by J. Franklin Jameson, in Original Narratives of Early American History. New York, Charles Scribner's Sons, 1910, pp. 71-73.

[King, Peter], An Enquiry into the Constitution, Discipline, Unity & Worship, of the Primitive Church. London, 1691. 2 vol.

Letter to an Eminent Clergy-man in the Massachusett's Bay, A. Boston, 1720. Also to be found in Colonial Currency Reprints, Vol. II, ed. by Andrew McFarland Davis, Prince Society Publications, XXXIII, 227-42.

Locke, John, Two Treatises of Government. London, Aunsham and John Churchill, 1694.

Massachusetts, Journal of the Honourable House of Representatives of His Majesty's Province of the Massachusetts Bay in New England. Boston, Samuel Kneeland, 1736, p. 97.

Massachusetts, Laws and Liberties. Reprinted from the copy of the 1648 edition in the Henry E. Huntington Library. Cambridge, Harvard University Press, 1929, pp. 11, 12, 29, 47.

Massachusetts Historical Society, Collections. Boston, 1st series, III, 126-38, V, 61-80, VIII, 1-34, IX, 275-80; 2d series, VI,

587-91, VIII, 166, X, 6-22; 3d series, IV, 291, VII, 255-69; 4th series, 587; 5th series, V, VI, VII; 6th series, I, II, IV, 5; 7th series, VII, VIII.

——Proceedings, 1st series, XII, 109.

Mather, Cotton, The Accomplished Singer. Boston, 1721.

——A Collection of Some of the Many Offensive Matters. Boston, Timothy Green, 1701.

——"An Essay on the Memory of My Venerable Master," Old South Leaflets. Boston, Directors of the Old South Work, Old South Meeting House, 1907, Vol. VIII, No. 177.

——Magnalia Christi Americana; or, the Ecclesiastical History of New-England. London, Thomas Parkhurst, 1702, Books III, IV, V.

——A Monitory Letter about the Maintenance of an Able and Faithful Ministry. Boston, 1700.

——Ratio disciplinae fratrum Nov-Anglorum. Boston, S. Gerrish, 1726.

——Theopolis Americana. Boston, B. Green, 1710.

——The Wonders of the Invisible World. London, John Russell Smith, 1862.

Mather, Increase, A Brief History of the War with Indians in New England. London, Richard Chiswell, 1676.

——A Disquisition concerning Ecclesiastical Councils. Boston, N. Boone, 1716.

——The Order of the Gospel. Printed at Boston in New-England, and Reprinted in London, and sold by A. Baldwin, 1700.

Murdock, Kenneth B., ed., Handkerchiefs from Paul. Cambridge, The Riverside Press, 1927. Introduction.

New Englands First Fruits. New York, Joseph Sabin, 1865, 23-36.

New England Historical and Genealogical Register, II, 104; V, 315, 320; X, 58; XIV, 220; XVIII, 72-73.

New news from Robinson Cruso's Island. . . in Colonial Currency Reprints, II, ed. by A. M. Davis, Prince Society Publications, XXXIII, 127-35.

Paine, Thomas, "A Discours" in Colonial Currency Reprints, II, ed. by A. M. Davis, Prince Society Publications, XXXIII, 279-301.

Pickering, Theophilus, A Bad Omen to the Churches of New-

England. Boston, Rogers and Fowle, 1747.

Platform of Church Discipline, A. Cambridge, Mass., Samuel Green, 1649.

Poole, Wm. Frederick, ed., The Witchcraft Delusion of 1692, by Gov. Thomas Hutchinson. Boston, Privately printed, 1870.

Present Melancholy Circumstances of the PROVINCE Consider'd. . . ,The, in Colonial Currency Reprints, ed. by A. M. Davis, Prince Society Publications, XXXII, 351-63.

Prince Society, Publications, Edward Randolph, VI, 307.

Pufendorf, Samuel, Of the Law of Nature and Nations. Oxford, A. and J. Churchill, 1710.

Roberts, Alexander and Donaldson, James, eds., The Ante-Nicene Fathers. New York, The Christian Literature Company, 1896, I, 309-13; III, 3-15; V, 267-74.

Saybrook (Conn.) Platform, The, A Confession of Faith. New London, Thomas Short, 1710.

Second Part of South-Sea Stock, The, in Colonial Currency Reprints, Vol. II, ed. by A. M. Davis, Prince Society Publications, XXXIII, 303-32.

Symmes, Thomas, The Reasonableness of Regular Singing; or, Singing by Note. Boston, Samuel Gerrish, 1720.

——Utile Dulci; or, Joco-Serious Dialogue concerning Regular Singing. Boston, B. Green, 1723.

Tertullian, The Select Works of Tertullian, ed. by F. A. March. New York, Harper & Brothers, 1876, pp. 153-56.

Toppan, Robert Noxon, ed., Edward Randolph; Publications of the Prince Society, XXV, 37-49; XXVII, 171-82.

Trumbull, J. Hammond, ed., The Public Records of the Colony of Connecticut, II, 76, 399-400, 402; III, 216.

Turell, Ebenezer, The Life and Character of the Reverend Benjamin Colman, D.D. Boston, Rogers and Fowle, 1749.

Tyng, Dudley Atkins, ed., Reports of Cases Argued and Determined in the Supreme Judicial Court of the Commonwealth of Massachusetts. Boston, Hilliard, Gray, and Company, 1836, XVI, 498-99.

Whitaker, Nathaniel, A Confutation of Two Tracts, Entitled A Vindication of the New England Churches; and the Churches Quarrel Espoused, Written by the Reverend John Wise. Boston,

Isaiah Thomas, near the Millbridge, 1774.

White, John, The Gospel Treasure in Earthen Vessels. Boston, N. Boone, 1725.

Whitmore, William H., ed., The Colonial Laws of Massachusetts. Boston, Rockwell and Churchill, 1889, pp. 190-91.

Wise, Jeremiah, Prayer for a Succession and Full Supply of Gospel Ministers. Boston, T. Fleet, 1731.

——Rulers the Minister of God for the Good of their People. Boston, T. Fleet, 1729.

——A Sermon Shewing the Suitableness and the Benefit of Prayer in Affliction. Boston, Nicholas Boone, 1717.

Wood, William, New Englands Prospect, ed. by Eben M. Boynton, Boston, 1898.

Woodbridge, Timothy, and others, The Gospel Order Revived. New York, William Bradford, 1700.

SECONDARY SOURCES

Adams, Brooks, Emancipation of Massachusetts. Boston, Houghton, Mifflin and Company, 1893, pp. 216-85.

Adams, James Truslow, "Benjamin Colman," Dictionary of American Biography. New York, Charles Scribner's Sons, 1930, IV, 311.

——"John Eliot," Dictionary of American Biography. New York, Charles Scribner's Sons, 1931, VI, 79-80.

——"John Wise," Dictionary of American Biography. New York, Charles Scribner's Sons, 1936, XX, 427-428.

——Revolutionary New England, 1691-1776. Boston, The Atlantic Monthly Press, 1923, pp. 97-98.

Allen, William, An American Biographical and Historical Dictionary. Boston, William Hyde & Company, 1832, p. 786.

Allibone, Samuel A., A Critical Dictionary of English Literature and British and American Authors Living and Deceased from the Earliest to the Latter Half of the Nineteenth Century Containing over Forty-Six Thousand Articles [authors]. Philadelphia, J. B. Lippincott & Company, 1872, Vol. III.

American Antiquarian Society, Proceedings. Worcester, Mass. Charles Hamilton, 1884, III (October, 1884), 293-99; V, 146.

Andrews, Charles M., The Fathers of New England. New Haven,

Yale University Press, 1919, pp. 166-94.

Bacon, Leonard W., The Story of the Churches. The Congregationalists. New York, The Baker and Taylor Company, 1904, pp. 97-101.

Baldwin, Alice M., The New England Clergy and the American Revolution. Durham, Duke University Press, 1928, pp. 28-30, 47-53.

Bancroft, George, History of the United States of America. New York, D. Appleton and Company, 1888, I, 585-86; II, 58-66, 180-82.

Barnes, Viola F., "Sir Edmund Andros," Dictionary of American Biography. New York, Charles Scribner's Sons, 1928, I, 300-301.

Blankenship, Russell, American Literature as an Expression of the National Mind. New York, Henry Holt and Company, 1931, pp. 103-04.

Byington, Ezra Hoyt, "John Eliot, The Apostle to the Indians," The Puritan as a Colonist and Reformer. Boston, Little, Brown, and Company, 1899, pp. 205-70.

Cambridge History of American Literature. New York, G. P. Putnam's Sons, 1917, I, 152, 425.

Carpenter, A. H., "Habeas Corpus in the Colonies," *American Historical Review,* VIII (October, 1902), 18-27.

Channing, Edward, A History of the United States. New York, The Macmillan Company, 1927, II, 179-85, 460-62, 490.

Clark, Joseph S., A Historical Sketch of Congregational Churches of Massachusetts. Boston, Congregational Board of Publication, 1858, pp. 73, 102, 106-07, 115-21.

Concise History of the First Church of Christ of Ipswich. Ipswich, L. H. Daniels, 1879.

Congregational Quarterly, The. Boston, Congregational Library Association, 1860, II, 207, 244, 340; 1861, III, 245; 1870, XII, 277-90; 1871, XIII, 297.

Cook, Sherwin L., "John Wise, the Preacher of American Insurgency," Proceedings of the Bostonian Society. Concord, N. H., The Rumford Press, 1925, pp. 28-41.

Cotton Mather and Witchcraft, Two Notices of Mr. Upham His Reply. Boston, T. R. Marvin & Son, 1870.

Crowell, E. P., "Historical Address," Celebration of the Two Hun-

dredth Anniversary of the Organization of the Congregational
Church & Parish in Essex, Mass. August 19-22, 1883. Salem,
J. H. Choate and Company, 1884, pp. 35-73.

Crowell, Robert, History of the Town of Essex from 1634 to 1700.
Boston, C. C. P. Moody, 1853, pp. 95-130, 137-45.

——A Sketch of the History of the Second Parish in Ipswich.
Andover, Flagg and Gould, 1815, pp. 11-18.

DeNormandie, James, "The Roxbury Latin School," *The New
England Magazine,* XII (June, 1895), 388-406.

Dexter, Franklin B., "The History of Connecticut, As Illustrated
by the Names of Her Towns," Proceedings of the American
Antiquarian Society, new series, III, 421-48.

Dexter, Henry M., "Address on Rev. John Wise," Celebration of
the Two Hundredth Anniversary of the Organization of the
Congregational Church & Parish in Essex, Mass., August 19-22,
1883. Salem, J. H. Choate and Company, 1884, pp. 113-39.

——The Congregationalism of the Last Three Hundred Years, As
Seen in Its Literature. New York, Harper and Brothers, 1880,
pp. 488-507.

Dillaway, Charles Knapp, A History of the Grammar School, or,
"the Free Schoole of 1645 in Roxburie." Roxbury, John
Backup, 1860.

Dorfman, Joseph, The Economic Mind in American Civilization
1606-1865. New York, The Viking Press, 1946, I, 3-205.

Drake, Samuel G., The History and Antiquities of Boston. Boston, Luther Stevens, 1856, p. 589.

Dunning, Albert E., Congregationalists in America. Boston, The
Pilgrim Press, 1894, pp. 207, 217-219.

Dunning, William Archibald, A History of Political Theories. New
York, The Macmillan Company, 1905, II, 14-23, 318-25.

Earle, Alice M., The Sabbath in Puritan New England. New
York, Charles Scribner's Sons, 1896.

Ellis, Charles M., The History of Roxbury Town. Boston, Samuel
G. Drake, 1847.

Ellis, George Edward, The Puritan Age in Massachusetts. Boston,
Houghton, Mifflin and Company, 1888, pp. 556-64.

Essex Institute Historical Collections, The. Salem, The Salem
Press, XXXVI (1900), 326, 330; LXVI (1930), 553-56.

Evans, Charles, American Bibliography. Chicago, Blakely Press, 1903, I-XIV.

Farmer, John, A Genealogical Register of the First Settlers of New England. Lancaster, Mass., Carter, Andrews, & Company, 1829, 325-26.

——Memorials of the Graduates of Harvard University in Cambridge, Massachusetts, Commencing with the First Class, MDCXLII. Concord, N. H., Marsh, Capen, and Lyon, 1833, pp. 14-19.

Felt, Joseph B., History of Ipswich, Essex and Hamilton. Cambridge, Mass., Charles Folsom, 1834, pp. 123-26, 257-60, 262.

Fiske, John, The Beginnings of New England. Boston, Houghton, Mifflin and Company, 1898, pp. 270-78.

——Witchcraft in Salem Village. Boston, Houghton, Mifflin and Company, 1923.

Fitz, Reginald H., "Zabdiel Boylston, Inoculator, and the Epidemic of Smallpox in Boston in 1721," *The Johns Hopkins Hospital Bulletin*, XXII (September, 1911), 314-27.

Foakes-Jackson, F. J., Eusebius Pamphili. Cambridge, Eng., W. Heffer and Sons, Ltd., 1933.

Fuess, Claude M., ed., The Story of Essex County. New York, The American Historical Society, Inc., 1935, II, 698, 810-11, 754-57; 849-53.

Gillett, Timothy P., The Past and the Present, in Secular and Religious History of the Congregational Church and Society of Branford. New Haven, Morehouse & Taylor, 1858.

Grahame, James, The History of the United States of America. Boston, Little, Brown, and Company, 1845, I, 401-14.

Greene, J. Evarts, The Roxbury Latin School. Worcester, Mass., Charles Hamilton, 1887.

Hale, Richard Walden, Jr., Tercentenary History of the Roxbury Latin School 1645-1945. Cambridge, The Riverside Press, 1946, pp. 1-70.

Hammatt, Abraham, Early Inhabitants of Ipswich, Mass. Ipswich, Augustine Caldwell, 1880, p. 272.

Hildreth, Richard, The History of the United States of America. New York, Harper and Brothers, 1856, II, 145-67.

Hill, Hamilton A., History of the Old South Church, Boston,

1669-1884. Cambridge, The Riverside Press, 1890, I, 308-13, 319-23.

Holmes, Abiel, The Annals of America. Cambridge, Hilliard and Brown, 1829, I, 425, 537.

Holmes, Pauline, A Tercentenary History of the Boston Public Latin School 1634-1935. Cambridge, Harvard University Press, 1935.

Hurd, D. Hamilton, History of Essex County, Massachusetts, with Biographical Sketches of Many of Its Pioneers and Prominent Men. Philadelphia, J. W. Lewis and Company, 1888, I, 163-65h; II, 995-98, 1162-65, 1180.

Hutchinson, Thomas, The History of the Colony and Province of Massachusetts Bay., ed. by Lawrence Mayo. Cambridge, Harvard University Press, 1936, I, 336-41, 459-67; II, 12-47.

Ipswich, Mass., Antiquarian Papers, I, No. X, July, 1880.

——Historical Society, Publications. Salem, Salem Observer Book and Job Printing, 1894, I, 1-30.

Jenks, Henry F., et al., eds., Records of the Church in Brattle Square, Boston, 1699-1872. Boston, The Benevolent Fraternity of Churches, 1902, pp. vii-xii, 4-25.

Jewett, Isaac A., Memorial of Samuel Appleton. Boston, Bolles and Houghton, 1850, pp. 13-15, 153-68.

Judd, Sylvester, History of Hadley, including the Early History of Hatfield, South Hadley, Amherst and Granby, Massachusetts. Northampton, Metcalf and Company, 1863, pp. 3-104.

Kimball, Everett, The Public Life of Joseph Dudley. New York, Longmans, Green, and Company, 1911.

Lecky, W. E. H., History of Rationalism in Europe. London and Bombay, Longmans, Green, and Company, 1919, I, Chapter I.

Longfellow, Henry W., "The New England Tragedies. Giles Cory of the Salem Farms," The Poetical Works of Henry Wadsworth Longfellow. Boston, Houghton, Mifflin and Company, 1882, III, 97-179.

Lothrop, Samuel K., A History of the Church in Brattle Street. Boston, Wm. Crosby and H. P. Nichols, 1851, pp. 1-60.

McElroy, Paul S., "John Wise: The Father of American Independence," The Essex Institute Historical Collections, LXXXI (1945), 201-26.

Mackaye, J. M., "The Founder of American Democracy," *The New England Magazine*, XXIX (September, 1903), 73-83.

Miller, Perry, Orthodoxy in Massachusetts 1630-1650. Cambridge, Harvard University Press, 1933.

Miller, Perry, and Thomas H. Johnson, *The Puritans*. New York, American Book Company, 1938.

Morison, Samuel Eliot, The Founding of Harvard College. Cambridge, Harvard University Press, 1935.

——Harvard in the Seventeenth Century. Cambridge, Harvard University Press, 1936, Vols. I, II.

——Three Centuries of Harvard. Cambridge, Harvard University Press, 1936.

Morris, John E., and George W. Ellis, King Philip's War, New York, The Grafton Press, 1906.

Morris, Richard B., Government and Labor in Early America. New York, Columbia University Press, 1946.

Murdock, Kenneth B., "Benjamin Tompson," Dictionary of American Biography. New York, Charles Scribner's Sons, 1936, XVIII, 584-85.

——Increase Mather. Cambridge, Harvard University Press, 1925.

Nason, Elias, "Essex," Standard History of Essex County, Massachusetts. Boston, C. F. Jewett & Company, 1878, p. 116.

Nevins, Winfield S., Witchcraft in Salem Village in 1692. Boston, Lee and Shepard, 1892.

Paige, Lucius R., History of Cambridge, Massachusetts, 1630-1877. Boston, Houghton and Company, 1877, pp. 225-26.

Palfrey, John Gorham, History of New England. Boston, Little, Brown and Company, 1892, III, 492, 520-29, 577-78; IV, 189-96.

Palmer, F. H. "Memorial Sermon," Celebration of the Two Hundredth Anniversary of the Organization of the Congregational Church & Parish in Essex, Mass. August 19-22, 1883. Salem, J. H. Choate & Co., 1884, pp. 9-34.

Papers Concerning the Attack on Hatfield and Deerfield. New York, 1859. Bradford Club, Series No. 1.

Parker, Theodore, The Trial of Theodore Parker. Boston, Printed for the author, 1855, p. 59.

Parrington, Vernon L., Main Currents in American Thought. New

York, Harcourt, Brace and Company, 1927, 1930, I, 118-25.

Pew, William Adams, "John Wise," The Essex Institute Historical Collections, LXVI (October, 1930).

Poole, Wm. Frederick, "Cotton Mather and Salem Witchcraft," *North American Review,* CVIII (April, 1869), 337-97.

Pope, Charles Henry, The Pioneers of Massachusetts. Boston, Published by the author, 1900, pp. 509, 524.

Potter, I. J., ed., Chronicle Report of the 250th Anniversary Exercises of Ipswich, August 16, 1884, Together with a Few Sketches About Town. Ipswich, Chronicle Press, 1884.

Quincy, Josiah, The History of Harvard University. Boston, John Owen, 1840, I, 24-144, 486-88, 502.

Robbins, Chandler, History of the Second Church, or Old North, in Boston. Boston, John Wilson and Son, 1852, pp. 40-50.

Rossiter, Clinton L., "John Wise: Colonial Democrat," *The New England Quarterly,* XXII (March, 1949), 3-32.

Savage, James, A Genealogical Dictionary of the First Settlers of New England Showing Three Generations of Those Who Came Before May, 1692 on the Basis of Farmer's Register. Boston, Little, Brown and Company, 1860, I, 21; II, 231; IV, 289, 614-15.

Shipton, Clifford K., "A Plea for Puritanism," *American Historical Review,* XL (April, 1935), 460-67.

——"The New England Clergy of the 'Glacial Age,'" Colonial Society of Massachusetts, Publications, XXXII (1933-1937), 24-54.

Shurtleff, Nathaniel B., ed., Records of the Governor and Company of the Massachusetts Bay in New England. Boston, William White, 1854, III, 126, 229.

Sibley, John Langdon, Biographical Sketches of Graduates of Harvard University. Cambridge, Harvard University Press, 1873, I, 277-79, 423-30; II, 169, 267-76, 428-41; III, 180-98, 200-07; IV, 120-37, 414; VI, 219-20. (Vols. IV and VI were compiled by Clifford K. Shipton.)

Simonds, J. Rupert, A History of the First Church and Society of Branford, Connecticut 1644-1919. New Haven, Tuttle, Morehouse & Taylor Co., 1919, pp. 1-42.

Smith, Abbot Emerson, Colonists in Bondage, 1607-1776, Chapel

Hill, University of North Carolina Press, 1947, pp. 3-20, 307-37.

Sparks, Jared, ed., The Library of American Biography. New York, Harper and Bros., 1844, VI, 163-350.

Spiller, Robert, ed., The Roots of National Culture. New York, The Macmillan Company, 1933, pp. 149-57, 704-05.

Sprague, William B., Annals of the American Pulpit. New York, Robert Carter and Brothers, 1857, I, 188-89.

Stone, Edwin M., History of Beverly. Boston, James Munroe and Company, 1843, p. 213.

Story, Irving C., "John Wise: Congregational Democrat," *Pacific University Bulletin*, XXXVI, 1939, No. 3.

Struik, Dirk J., Yankee Science in the Making. Boston, Little, Brown and Company, 1948, pp. 3-36.

Tapley, Charles S., Rebecca Nurse, Saint but Witch Victim. Boston, Marshall Jones Company, 1930.

Temple, J. H., History of the Town of Whately, Mass. Boston, T. R. Marvin & Son, 1872, pp. 7-53.

Thwing, Walter Eliot, History of the First Church in Roxbury, Massachusetts, 1630-1904. Boston, W. A. Butterfield, 1904, pp. 1-65.

Tyler, Moses Coit, A History of American Literature: 1607-1765. New York, G. P. Putnam's Sons, 1878, II, 104-16.

Upham, Charles W., History of the Salem Witchcraft. Boston, Wiggin and Lunt, 1867, I, II.

——Salem Witchcraft and Cotton Mather. Morrisania, N. Y., Privately printed, 1869.

Upham, Wm. P., House of John Procter. Peabody, Mass., Press of C. H. Shepard, 1904.

Walker, Williston, The Creeds and Platforms of Congregationalism. New York, Charles Scribner's Sons, 1893, pp. 470-94.

——A History of the Congregational Churches in the United States. New York, The Christian Literature Company, 1894, pp. 198-213.

Washburn, Emory, Sketches of the Judicial History of Massachusetts from 1630 to the Revolution in 1775. Boston, Charles C. Little and James Brown, 1840, pp. 105-07.

Waters, Thomas Franklin, An Historical Address Delivered on the 140th Anniversary of the Organization of the South Church.

Ipswich, 1887, p. 91 and note.

——Ipswich in the Massachusetts Bay Colony. Ipswich, The Ipswich Historical Society, 1905, I, 237-71, 287-300, Appendix G.; 1917, II, 20-30, 33, 141-48, 227-28, 301.

——"Two Ipswich Patriots: John Wise of Chebacco," Ipswich Historical Society, Publications, XXVI (1927), 1-23.

Weeden, William B., Economic and Social History of New England 1620-1789. Cambridge, The Riverside Press, 1890, II, 479-80.

Wells, Daniel W., and Reuben F. Wells, A History of Hatfield, Massachusetts, Springfield, Mass., F. C. H. Gibbons, 1910, pp. 11-107.

Wendell, Barrett, Cotton Mather. New York, Dodd, Mead and Company, 1891.

Wilson, James G., and John Fiske, eds., Appletons' Cyclopaedia of American Biography. New York, D. Appleton and Company, 1899, VI, 464-65, 580-81.

Winsor, Justin, ed., The Memorial History of Boston. Boston, James R. Osgood and Company, 1881, II, 131-72, 216, 331, 350-51, 425; III, 122.

Wirner, James A., Events in Indian History. Lancaster, Mass., G. Hills & Co., 1843, pp. 31-32, 47-48.

Wright, Thomas G., Literary Culture in Early New England 1620-1730. New Haven, Yale University Press, 1920.

Yearbook, Charleston, S. C., 1899, pp. 149-54.

Index